IMAGES
of America

WASHINGTON, DC, JAZZ

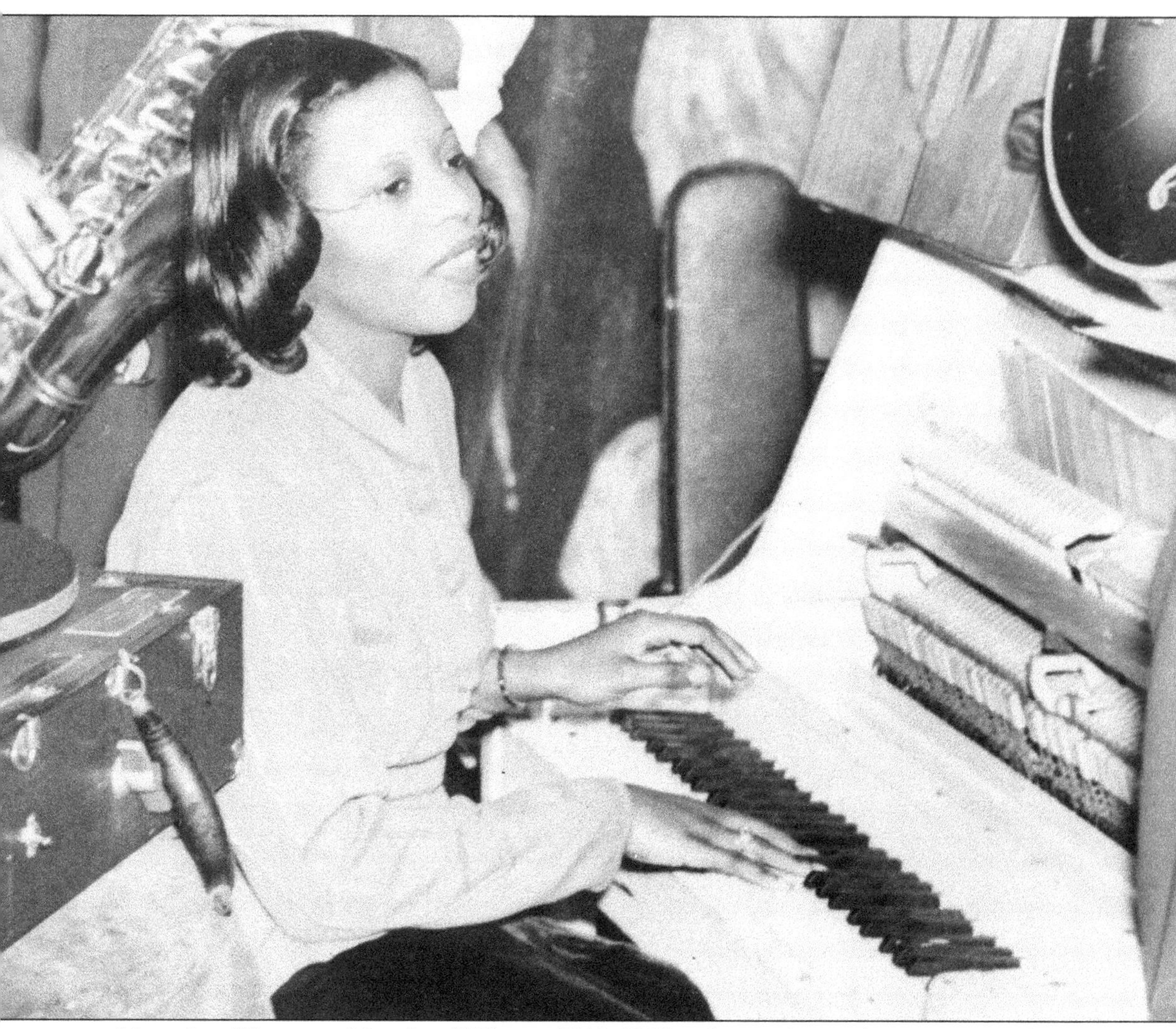

Mary Lou Williams. Mary Lou Williams (1910–1981) is shown playing the piano at Washington's Howard Theatre around 1947. A child prodigy, she went on to enjoy great success as a woman in a male-dominated profession. As a prolific composer, she created works for Benny Goodman, Duke Ellington, Dizzy Gillespie, and numerous other jazz artists. Following a religious conversion in the 1950s, she focused increasingly on liturgical music, including "Mary Lou's Mass," which was originally known as "Music for Peace." Williams is also remembered as the founder of the Bel Canto Foundation, an organization that engaged in charitable work for the benefit of musicians. In 1996, Dr. Billy Taylor founded the John F. Kennedy Center's annual Mary Lou Williams Women in Jazz Festival to both honor this musical genius and showcase the talents of some of the world's most accomplished women in jazz. (Photograph by William P. Gottlieb; courtesy of the William P. Gottlieb / Ira and Leonore S. Gershwin Fund Collection, Music Division, Library of Congress.)

On the Cover: Saxophonists and native Washingtonians Ron Holloway (left) and Roger Wendell "Buck" Hill perform at Blues Alley, a popular DC jazz club. (Photograph by Michael Wilderman.)

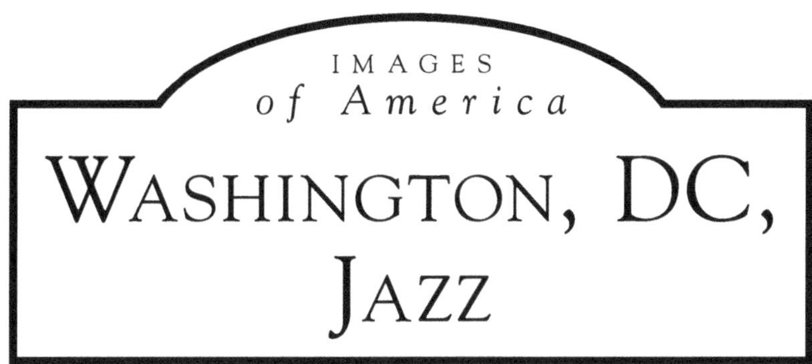

Dr. Regennia N. Williams and
Rev. Dr. Sandra Butler-Truesdale
Foreword by Willard Jenkins

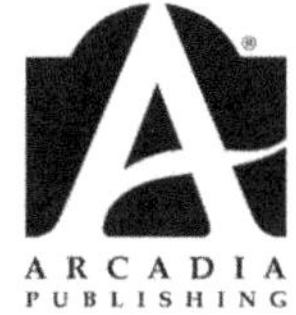

ISBN 978-1-4671-2783-7

Published by Arcadia Publishing
Charleston, South Carolina

Library of Congress Control Number: 2017945295

For all general information, please contact Arcadia Publishing:
Telephone 843-853-2070
Fax 843-853-0044
E-mail sales@arcadiapublishing.com
For customer service and orders:
Toll-Free 1-888-313-2665

Visit us on the Internet at www.arcadiapublishing.com

To Roger Wendell "Buck" Hill and Denyse Pearson-Williams, Washington, DC, jazz artists who joined the ancestors in 2017.

CONTENTS

FOREWORD

Washington, DC—befitting our nation's capital—holds an indelible place in the pantheon of cities that have contributed historically to both the development of great jazz musicians and the extraordinary arc of the music itself. Part of this book's achievement is the intertwined nature of the development of jazz in the city with the very development of the city as a major metropolis. History shows that there was a time in the first half of the 20th century when the level of activity and the sheer number of vibrant homes to jazz music's development in DC rivaled that of the more storied historic Harlem community of New York, for decades considered the figurative capital of black America. After all, DC's fabled U Street corridor and surrounding environs were once quite accurately nicknamed "Black Broadway" as a signifier of its pulsating nature as an entertainment district.

But this book is not about making specious comparative analysis; *Washington, DC, Jazz* is about highlighting and enlightening its readers on DC's true place in the list of celebrated jazz cities, a list that arguably begins with New Orleans and includes Chicago, New York, Los Angeles, Philadelphia, and Detroit. *Washington, DC, Jazz* certainly makes the case for DC's inclusion as part of that jazz circuit.

Chock full of richly illustrative historic photographs, *Washington, DC, Jazz* achieves this goal in both its sense of reportage and in the wonderful images represented here. Another laudable element of this book is how neatly it achieves a sense of gender balance in highlighting the contributions of DC's jazz men *and* its women! And that is certainly no mean feat, though if you know or recognize the high standards of the work of its chroniclers—Regennia N. Williams and Sandra Butler-Truesdale—then that sense of gender balance comes as no surprise.

Readers of this book will not only derive a greater sense of DC's jazz history, c. 1917–2017, but will achieve a better sense of its key contributors, classic to contemporary—literally from the ancestors Duke Ellington, Keter Betts, and Shirley Horn to current contributors Ron Holloway, Sharón Clark, Kush Abadey, and their contemporaries on the DC jazz scene.

In addition, readers of *Washington, DC, Jazz* will gain a greater sense of the places significant to jazz music–making on the DC scene, from the Howard Theatre, Lincoln Colonnade, and Bohemian Caverns (in both its classic and contemporary iterations) to Blues Alley, Westminster Presbyterian Church, and the DC Jazz Festival. Readers of this book should be prepared to experience Washington jazz through enlightened eyes after exploring its pages.

—Willard Jenkins

Acknowledgments

Grateful acknowledgment is given to the following individuals and organizations for their support:

Meaghan A. Alston, Moorland Spingarn Research Center, Howard University
Larry Apelbaum, Library of Congress
Caitrin Cunningham, senior title manager, Arcadia Publishing
Rachel Elwell, The Felix E. Grant Jazz Archives, University of the District of Columbia
DC Legendary Musicians Inc., governing board and members
The Rev. Brian Hamilton, Westminster Presbyterian Church
Karen Harris, Historical Society of Washington, DC
Rusty Hassan, WPFW 89.3 FM
John Edward Hasse, curator emeritus, National Museum of American History, Smithsonian Institution
Jim Kempert, senior editor, Arcadia Publishing
Kennith Kimery, Smithsonian Jazz, National Museum of American History
Judith Korey, The Felix E. Grant Jazz Archives, University of the District of Columbia
Lauren Martino, Washingtoniana Collection, DC Public Library
Lora Moinkoff, Gibson Inc., Entertainment Relations
Kelly Elaine Navies, National Museum of African American History and Culture
Rock Newman, WHUR TV
Pamela S. Perkins, Human Communications Institute LLC
Lawrence A. Randall, photographer
The RASHAD Center Inc., Dr. Regennia N. Williams, founder and director
Nathaniel Rhodes, photographer and project consultant
Blair Ruble, The Woodrow Wilson Center
Jessica Smith, Historical Society of Washington, DC
Katea Stitt, WPFW 89.3 FM
Michael Wilderman, jazzvisionsphotos
James Zimmerman, Smithsonian Jazz, National Museum of American History

The 24 interviewees and one informant (Rainy Williams, daughter of the late Shirley Horn) for the 2017–2018 Washington, DC, Jazz Oral History Project and one interviewee (Queen Esther Marrow) for the Praying Grounds Oral History Project. The directors of the RASHAD Center Inc. and DC Legendary Musicians Inc. have agreed to place both the recorded interviews and the interview transcripts for the following narrators in a public archive, where the material can be accessed and used for educational and research purposes.

Kush Abadey
Nasar Abadey
Brother Ah (Robert Northern III)
Nia Elaine Marie Alsop
The Rev. Dr. Sandra Butler-Truesdale
Howard Chichester
The Rev. Dr. Ginger Cornwell
Donald "Big Foot" Edwards
Roy "Chip" Ellis
Keanna Faircloth
Janine Gilbert-Carter
Je'Lan Harwell
Ron Holloway
Corcoran Holt
Kim Jordan
Manuel "Manny" Kellough
Queen Esther Marrow
Mark Meadows
Aaron Myers
Jeffrey J. "Left Hand" Neal
Lavenia Nesmith
Herbert James Scott
Jawoed Mosché Snowden
Coniece Washington
Lori Williams
Rainy Williams

INTRODUCTION

Since the era of World War I, the life stories of some of the greatest musicians in the history of jazz have been intertwined with the history of the District of Columbia; Washington, DC, the nation's capital, the seat of government, and the Federal City. Thus, the focus here is on jazz history, c. 1917–2017. Washington was, for at least part of the subject period for this book, also affectionately known as the "Chocolate City," and, in the early 20th century, the combined populations of its vibrant African American neighborhoods rivaled that of megacity New York's Harlem, home to one of the world's largest contiguous "Chocolate" communities.

In the Shaw-Howard community, the popularity of the music emanating from the clubs along the U Street corridor—and the caliber of performances at the historic Howard Theatre and other venues—suggested to many that the District of Columbia was, to invoke yet another popular New York comparison, home to "Black Broadway." It must be stated, however, that, as was the case on New York's Broadway during the subject era, an incredibly diverse group of Americans performed, contributed to, and consumed jazz in Washington. Moreover, many of the aforementioned individuals, including legendary pianist and North Carolina native John Malachi (1919–1987)—whose portrait by William P. Gottlieb graces the cover of *DC Jazz: Stories of Jazz Music in Washington, DC* (Georgetown University Press, 2018)—migrated to the city during the subject era.

Our primary purpose for writing *Washington, DC, Jazz* was to invite readers to join us in placing Washington front and center in an illustrated account of one important aspect of its rich and complex music history, while considering the contributions of some of the men, women, and children who have long been steeped in the traditions associated with jazz. In so doing, we were not as concerned with comparing Washington, DC, to other cities as we were with highlighting those individuals and institutions that have made it possible for students of history and music lovers alike to see Washington as a jazz center in its own right; one where both native-born Washingtonians and migrants from other states and countries have chosen to establish their musical homes, whether they reside in DC proper or in another part of the Washington metropolitan area, known to many as the "DMV" (for the District, Maryland, and Virginia.) This book considers the work of a select few of those artists.

In the larger discussion of both the complex history of jazz and that of Washington, DC, geography, a sense of community, acquired knowledge, and shared understanding take on special meaning for musicians. Within Washington's 21st-century jazz community, there appears to be a general consensus among many musicians that jazz is black music that is rooted in the rhythms, cultures, and spiritual traditions of West Africa.

During interviews for the 2017–2018 Washington, DC, Jazz Oral History Project phase of our research for this book, our narrators let us know that, "jazz is class . . . jazz is sacred, spiritual, and secular . . . jazz is 'oxygen for the ears'. . . jazz is great black music . . . and many Washington, DC, musicians are multi-talented, multi-instrumentalists, multi-genre artists, or genreless." To borrow a line from Duke Ellington, DC's musicians and their music are "beyond category!" In academic circles—and the academic and musicians' circles are not always mutually exclusive—one finds a number of definitions in scholarly literature about the roots and evolving meanings of jazz.

James McCalla, author of *Jazz: A Listener's Guide*, wrote: "There is no generally accepted definition of the word "jazz," nor do we know where the word came from or what it originally meant." *The Smithsonian Collection of Classic Jazz* includes the following statements on the music:

> Jazz music has been called an American art, America's contribution to the arts, and even an explosion of genius. . . . Composer and critic Virgil Thomson has described it as "the most astounding spontaneous musical event to take place anywhere since the Reformation."

> Jazz is a major contribution of American black men to contemporary culture. It was they who created it and they who have provided its greatest innovations. At the same time, it has always been a meeting ground: white men have participated since its beginnings, and some of them have contributed with excellence.

As a result, perhaps, of the factors described in the above passages, musicologist Grover Sales defined jazz as "America's classical music." A product of the synthesis of European instrumentation, West African performance styles, and the coincident creolization of cultures, jazz emerged as a uniquely American music in New Orleans, Louisiana, and other Southern cities at the turn of the 20th century. This new music also helped shape the artistic visions of countless performing artists outside the Deep South, including Edward Kennedy "Duke" Ellington, a native of Washington, DC, and a former student at the city's Armstrong High School.

The above definitions are applicable, certainly, to part of the music created and performed during Duke Ellington's lifetime (1899–1974). However, it is also important to note that, from the earliest period of the "straight-ahead" jazz discussed at length by several of the narrators for our companion Washington, DC, Jazz Oral History Project through the present time, women have made significant contributions to the music. Readers should not be surprised, then, to see that Mary Lou Williams, Pearl Bailey, Shirley Horn, Kim Jordan, Lori Williams, Janine Gilbert-Carter, Connaitre Miller, and other women are among the artists discussed herein. Gender is one of several significant factors associated with diversity in North American jazz communities that have long been influenced by Caribbean and Latin American cultures.

Ted Gioia, author of *The History of Jazz*, considers the impact of the above-referenced diversification of the communities of jazz artists on the seemingly continual evolution of the music. In his discussion of "The Fragmentation of Jazz Styles" in the decades following World War II, Gioia mentions the emergence of swing, traditional jazz, bebop, cool jazz, hard bop, West Coast jazz, soul jazz, third stream jazz, fusion, and free jazz—and the evolution and simultaneous acceptance and rejection of certain styles among individual artists who chose to "follow their own muse." In "Jazz in the New Millennium," the final chapter of his book, Gioia offers a thought-provoking analysis of a marked "new earnestness in the post-millennial jazz scene" among female vocalists, even as he sounds a cautionary note regarding the tendency to apply "narrow definitions" to jazz. He states, in part:

> The three most commercially successful singers of jazz-oriented material during the opening years of the new century have been Norah Jones, Diana Krall, and the late Eva Cassidy. Yet their vocal work is so cleansed of the skippety-ippety-doo pyrotechnics of the previous generation, so introspective and austere, that some critics would contend that they aren't real jazz singers at all. A tempting verdict—except that the history of jazz teaches us that attempts to exclude whole groups of performers by the applications of narrow definitions are usually a sign that something important is underway in the art form. Certainly a different aesthetic sensibility is rising to the fore here.

Those differences notwithstanding, interest in the various styles—of both the 20th and 21st centuries—is still evident, although some educators and musicians lament the fact that jazz is becoming the "music of the museum." More than 40 years after his death, Duke Ellington is still one of Washington's favorite sons, one of America's greatest and most prolific composers, and one of the most written-about artists of any race, class, gender, or musical genre. In a similar fashion, sales of the recordings of vocalist and guitarist Eva Cassidy, another native Washingtonian, skyrocketed following her untimely death in 1996 at the age of 33.

It is also true that interest in the early-20th-century Jazz Age and the related "New Negro" movement remains high, and cultural historians and students of all ages are among those engaged in the examination of the lives and legacies of many notable Southern-born African American artists, their reasons for migrating to urban areas in the 1910s and 1920s, and their contributions to the cultural renaissance movements in New York, Chicago, and Washington, DC. With regard to what is often described as the first self-conscious cultural movement among African Americans during the Jazz Age, Washingtonians seem to take great pride in the fact that many of the most celebrated artists and scholars associated with the movement were, for a time, educated and/or employed in Washington, including Langston Hughes, Zora Neale Hurston, Alain Locke, Carter G. Woodson, and Duke Ellington.

Ellington's post-1923 successes in Harlem's extremely competitive world of arts and entertainment were directly related to his earlier educational, cultural, and professional experiences in Washington. He and fellow Washingtonian Shirley Horn were two of the many DC artists who won critical acclaim for their contributions to jazz and whose work is documented in the extensive collections (manuscript materials and oral histories) at the Smithsonian Institution's National Museum of American History (NMAH) in Washington. In addition, NMAH is—due in no small measure to the invaluable work of the museum's curator emeritus of American music, Dr. John Edward Hasse—home to the Smithsonian Jazz Masterworks Orchestra and the headquarters for the annual Jazz Appreciation Month celebration, which the museum launched in 2002.

These Washington-based research and programming activities have enhanced classroom teaching activities at all levels and inspired related campus and community-based concerts and other special events, including the popular Jazz Night concerts at Westminster Presbyterian Church. Far from simply being "the music of the museum," it appears that jazz is thriving—in church sanctuaries, in clubs from Georgetown to the Shaw-Howard community, and in classrooms at the Duke Ellington School of the Arts, Howard University, the University of the District of Columbia, the Peabody Institute of The Johns Hopkins University, and other educational institutions. Indeed, the roots of jazz run deep in "Duke Ellington's Washington," but Washington, DC, jazz has also transformed cultural landscapes and individual lives throughout the mid-Atlantic region, the nation, and the world.

The importance of jazz has not escaped the notice of Washington's public servants and public administrators. Marion S. Barry, DC's "Mayor for Life;" Congressman John Conyers Jr.; and their colleagues saw to it that jazz would be celebrated in their lifetimes and preserved for future generations. As the April 30, 2016, UNESCO International Jazz Day Celebration at the White House demonstrated, the eyes of the jazz world have good reason to look to Washington.

While government support has played a crucial role in the history of American jazz, and the Library of Congress, the world's largest library, remains an invaluable repository of primary and secondary sources for those conducting research on the music, individual donors, corporate and family foundations, and other funders are vital to the lives of the annual jazz festivals that further enhance DC's reputation as a destination city for those in search of excellence in the performing arts. Thus, librarians, archivists, politicians, funders, and the artists, artistic directors, producers, and audiences have also secured their places in the history of Washington, DC, jazz.

Limitations of time and space (128 pages for the books in this series) ensured that this work would not and could not be a comprehensive study of the cultural expressions that drummer Jimmy "Junebug" Jackson (1957–2012) described as "oxygen for the ears." No one book, regardless of its size, will ever be able to do that. Nevertheless, it is our hope that this slim volume will serve as a catalyst for further research—on Latin jazz, "JoGo" (jazz combined with go-go, as performed by DC's Elijah Jamal Balbed and the JoGo Project), and other jazz styles that are part of the District of Columbia's cultural heritage.

One

Roots Music

Washington, DC, and the Early History of Jazz

This chapter considers several musical styles that predate the popular music of the 1920s Jazz Age and some key purveyors (if not inventors) of those styles that had ties to Washington, DC. Ethnomusicologists are quick to remind readers that enslaved African Americans created the instruments and performance styles associated with antebellum gatherings in Congo Square in New Orleans, arguably the birthplace of jazz. In freedom, African Americans continued to establish the musical foundation upon which 21st-century jazz artists stand.

Today, of course, jazz musicians from across the globe are bringing to their music a sense of who they are as creative artists, and race, class, ethnicity, nationality, and cultural background continue to transform the music and the messages that are transmitted through it. Evidence in both scholarly studies and primary sources also suggests that jazz has, since the earliest period of its history, been a hybrid style of music, with musicians of various backgrounds borrowing freely from each other and blending several artistic traditions to produce something new.

One example of this practice is reflected in the work of Jelly Roll Morton (1890–1941). A legendary pianist, composer, and pioneering jazz recording artist, Morton lived in Washington in the 1930s, performing at the Jungle Inn nightclub on U Street. He also became cocreator (with Alan Lomax) of one of the first oral histories of jazz in 1938. Born Ferdinand Joseph LaMothe, Jelly Roll let the world know that he was fiercely proud of his Creole culture, his French ancestry, and his work with other Creole, black, and white musicians in New Orleans. The first-person narrative of the self-proclaimed "Inventor of Jazz" is one of the thousands in library collections in Washington. Other Library of Congress collections, including those containing sheet music and studio recordings, identify several musical tributaries (some African and some European American) that flowed into early jazz.

European influences notwithstanding, Lawrence Levine's seminal book *Black Culture and Black Consciousness* (1976) revealed that black music in performance, including jazz, has retained the following distinctive characteristics: the primacy of rhythm and polyrhythms, the marriage between movement and music, the importance of call-and-response / antiphony, improvisation, collective participation that does not distinguish between performers and their audiences, and the functionality of the music. These characteristics, according to Levine, suggest that black music, while influenced by the music of Western Europe, was more closely related to the music of West Africa and the Caribbean than it was to other musical expressions of the Americas or Europe.

Levine, citing the work of W.E.B. Du Bois and other early-20th-century writers, also suggested that blacks were, of necessity, at least bicultural in Jim Crow America, when knowledge of the wider society's beliefs about acceptable behavior could mean the difference between life and death. In the history of Washington, DC, jazz and in subsequent scholarly works by Portia Maultsby and others, however, one sees more than the "two-ness" ("an American, a Negro") made famous in Du Bois's *The Souls of Black Folk* (1903), since musicians continually engaged in ongoing and often controversial cultural exchanges throughout the 20th century.

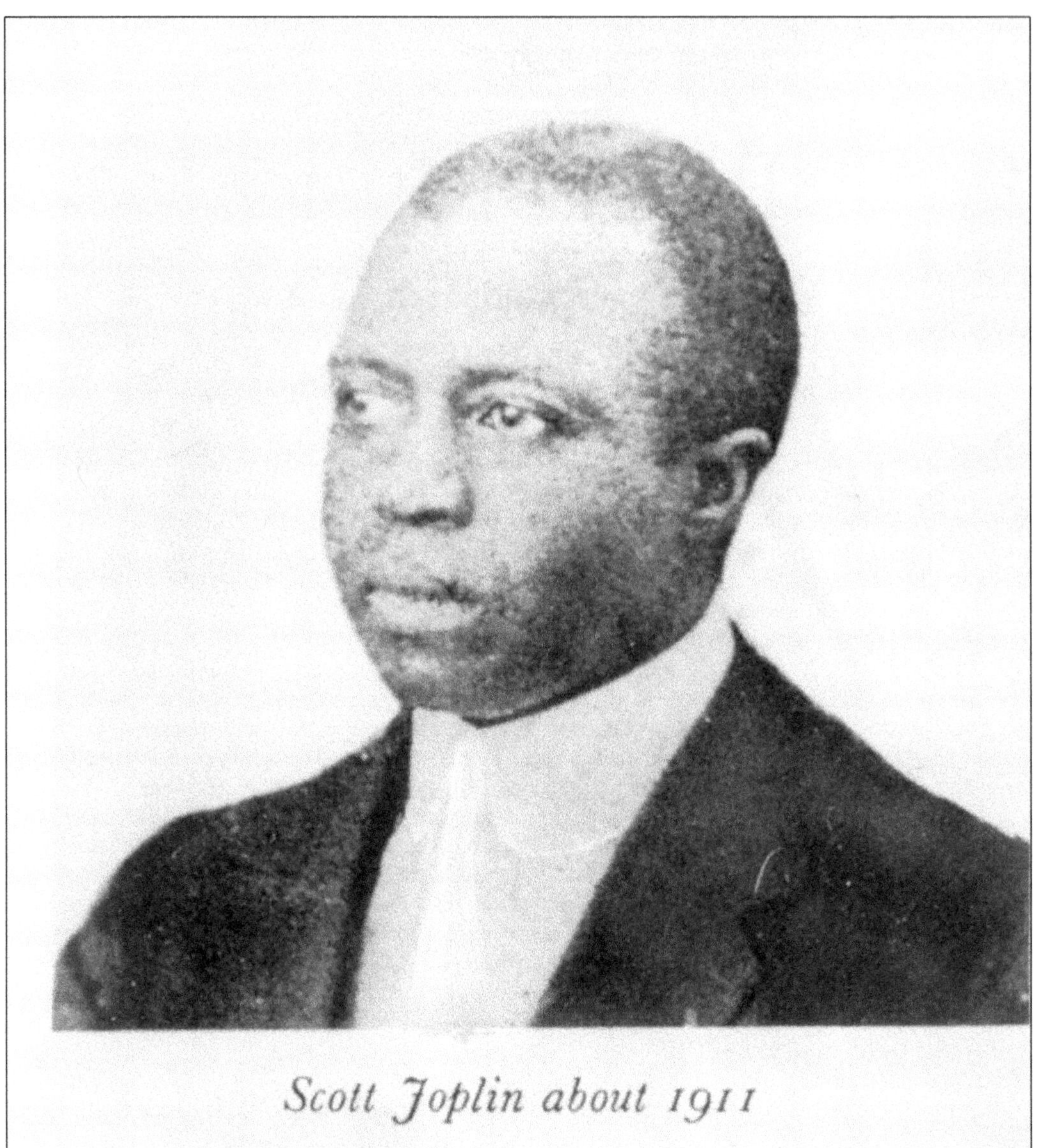

Scott Joplin. Pianist-composer Scott Joplin (1868–1917), the "King of Ragtime," embodied many of the aspirations of African Americans during the post–Civil War era. A trained musician, piano teacher, composer, and publisher of sheet music, he enjoyed some financial success in Sedalia, Missouri. He published the best-selling "Maple Leaf Rag" in 1899, the year of Duke Ellington's birth. Like Ellington, Joplin experimented with composing larger works based on African American folk themes, including his opera *Treemonisha*, which explored the evolving roles of folk beliefs and education in African American cultural history. (Courtesy of the Historical Society of Washington, DC.)

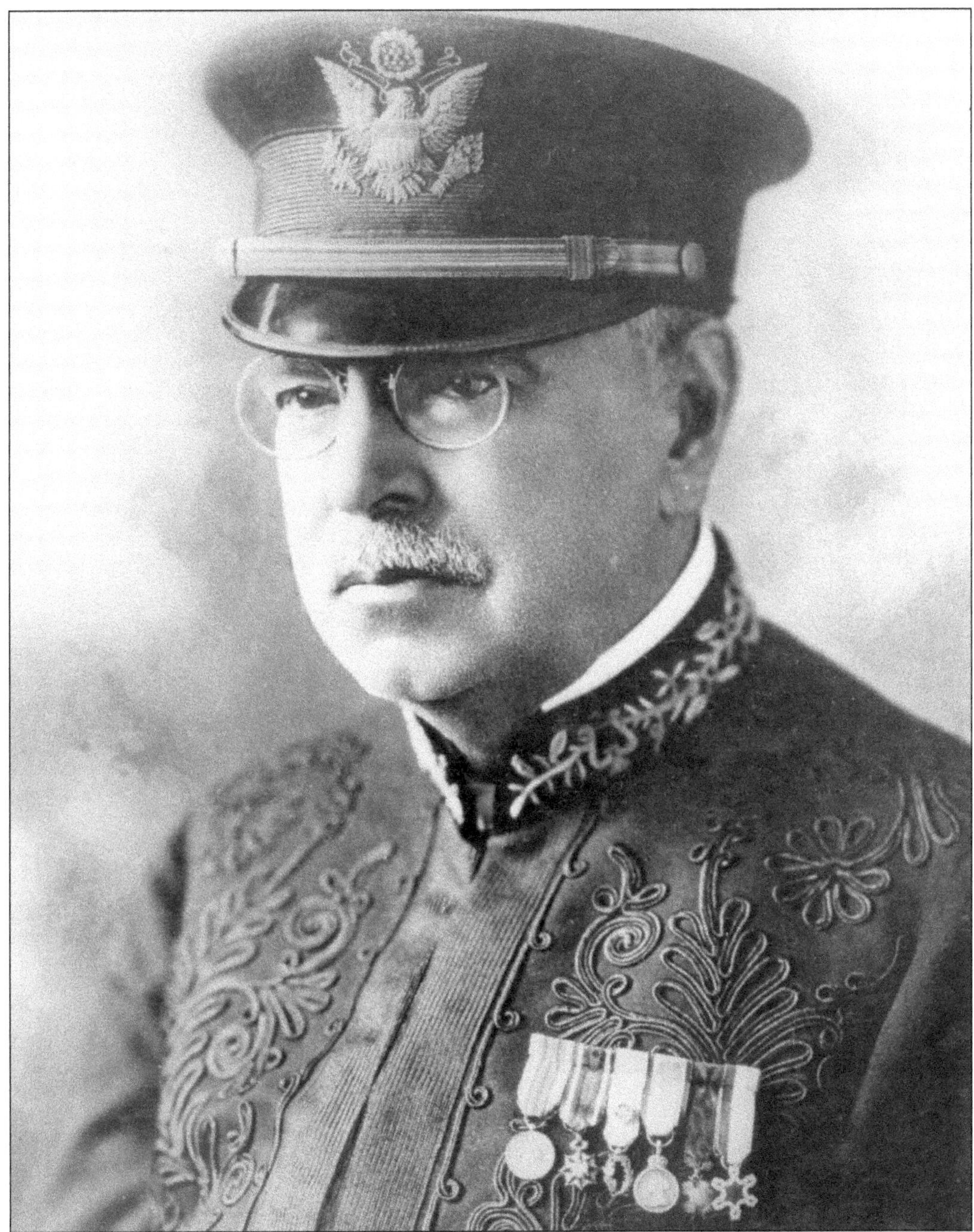

JOHN PHILIP SOUSA IN THE UNIFORM OF HIS CIVILIAN BAND, C. 1921. A native Washingtonian, Sousa formed his own marching band in 1892, and in the era of World War I, he led the Naval Band on fundraising tours to benefit the war effort and the Red Cross. Sousa is best known as the composer of numerous marches, including "The Stars and Stripes Forever," but his bands also performed European classical music, ragtime, and jazz. (Courtesy of the Historical Society of Washington, DC.)

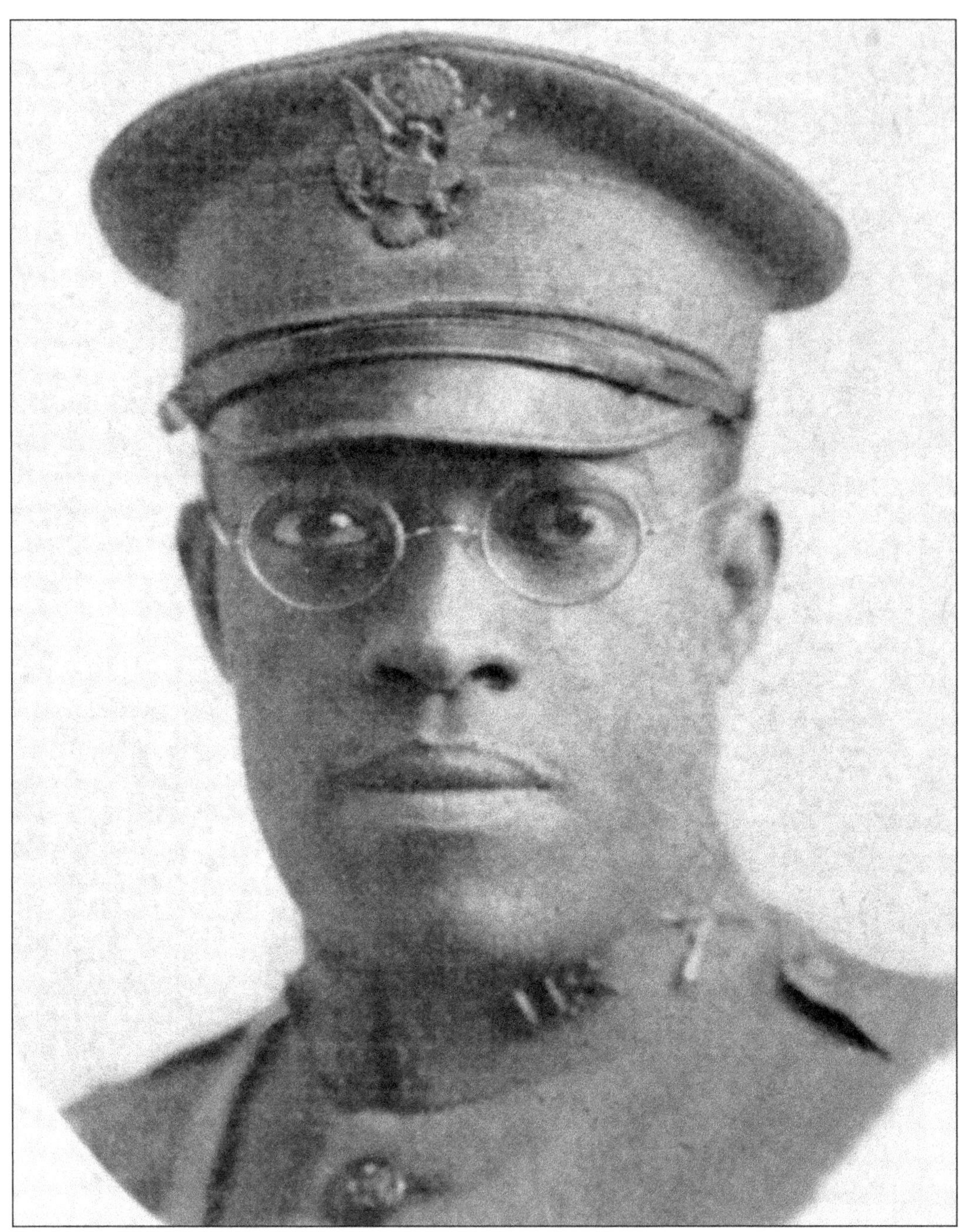

James Reese Europe. Born in Alabama in 1881, James Reese Europe moved to Washington, DC, when he was 10 years old and spent 14 formative years in the nation's capital, where he found his voice as a musician and champion of the music of African American people. After moving to New York in 1904, he founded and served as president of the Clef Club, home to performing ensembles and a union for African American professional musicians. In 1912, Europe's Clef Club Orchestra made its Carnegie Hall debut performing "A Concert of Negro Music." Many audio and print examples of his compositions and arrangements are available at the Library of Congress. (Courtesy of the Library of Congress.)

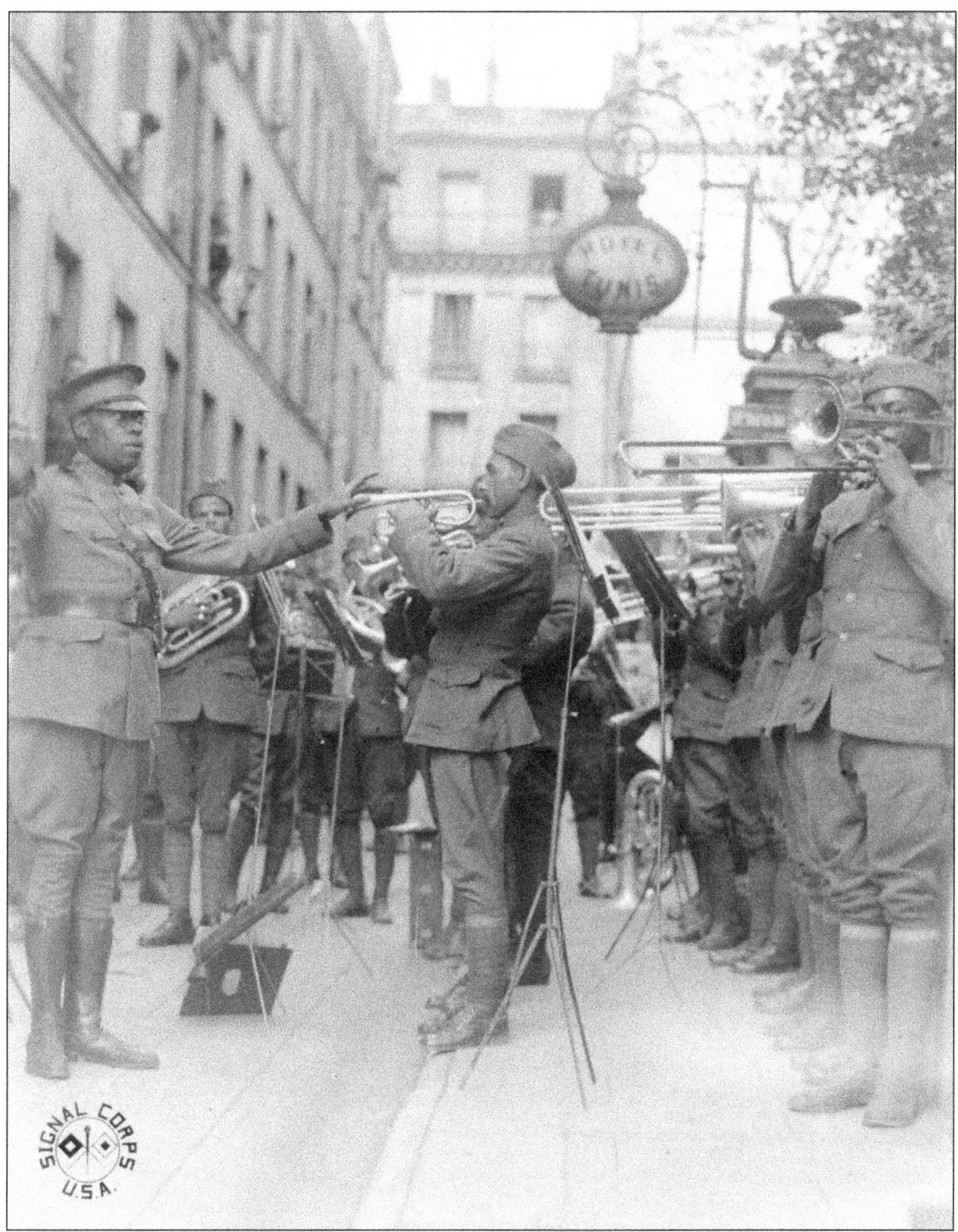

THE JAMES REESE EUROPE ORCHESTRA OF THE 369TH REGIMENT IN FRANCE, 1917. During World War I, James Reese Europe formed a regimental band that won critical acclaim in the United States and in Europe. As a composer-director, he continually emphasized the importance of musical expressions that reflected the unique experiences of African Americans. Because of his nationalistic thinking, his early success composing for and conducting large instrumental ensembles, and his rhythmically complex works that reflected the influence of ragtime, many musicologists consider him to be one of the most significant artists in shaping the history of the music that would come to be known as jazz. (Courtesy of the Library of Congress.)

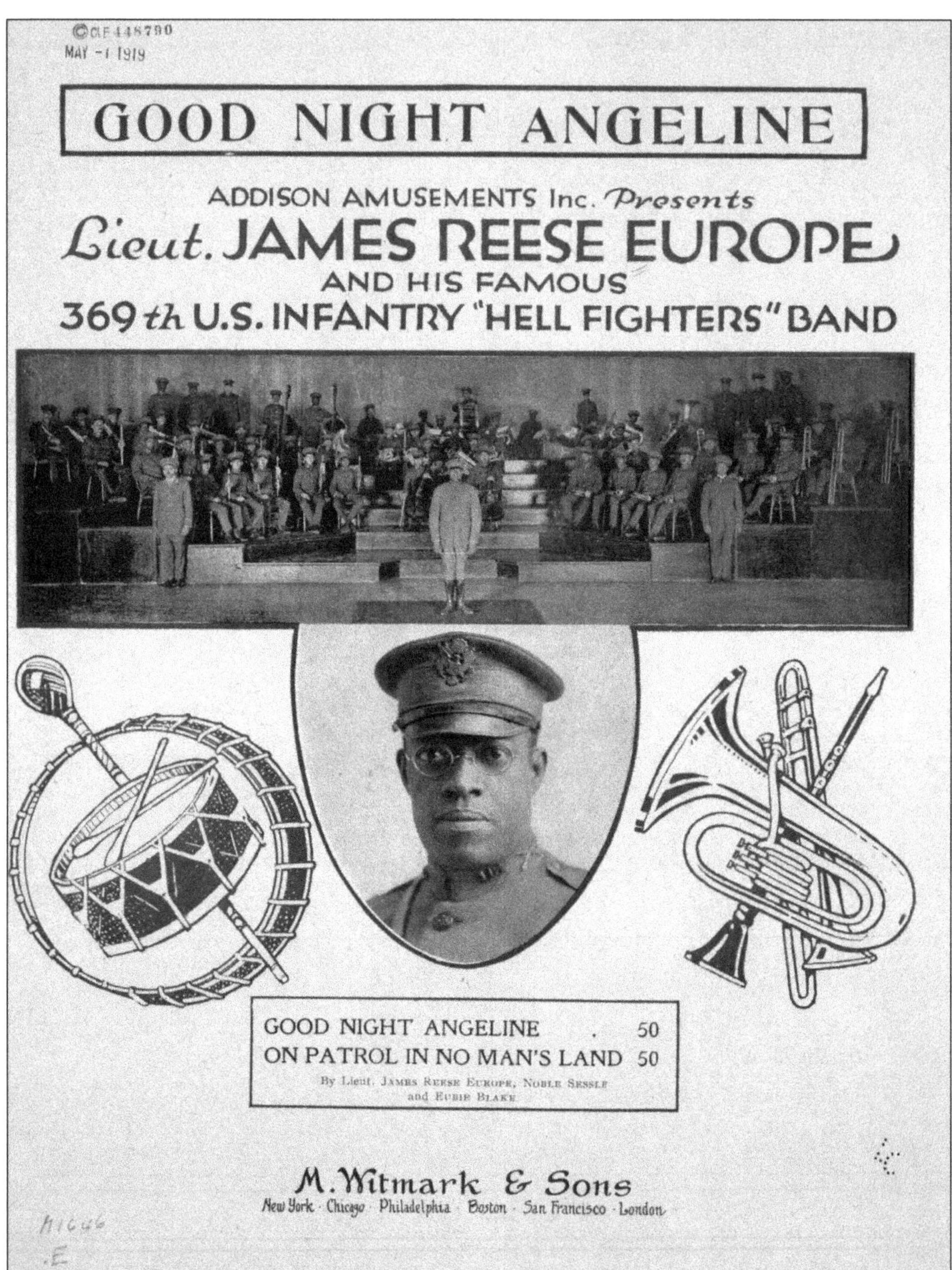

Sheet Music for "Good Night Angeline" by James Reese Europe. The music of James Reese Europe remained popular long after his death in 1919. (Courtesy of the Library of Congress.)

Two

Black Broadway

From the Jazz Age Renaissance through the Era of the Great Depression

For Americans, the second decade of the 20th century was characterized by internal migration and disruptions due to global warfare. Regardless of the causes of the seismic changes associated with this decade, it is worth noting that African Americans carried their music with them, during voluntary and involuntary migrations and in times of war and peace, both at home and abroad. After the Great Migration, they shared their cultural expressions in more urban communities in the American North and, to the delight of European listeners, James Reese Europe shared ragtime and other precursors to jazz during the Great War, in which members of the 369th Regiment and other African American men fought to "make the world safe for democracy." In Washington, DC, a teenaged Duke Ellington, inspired by his family, church, teachers at Armstrong Manual Training High School (later known as just Armstrong High School), pool sharks, and pianists, began trying his hand at graphic arts and musical arts.

DC's Shaw-Howard community also witnessed the emergence of Carter G. Woodson, founder of the Association for the Study of Negro Life and History (now the Association for the Study of African American Life and History) and Howard University professor Alain Leroy Locke as celebrated educators, public scholars, and catalysts for a DC–based renaissance in arts and letters. These activities had direct ties to the companion "New Negro" movement and Harlem Renaissance in New York.

From its heyday in the 1920s through the Great Depression of the 1930s and the United States' entry into World War II in the 1940s, Washington's U Street was the home to "Black Broadway," and artists hailing from Virginia, Maryland, and beyond joined DC natives and earlier transplants in making the greater U Street community an entertainment mecca. Local branches of the National Association for the Advancement of Colored People and the National Urban League joined various literary, fraternal, and benevolent groups in working to improve the quality of life, art, and entertainment in DC, especially when race riots and economic downturn threatened in the postwar era. At times, it seemed that almost nothing—short of civil unrest, war, and economic disaster—could dampen the creative spirits of Washington, DC's jazz artists.

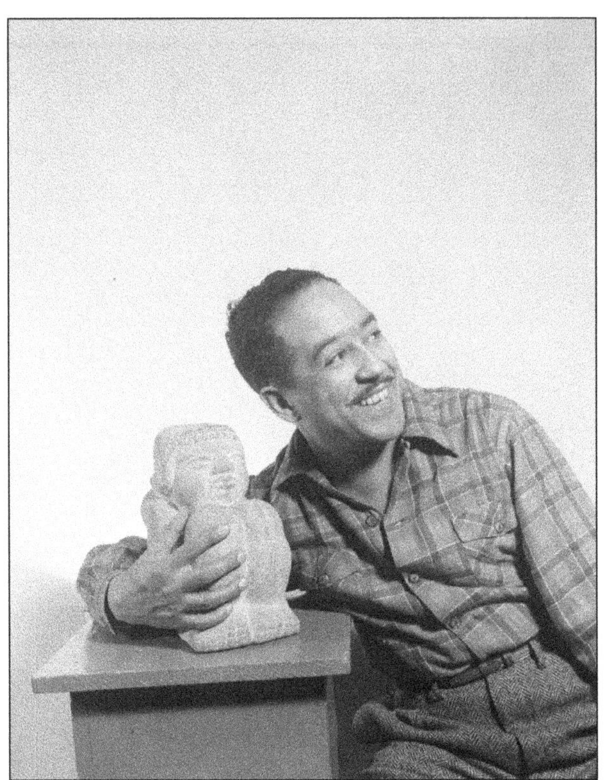

Langston Hughes. Writer James Mercer Langston Hughes (1902–1967) was a leading light during the Jazz Age / Harlem Renaissance and a champion of both blues and jazz influences in America's musical and literary arts. During the 1920s, the aspiring poet lived in Washington, DC, working for a time as a busboy at the Wardman Park Hotel, where, according to a popular legend, he was "discovered" by poet Vachel Lindsay. Hughes published his first volume of poetry, *The Weary Blues*, in 1926. Honoring Hughes's Washington ties, artist and restaurateur Anas "Andy" Shallal chose the name Busboys and Poets for his DC–based business. (Courtesy of the Library of Congress, Carl Van Vechten Collection.)

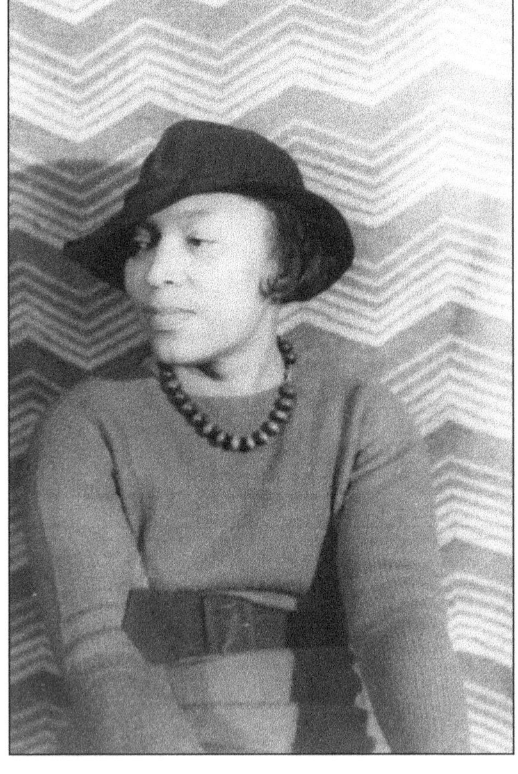

Zora Neale Hurston. Cultural anthropologist and novelist Zora Neale Hurston attended Washington, DC's Howard University, where she cofounded the *Hilltop* student newspaper in 1924. During and beyond the Jazz Age / Harlem Renaissance of the 1920s and 1930s, she collected, studied, anthologized, and was continually inspired by African American cultural expressions, including folktales, spirituals, blues, and jazz. She published her most famous novel, *Their Eyes Were Watching God*, in 1937. (Courtesy of the Library of Congress, Carl Van Vechten Collection.)

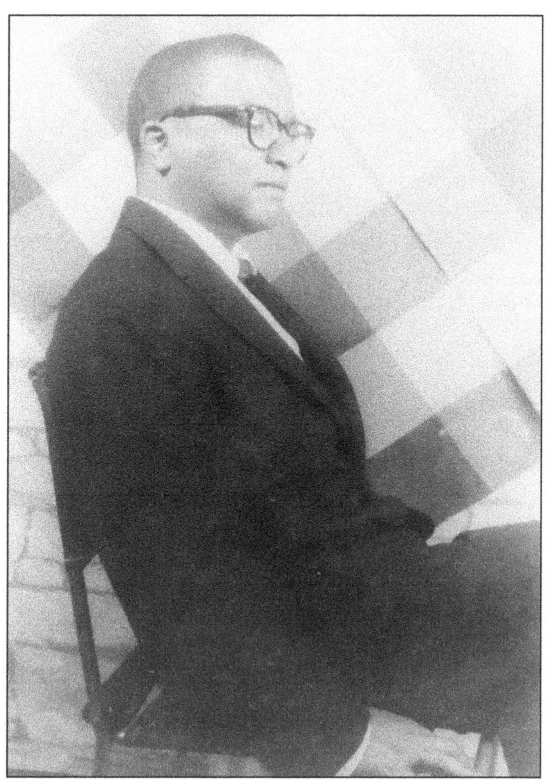

Billy Strayhorn, 1958. Pianist, composer, and arranger William Thomas "Billy" Strayhorn (1915–1967) was a native of Dayton, Ohio. Raised in Pittsburgh, Pennsylvania, he graduated from Westinghouse High School and, by the late 1930s, had established a close working relationship with Duke Ellington. Strayhorn worked with the Ellington Orchestra for more than two decades, composing its signature song, "Take the A Train," in 1939. Among his other well-known works are "Lush Life" and "Something to Live For." On November 29, 2018, the 103rd anniversary of Strayhorn's birth, the Library of Congress announced the acquisition of the Billy Strayhorn Collection, which contains nearly 18,000 documents. Researchers can access the collection by visiting the Library of Congress in Washington, DC. (Courtesy of the Library of Congress, Carl Van Vechten Collection.)

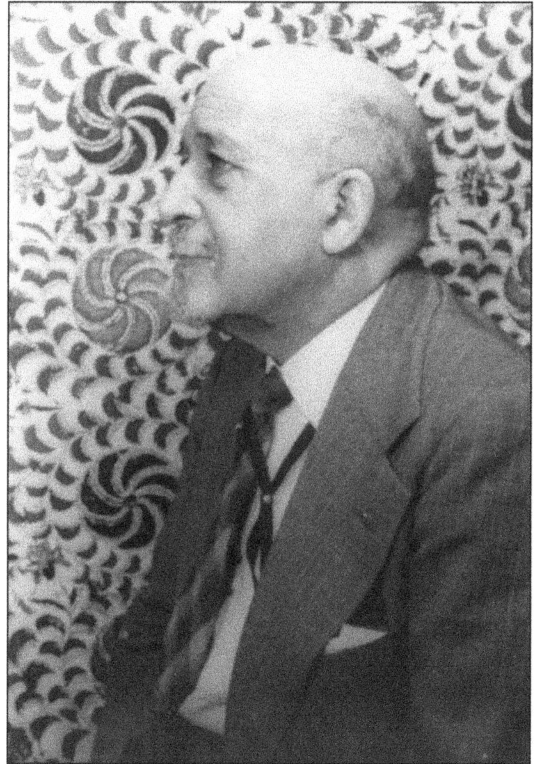

William Edward Burghardt Du Bois. A distinguished historian and sociologist, W.E.B. Du Bois was the first African American to earn a doctorate at Harvard University. In his capacity as the founding editor of the National Association for the Advancement of Colored People's *Crisis Magazine*, he helped advance the careers of Langston Hughes, Zora Neale Hurston, and other writers during the Jazz Age / Harlem Renaissance. (Courtesy of the Library of Congress, Carl Van Vechten Collection.)

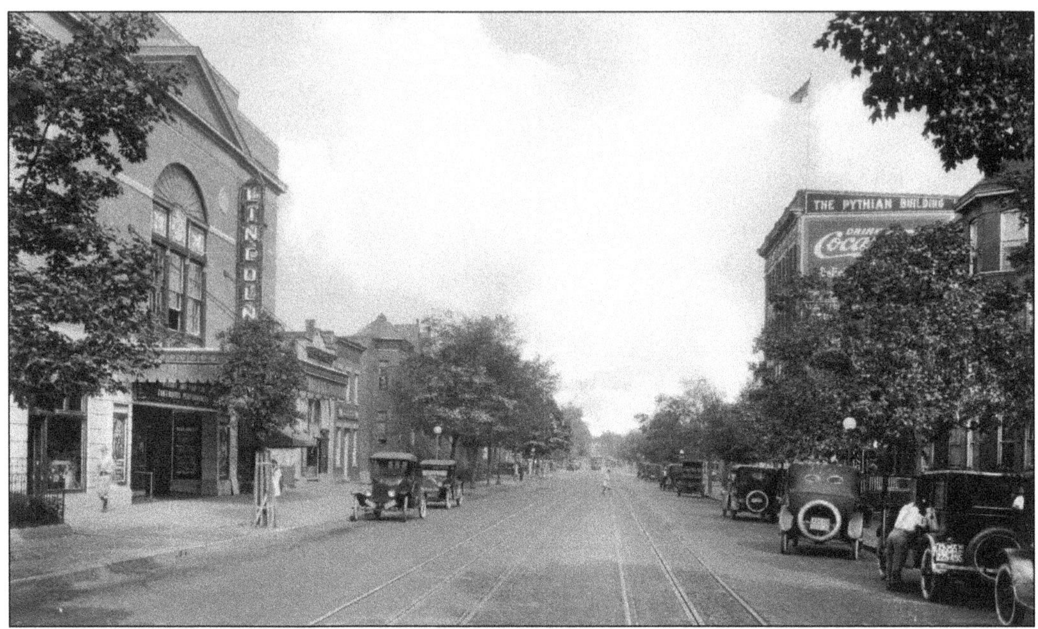

The Lincoln Theatre. Founded in 1922, the Lincoln Theatre (left) is located on U Street and was one of the most popular venues along Washington's fabled "Black Broadway." (Courtesy of the Historical Society of Washington, DC.)

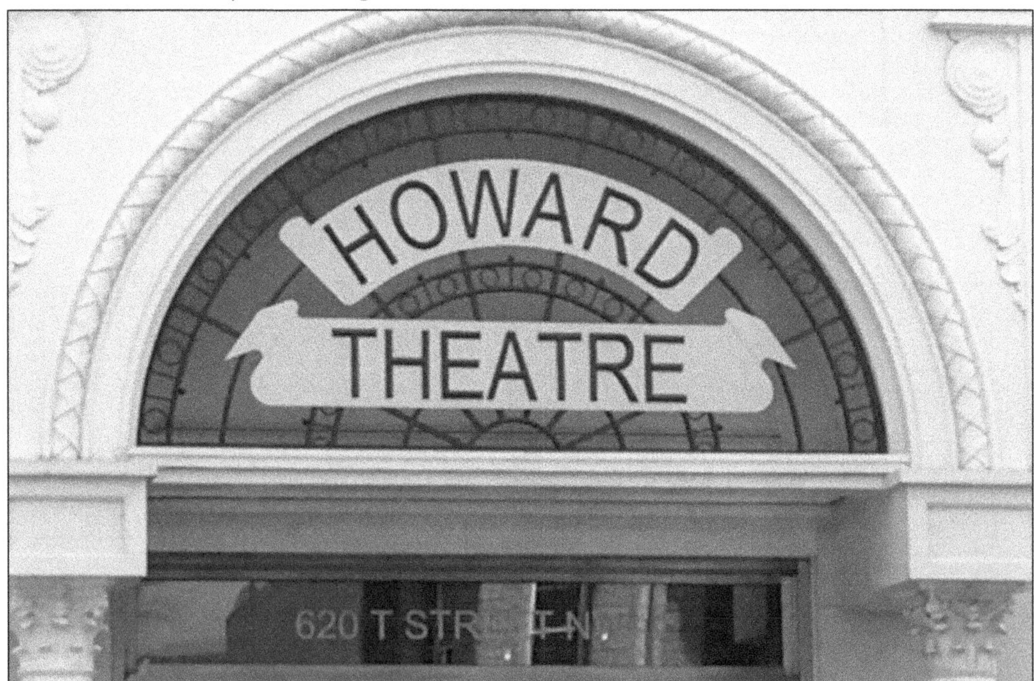

The Howard Theatre Sign. Located on T Street in the Shaw-Howard community, the Howard Theatre opened in 1910. The theater hosted many of the top acts of the 20th century, from Duke Ellington's Orchestra in the 1930s to the Temptations in the 1960s. After a period of dormancy following the riots of 1968 and related neighborhood decline, the beautifully restored theater reopened in a rapidly gentrifying Shaw-Howard community in 2012. (Photograph by Regennia N. Williams.)

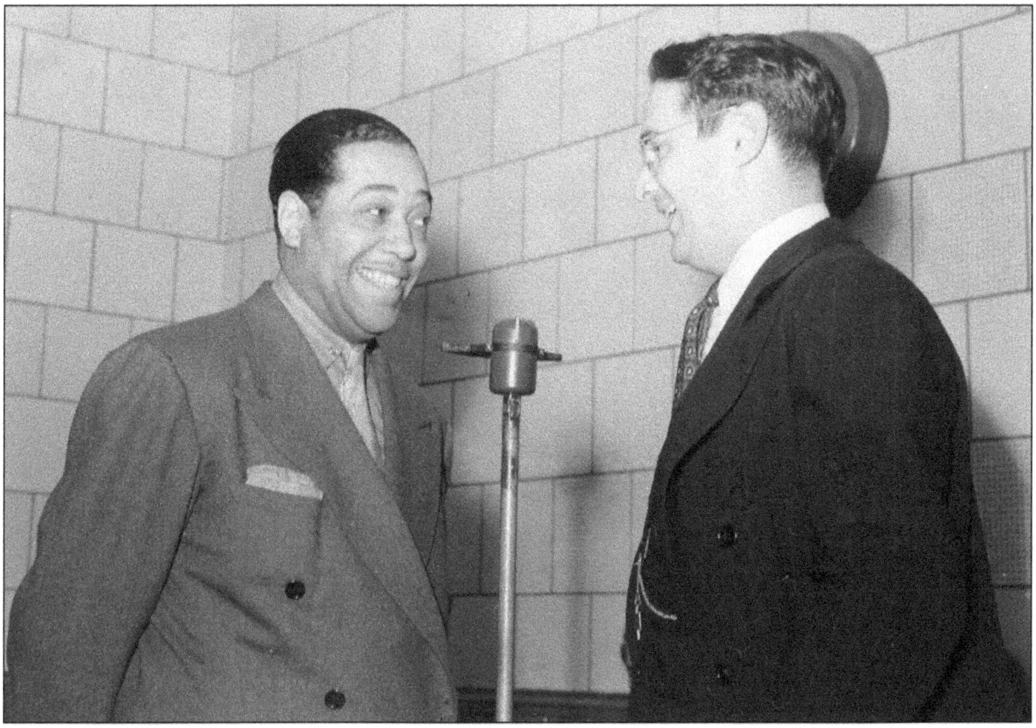

Duke Ellington and William Gottlieb. Duke Ellington (left) is shown here at Washington, DC's WINX radio station with photojournalist William Gottlieb, whose work appeared in the *Washington Post*, *Downbeat* magazine, and other publications. (Courtesy of the William P. Gottlieb / Ira and Leonore S. Gershwin Fund Collection, Music Division, Library of Congress.)

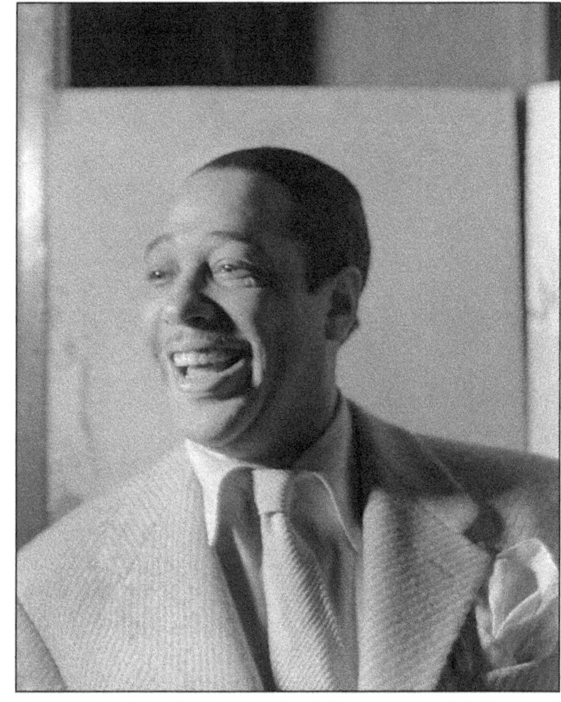

Edward Kennedy "Duke" Ellington. Born in Washington, DC, in 1899, Duke Ellington launched his career as a professional musician while a student at Armstrong Manual Training High School, where he studied art and design. During his orchestra's successful residency at Harlem's Cotton Club and the related Cotton Club radio broadcasts, Ellington gained the national exposure that would propel his group to international fame. In 1943, the orchestra had its Carnegie Hall debut in a performance that included the world premiere of "Come Sunday" in *Black, Brown, and Beige.* Years later, Ellington began to create entire concerts of sacred music, with the first one taking place at San Francisco's Grace Cathedral in 1965. (Courtesy of the William P. Gottlieb / Ira and Leonore S. Gershwin Fund Collection, Music Division, Library of Congress.)

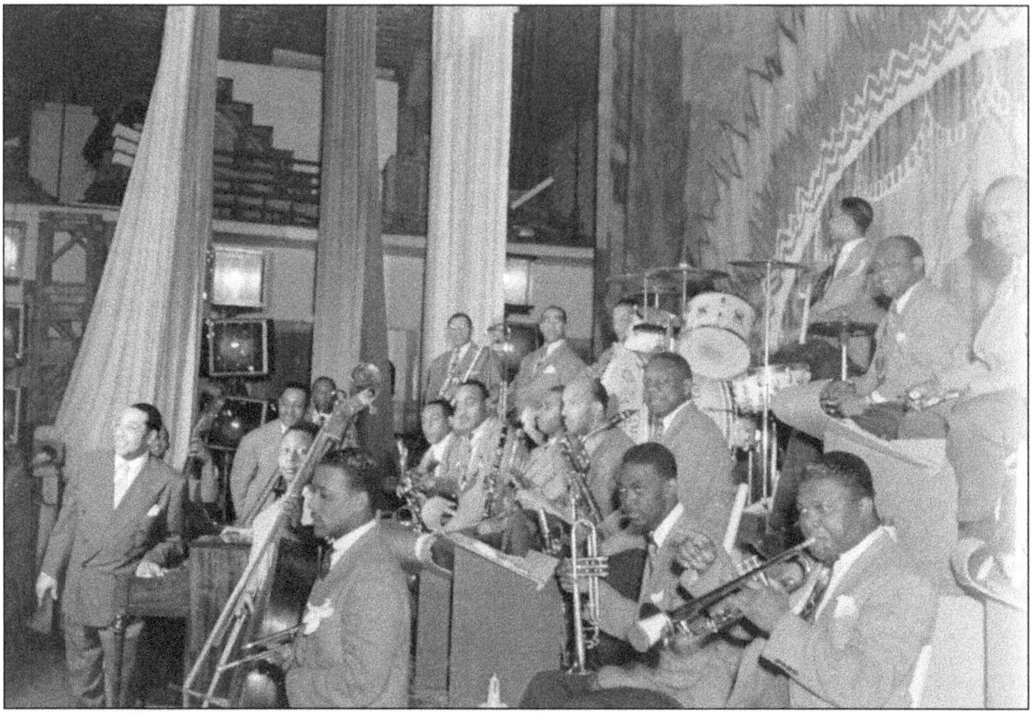

The Duke Ellington Orchestra on the Howard Theatre Stage, Early 1940. One of Washington's favorite sons, Duke Ellington returned often to the city that helped launch his career as a professional bandleader. (Courtesy of the William P. Gottlieb / Ira and Leonore S. Gershwin Fund Collection, Music Division, Library of Congress.)

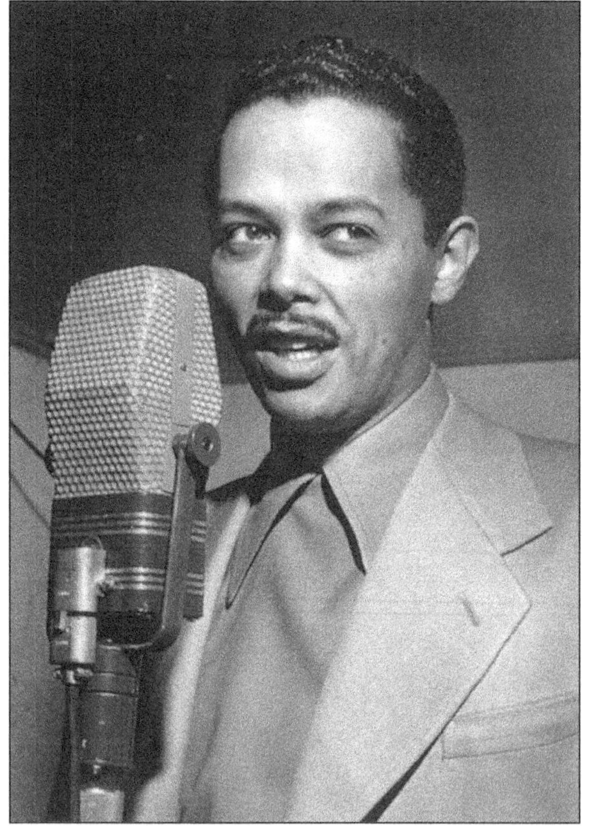

Billy Eckstine. Born in Pittsburgh, William "Billy" Clarence Eckstine (né Eckstein) attended both Armstrong Manual Training School and Howard University in Washington, DC. After achieving local success, he moved to Chicago and for four years served as lead vocalist for the Earl Hines Band. In 1943, he launched the Billy Eckstine Band, one of the first to experiment with bebop arrangements for large groups. (Courtesy of the William P. Gottlieb / Ira and Leonore S. Gershwin Fund Collection, Music Division, Library of Congress.)

Three

Vocalists and Instrumentalists

World War II and the Post–World War II Era

World War II and the beginning of the Cold War era helped set the stage for what would be a transformative period in the history of jazz. Many Washingtonians supported the "Double V Campaign" and joined other Americans in fighting to secure victory over fascism abroad and victory over racism at home. As was the case during World War I, African Americans also joined others in migrating out of the rural South and heading to the urban North and West in search of a better quality of life and improved employment opportunities, which they frequently found in the government sector and in defense industries.

From 1940 to 1950, DC's population increased from 663,091 to 802,178, and the black population for this period rose from 28.2 percent in 1940 to 35 percent in 1950. By comparison, blacks were 9.8 percent of the nation's population in 1940 and 10 percent by 1950. By mid-century, the growing concentration of blacks in Washington, DC, would have a tremendous impact on the jazz scene of the "Chocolate City," and blacks, who would continue to be creators, producers, and consumers of jazz, were not the only beneficiaries of these developments.

Nesuhi and Ahmet Ertegun, sons of the Turkish ambassador to the United States, became two of the most supportive fans and innovative producers of jazz in Washington. As the research of Dr. Maurice Jackson and others shows, the Ertegun brothers also engaged in one of the most obvious and deliberate efforts to celebrate the racial and ethnic diversity of the growing community of jazz musicians in the District of Columbia and the country.

During and after the war years, live performances, recordings, and radio broadcasts made it possible for jazz to be heard in places that had heretofore not been introduced to it. As a result, "America's classical music" was exported, exchanged, blended, reimagined, and, in the process, transformed. Native Washingtonians Buck Hill and Shirley Horn joined the migrant and transient members of Washington's community of musicians—and Miles Davis, Charlie Parker, and Quincy Jones, among other musical giants—in creating new musical styles for global audiences.

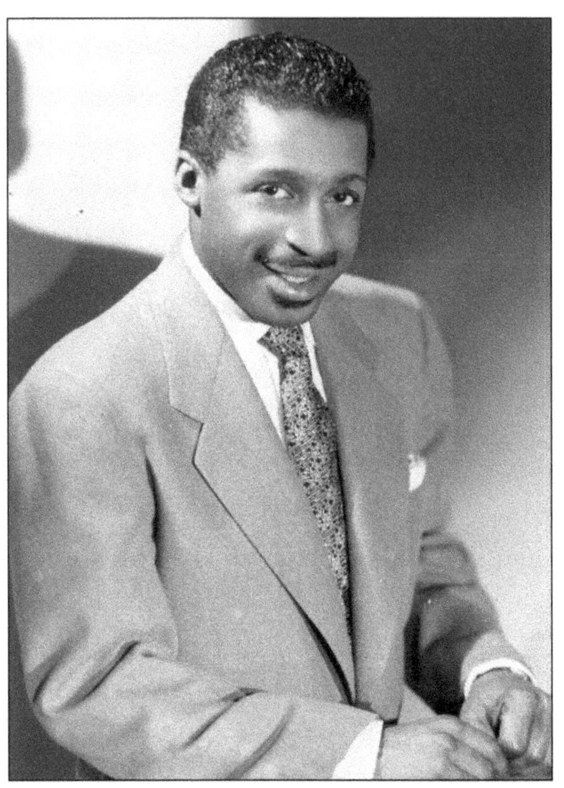

ERROLL GARNER. Pittsburgh-born and largely self-taught, award-winning pianist Erroll Louis Garner (1921–1977) was greatly admired in Washington, DC, jazz circles and across the globe. In a 1990 interview for Dutch television, DC native Shirley Horn identified Erroll Garner as the first pianist who "really blew [her] away" and confessed that she admired his music so much that she would listen to it and play it note for note. (Courtesy of the Pittsburgh Courier Collection–Washington Bureau, Moorland-Spingarn Special Collections, Howard University.)

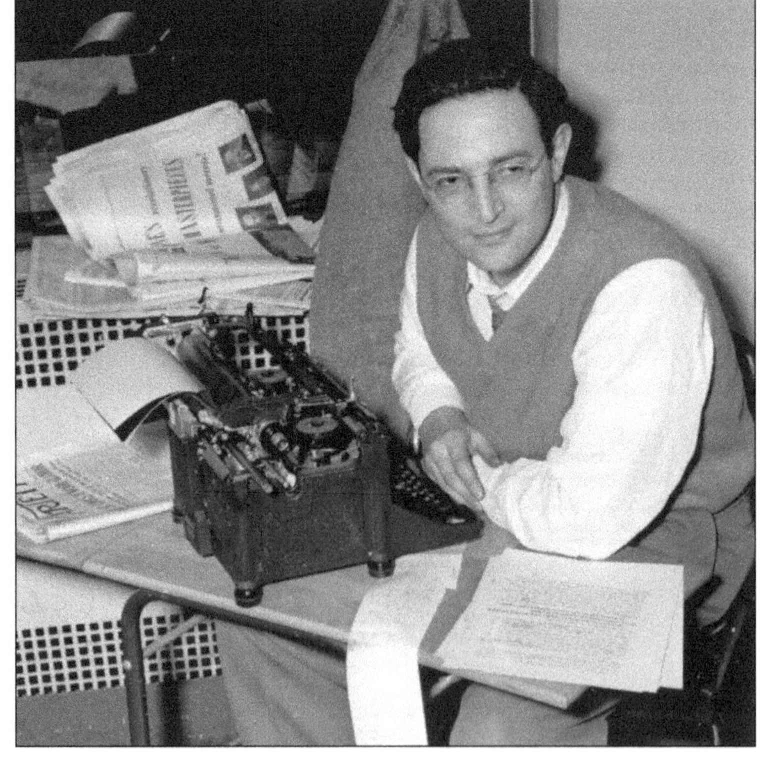

WILLIAM P. GOTTLIEB. Photojournalist William P. Gottlieb was a frequent contributor to the *Washington Post*, *Downbeat* magazine, and other popular publications. His collection, which is now housed at the Library of Congress, includes iconic images of Billie Holiday, Ella Fitzgerald, and other artists of the "Golden Age of Jazz" (c. 1938–1948). (Courtesy of the William P. Gottlieb / Ira and Leonore S. Gershwin Fund Collection, Music Division, Library of Congress.)

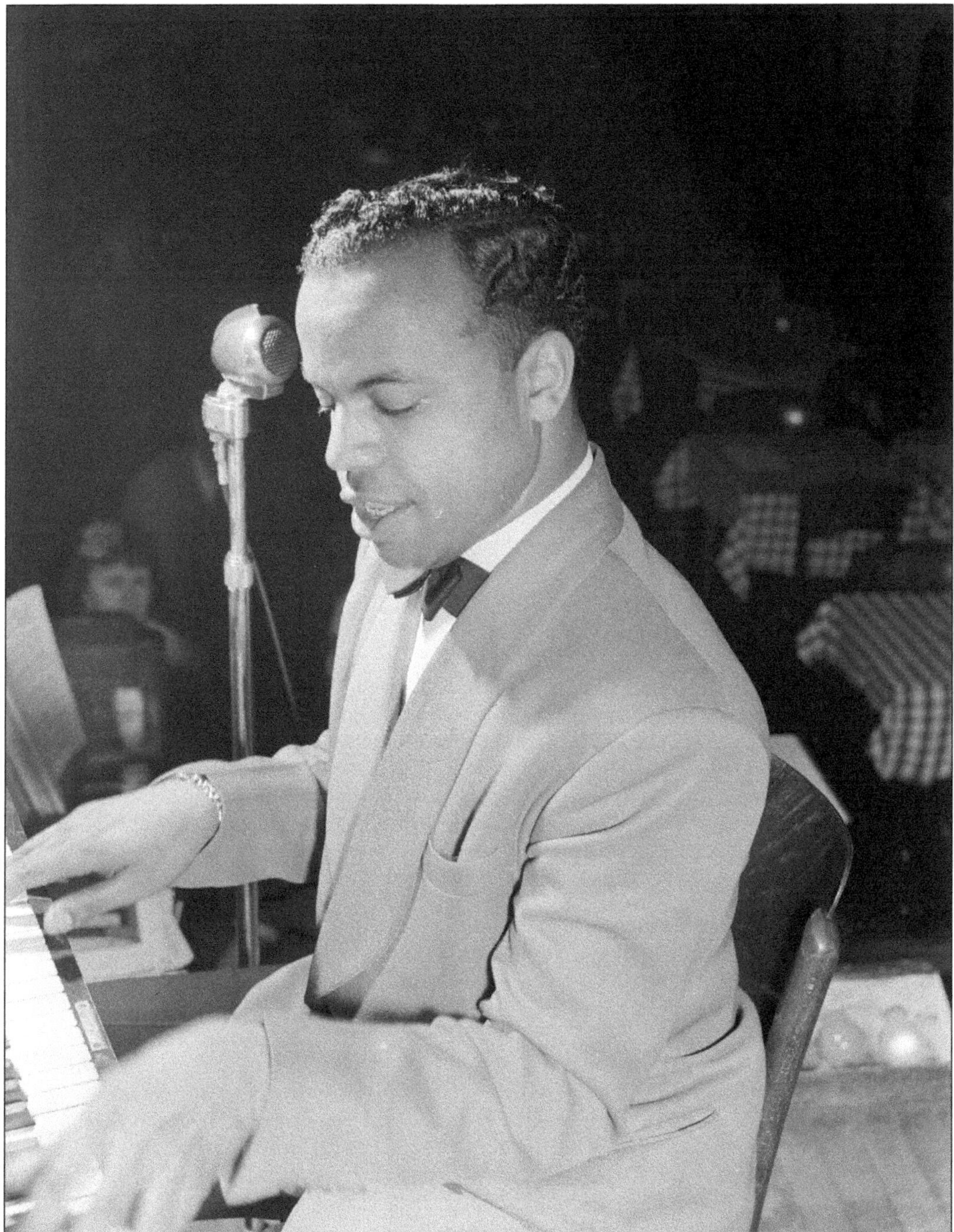

ERSKINE BUTTERFIELD, C. 1942. This image of pianist and vocalist Erskine Butterfield, which appeared in the *Washington Post* in March 1942, is believed to have been taken in the Brown Derby in Washington, DC. Born in Syracuse, New York, in 1913, Butterfield's AllMusic biographer, Eugene Chadbourne, credits the artist with the style known as "cocktail piano," but his recordings also include works in the boogie-woogie and swing styles. He recorded with his Blue Boys ensemble, among others. (Courtesy of the William P. Gottlieb / Ira and Leonore S. Gershwin Fund Collection, Music Division, Library of Congress.)

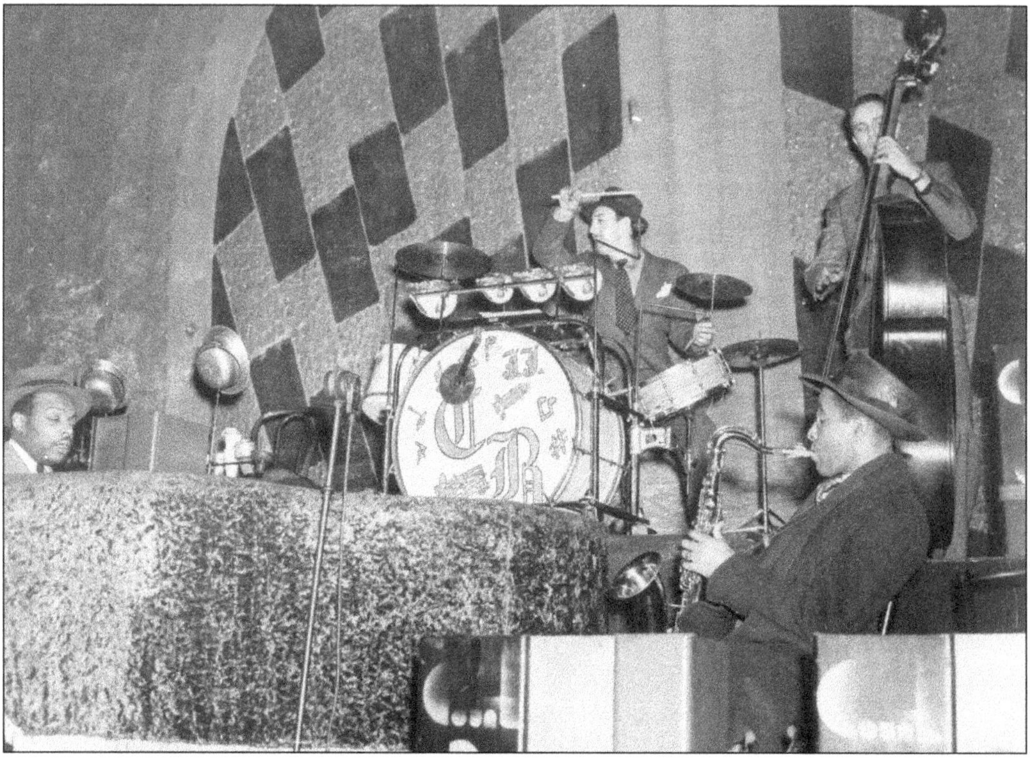

Count Basie at the Howard Theatre, c. 1941. Pianist, composer, and arranger William "Count" Basie (1904–1984) led one of the most influential jazz orchestras of the mid-20th century. A New Jersey native, he recorded with Ella Fitzgerald, Dizzy Gillespie, and many other jazz legends and went on to become a multiple Grammy Award–winning artist. Basie (far left) is pictured with drummer Ray Bauduc, saxophonist Herschel Evans, and bassist Bob Haggart. (Courtesy of the William P. Gottlieb / Ira and Leonore S. Gershwin Fund Collection, Music Division, Library of Congress.)

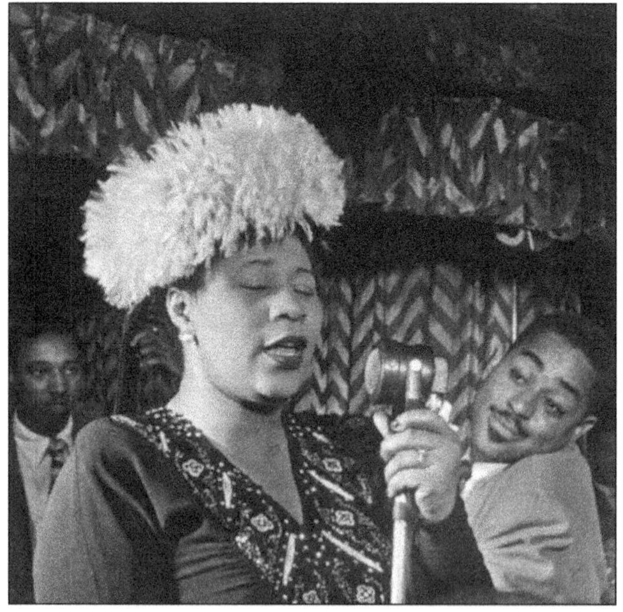

Ray Brown, Ella Fitzgerald, and Dizzy Gillespie, c. 1947. Newport News, Virginia, native Ella Fitzgerald is shown here with bassist Ray Brown (left) and trumpeter Dizzy Gillespie at New York's Downbeat Club. Fitzgerald's manuscript materials are among the many jazz-related collections at the Smithsonian Institution's National Museum of American History. (Courtesy of the William P. Gottlieb / Ira and Leonore S. Gershwin Fund Collection, Music Division, Library of Congress.)

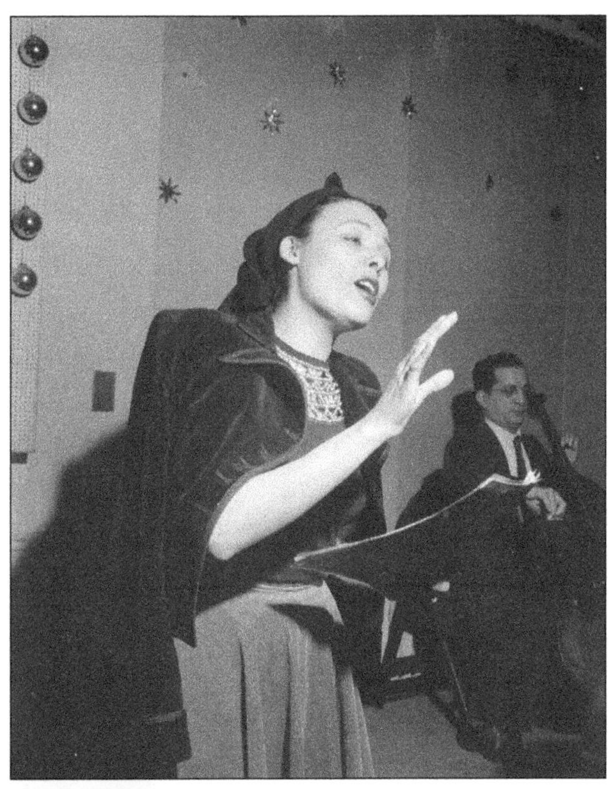

Lena Horne, c. 1946. Vocalist and actress Lena Mary Calhoun Horne (1917–2010) became one of the highest-paid African Americans in Hollywood in the 1940s. A Cotton Club alumna, she won popular acclaim for her role in *Stormy Weather*, and the theme song from that 1943 wartime classic remained in her repertoire for decades. In the 1960s, she became a vocal supporter of the civil rights movement, participating in the 1963 March on Washington and other protests in the Deep South. Her rendition of "A Christmas Surprise" (with piano accompaniment by close friend Billy Strayhorn) is included on the CD for Duke Ellington's *Concert of Sacred Music*, part of *Duke Ellington, The Centennial Edition: Complete RCA Victor Recordings: 1927–1973*. (Courtesy of the William P. Gottlieb / Ira and Leonore S. Gershwin Fund Collection, Music Division, Library of Congress.)

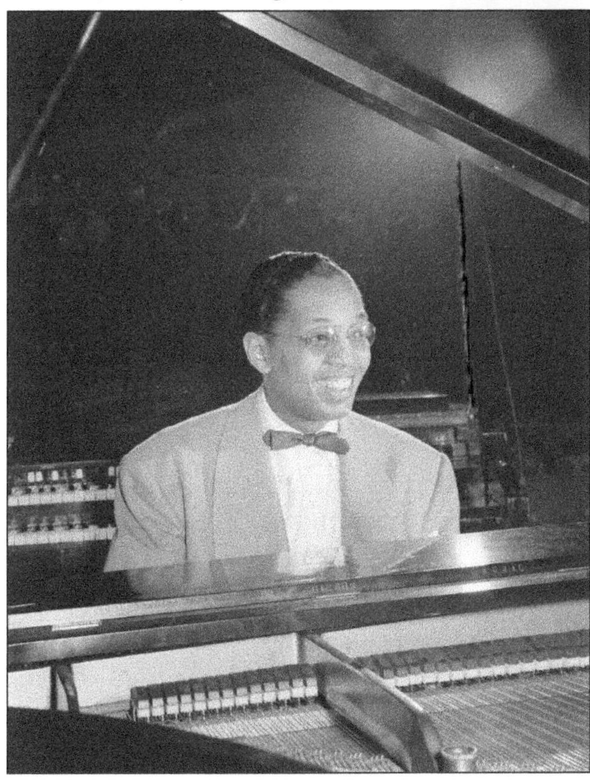

Dr. Billy Taylor, c. 1947. A native of North Carolina, Billy Taylor was a longtime resident of Washington, an award-winning pianist and educator, a prolific composer, and a jazz advocate in the truest sense of the word. He attended Paul Laurence Dunbar High School in Washington, DC, and completed his undergraduate studies at Virginia State College. A producer of jazz programming for radio and television, Taylor was the recipient of two Peabody Awards and an Emmy Award. For many years, he was the artistic director for jazz at the John F. Kennedy Center for the Performing Arts. (Courtesy of the William P. Gottlieb / Ira and Leonore S. Gershwin Fund Collection, Music Division, Library of Congress.)

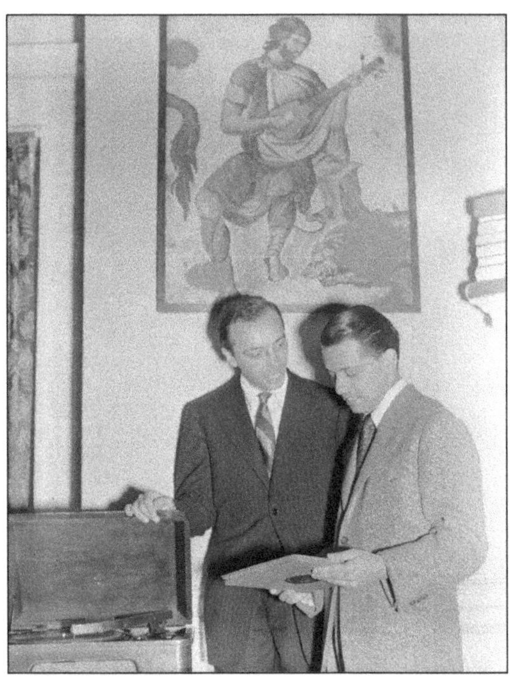

The Ertegun Brothers at the Turkish Embassy. When Ahmet (right) and Nesuhi Ertegun moved to Washington, DC, in 1935, these sons of the Turkish ambassador had already been introduced to the music of such artists as Duke Ellington and Cab Calloway. Born in Istanbul, Turkey, the brothers fell in love with African American music, including gospel and jazz, and frequented the DC venues where they could hear the music performed live. In 1947, Ahmet cofounded (with Herb Abramson) Atlantic Records, one of the most important labels for jazz and rhythm and blues. (Courtesy of the William P. Gottlieb / Ira and Leonore S. Gershwin Fund Collection, Music Division, Library of Congress.)

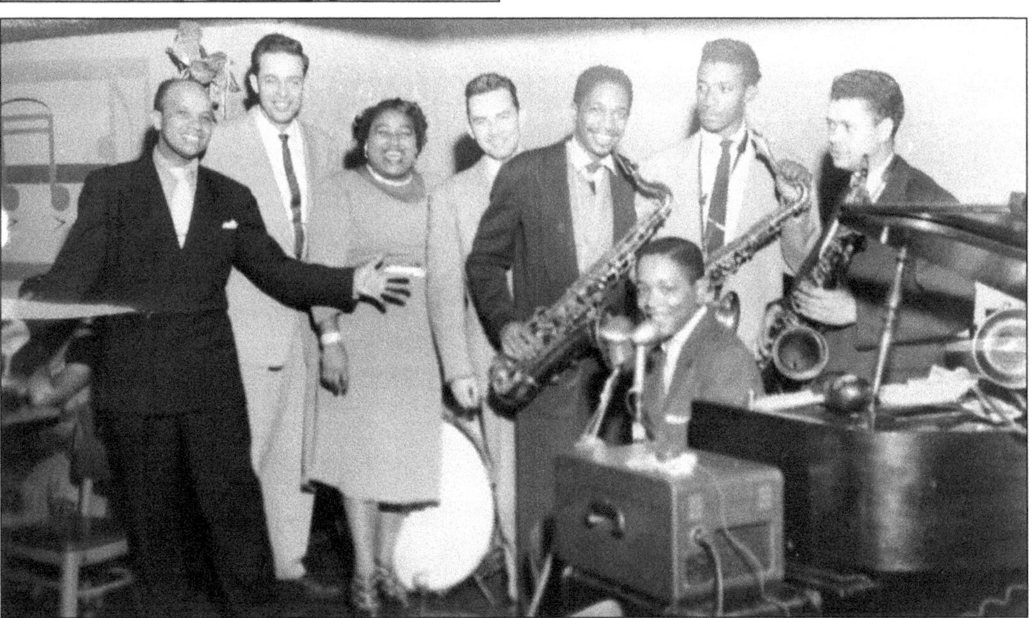

Buck Hill. Saxophonist Roger Wendell "Buck" Hill (far right) is shown after a "Battle of the Sax's" (sic) event at DC's Club 20-11 at 17th Street NW. With him are the other contestants, along with Harold "Hal" Rosen (second from left), who was the entertainment columnist for the *Washington Daily News*, and members of the newspaper's staff. Born in Washington in 1927, Hill studied both piano and saxophone as a child. He graduated from Armstrong Technical High School in 1945 and served in the US Army as "Bandsman Saxophone No. 349" through 1946. Hill went on to perform with many other jazz greats, including Dizzy Gillespie, Max Roach, the Shirley Horn Trio, and Miles Davis. (Courtesy of the Pittsburgh Courier Collection–Washington Bureau, Moorland-Spingarn Special Collections, Howard University.)

ADELE GIRARD, 1930. Harpist Adele Girard is shown here performing at the Turkish Embassy in Washington, DC, at a jazz event hosted by the Ertegun brothers. She was one of the first harpists to have a successful career in jazz. In 1937, she married clarinetist Joe Marsala, and they both continued to perform and record through the late 1940s. (Courtesy of the William P. Gottlieb / Ira and Leonore S. Gershwin Fund Collection, Music Division, Library of Congress.)

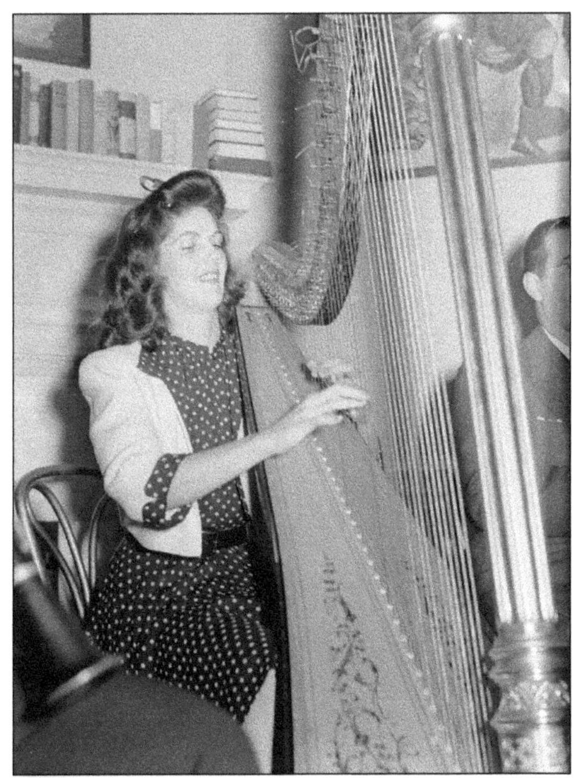

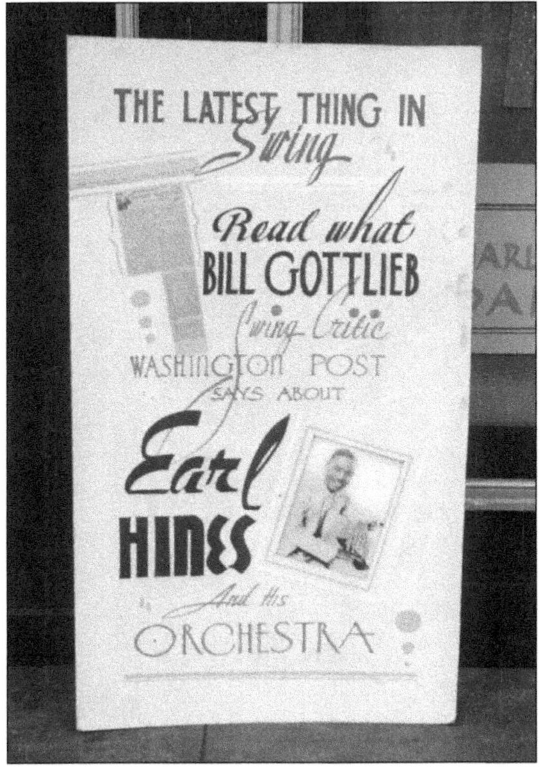

POSTER ADVERTISING PERFORMANCE BY EARL HINES. Earl "Fatha" Hines, a Pennsylvania native, was one of the earliest national artists to emerge from the Pittsburgh jazz scene and one of the greatest jazz pianists of the 20th century. The band that he led for more than 20 years helped launch the career of former Washingtonian Billy Eckstine and other top artists. (Courtesy of the William P. Gottlieb / Ira and Leonore S. Gershwin Fund Collection, Music Division, Library of Congress.)

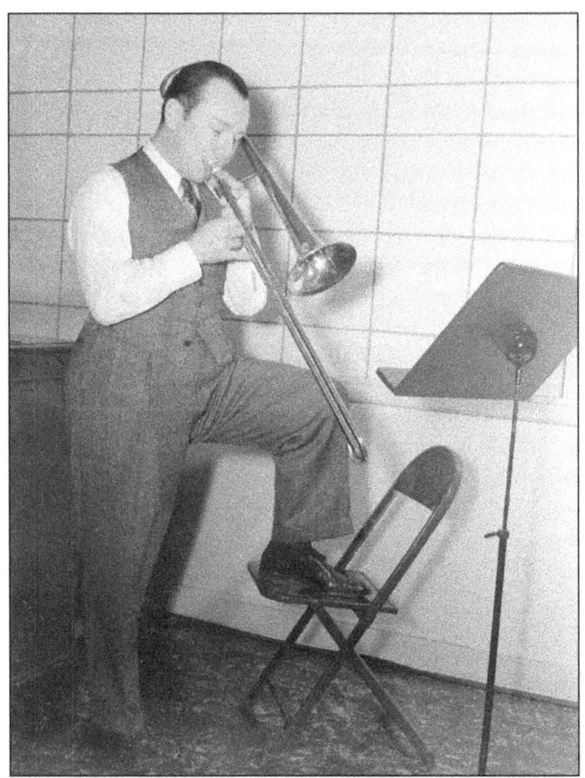

Toby Tyler. This image of saxophonist Toby Tyler appeared in the *Washington Post* in December 1941. He recorded with The Band that Played the Blues and Woody Herman and His Orchestra. (Courtesy of the William P. Gottlieb / Ira and Leonore S. Gershwin Fund Collection, Music Division, Library of Congress.)

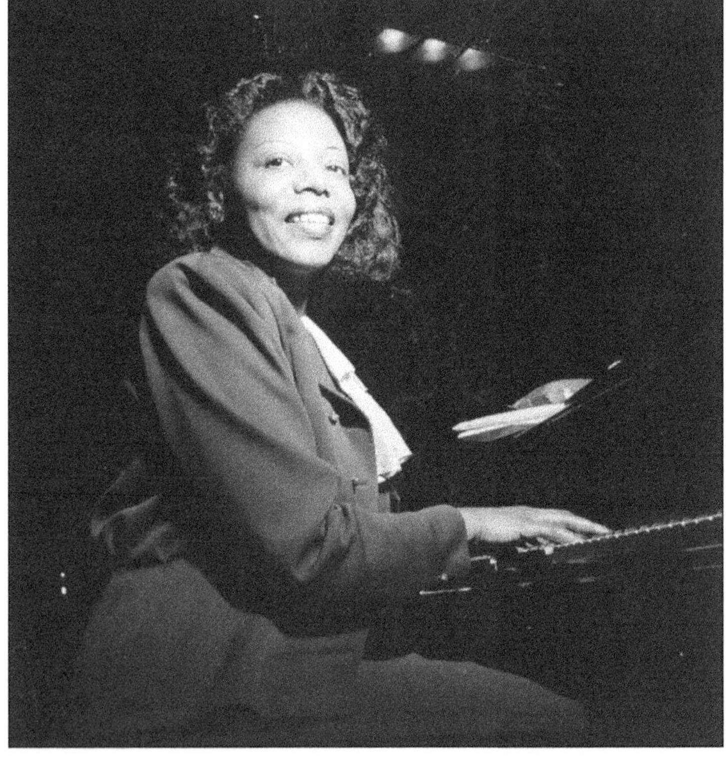

Mary Lou Williams at the Howard Theatre. Born in Atlanta, Georgia, in 1910, Mary Lou Williams was a prolific composer and arranger of blues and jazz. Like Duke Ellington, toward the end of her life, she composed liturgical works in the jazz idiom. (Courtesy of the William P. Gottlieb / Ira and Leonore S. Gershwin Fund Collection, Music Division, Library of Congress.)

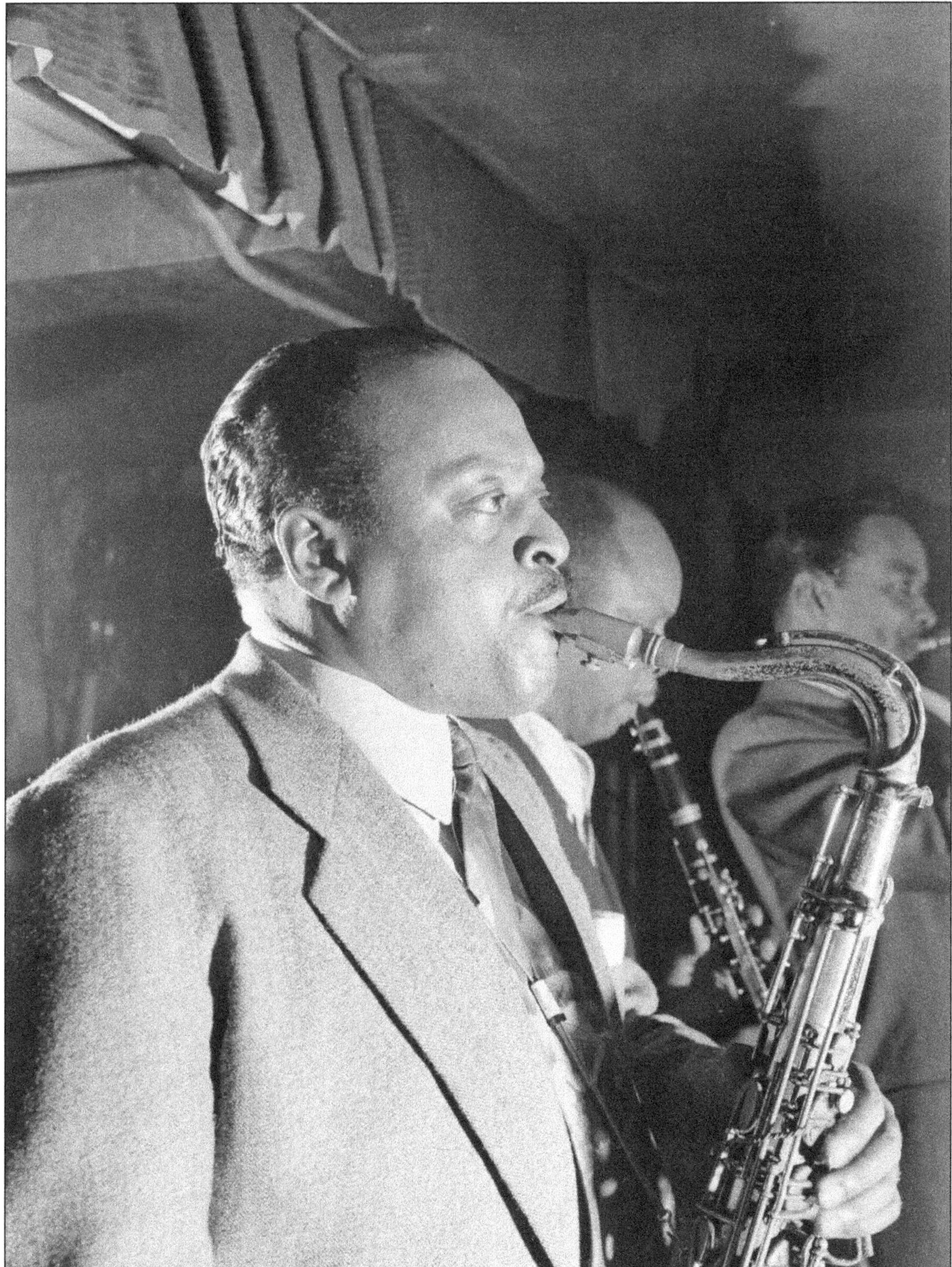

BEN WEBSTER PERFORMS AT CLUB BENGASI, 1946. Ben Webster (1909–1973) became the lead tenor saxophonist for the Duke Ellington Orchestra and performed with the group from 1940 to 1943. (Courtesy of the William P. Gottlieb / Ira and Leonore S. Gershwin Fund Collection, Music Division, Library of Congress.)

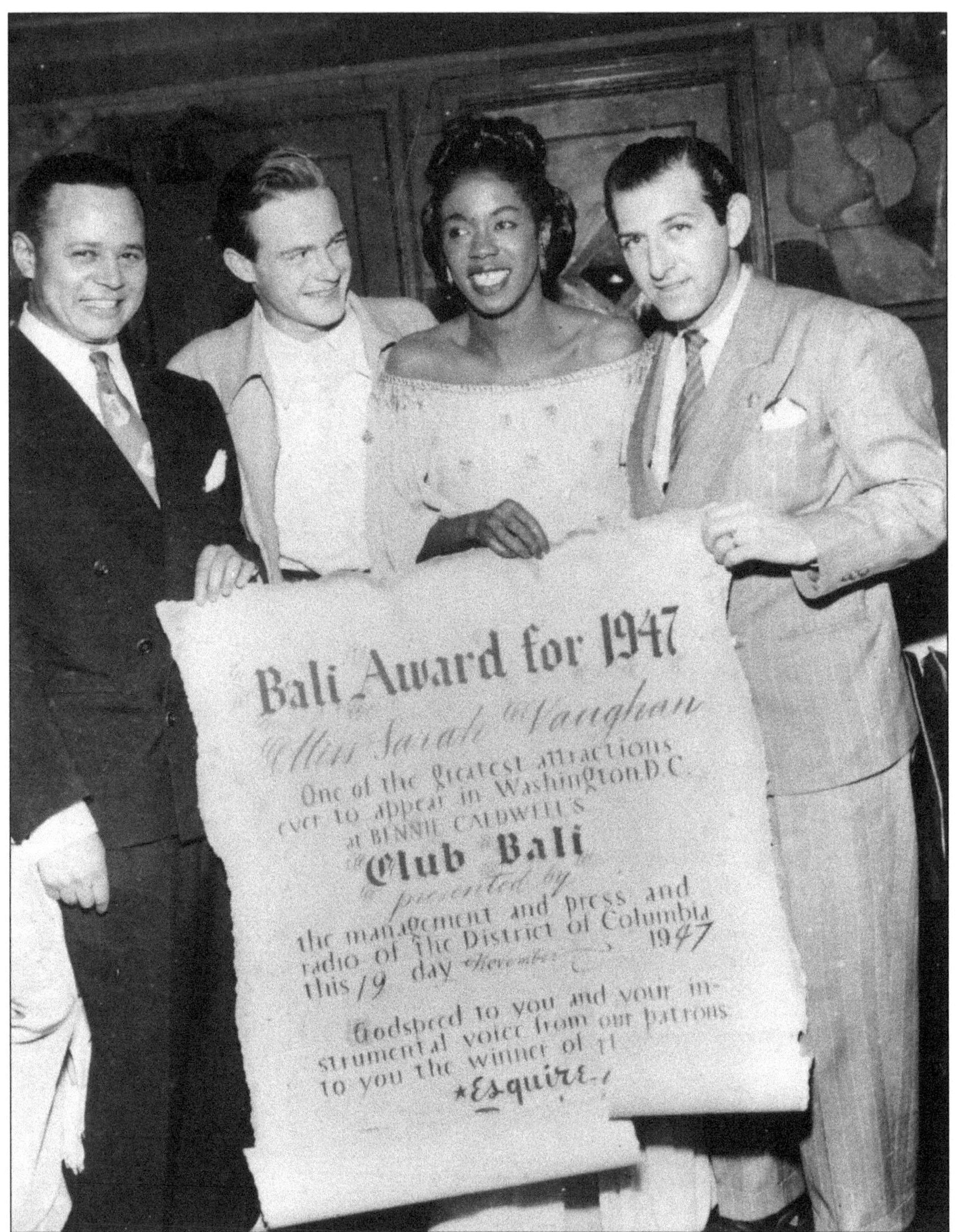

SARAH VAUGHAN ACCEPTING AWARD AT CLUB BALI, 1947. During the 1940s, vocalists Sarah Vaughan and Billy Eckstine performed with the Earl Hines Band. After Eckstine left the Hines group, Vaughan joined Eckstine's new group in 1944 and then launched her solo career in 1945. Known to fans as "Sassy" and "The Divine One," Vaughan went on to become an award-winning soloist, receiving multiple Grammy Awards and the Jazz Master Award from the National Endowment for the Arts. (Courtesy of the Pittsburgh Courier Collection–Washington Bureau, Moorland-Spingarn Special Collections, Howard University.)

Four

"Is That Jazz?" Cultural Nationalism, Revolutionary Rhetoric, and Musical Metamorphoses

In the wake of World War II and during the subsequent Cold War era, the seeds for cultural, political, and social revolutions were sown, especially among African Americans. At the same time, a brilliant team of legal experts with ties to Howard University helped to make Washington, DC, the headquarters for a national struggle to end discrimination in education, housing, and employment. If the unanimous 1954 Supreme Court ruling in the case of *Brown v. Board of Education* signaled the end of legally sanctioned Jim Crow segregation in public schools, then it can be said that the Civil Rights Act of 1964 and the founding of the Black Panther Party in 1966 were indicative of the strained relations between and differing perspectives of integrationist and nationalist groups in the United States.

Americans were not alone in grappling with these matters, since many African and Asian peoples were anxious to throw off the yoke of colonialism. In Asia, the escalation of the Vietnam War continued through the 1960s, and the growing Anti-Apartheid Movement in South Africa meant that Americans of all races had reason to be concerned about social, political, and cultural change in other parts of the world.

In the second half of the 20th century, American music mirrored many of the changes mentioned above, and Washington's jazz was no exception. The changes were evident as individual jazz musicians used art to protest perceived injustices at home and abroad or explored Eastern religions and philosophies while pursuing enlightenment and peace. Interestingly, at the urging of Congressman Adam Clayton Powell, the US State Department chose to place jazz at the center of a Cold War–era propaganda campaign that allowed jazz luminaries to serve as cultural ambassadors, traveling the world and sharing their music with new audiences and, as some critics have suggested, putting a happy face on American race relations.

No amount of propaganda could quell the urban unrest of the late 1960s, however, as more than 100 race riots erupted across the country. In the unrest that engulfed the Shaw-Howard community in the immediate aftermath of the April 4, 1968, assassination of the Rev. Dr. Martin Luther King Jr., Washingtonians mourned the loss of a dozen lives, millions of dollars in property damage, and perhaps an equal amount in lost revenue from travel and tourism. Healing would come slowly, but in time, DC jazz experienced a renaissance of its own. From "The Godfather of Soul" James Brown's "Say it Loud, I'm Black and I'm Proud" (1968) to bluesologist Gil Scott-Heron's "Johannesburg" (1975) and "Is That Jazz?" (1981), the genre-crossing messages in black music of the time continue to inspire and influence Metro DC performers and listeners alike. The artists pictured in this chapter were among those who lived, made, and/or continue to make some of the music history associated with this era.

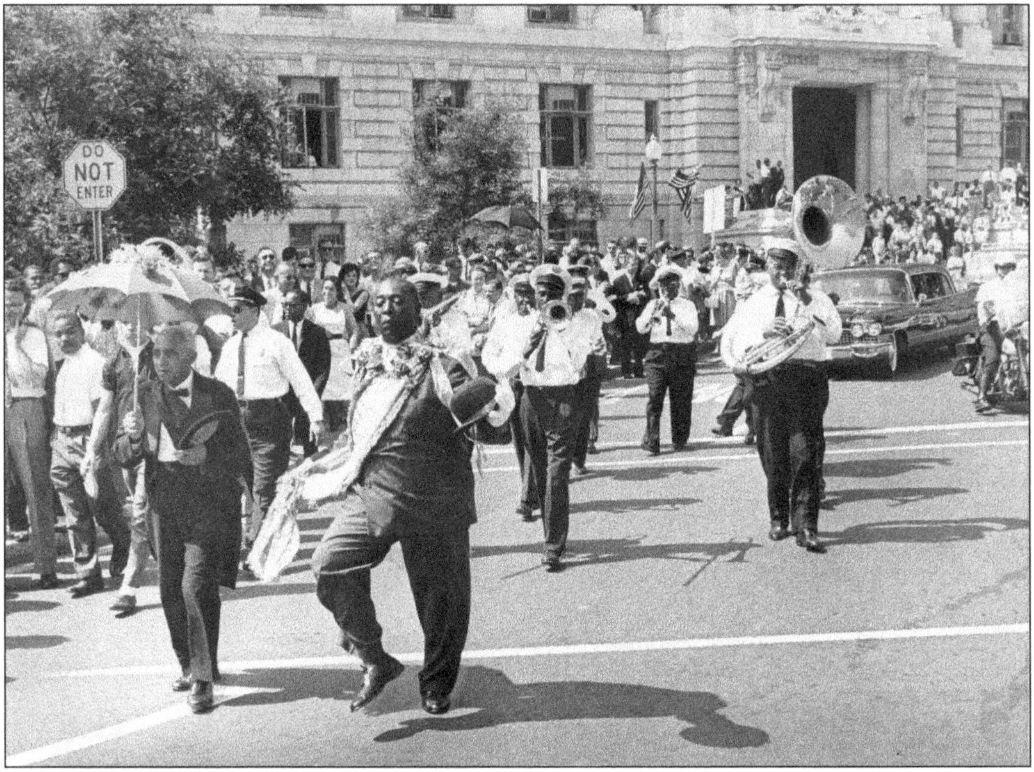

THE EUREKA JAZZ BAND MARCHES TO THE WHITE HOUSE, 1962. The Eureka Jazz Band of New Orleans leads the march during the parade for the May 1962 International Jazz Festival. (Courtesy of the DC Public Library, Washington Star Newspaper Collection.)

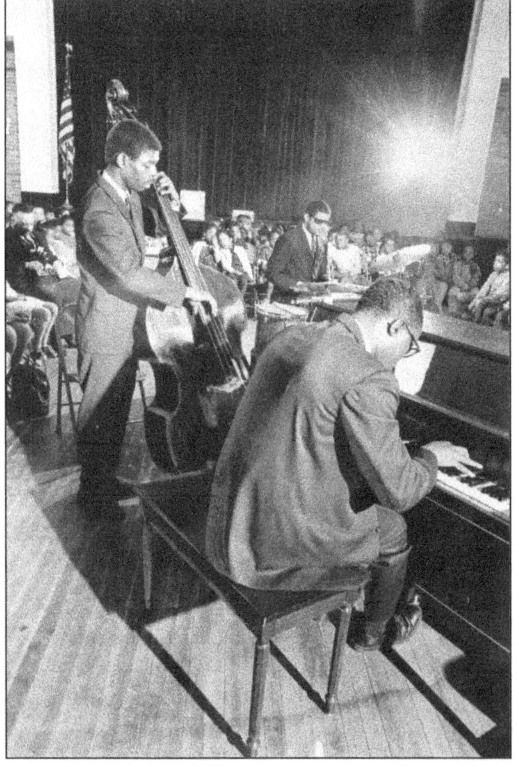

THE MARSHALL HAWKINS JAZZ TRIO, 1967. Bassist Marshall Hawkins, drummer Harold Chavis, and pianist Frank Maxwell perform at the Petworth Public School in February 1967. (Courtesy of the DC Public Library, Washington Star Newspaper Collection.)

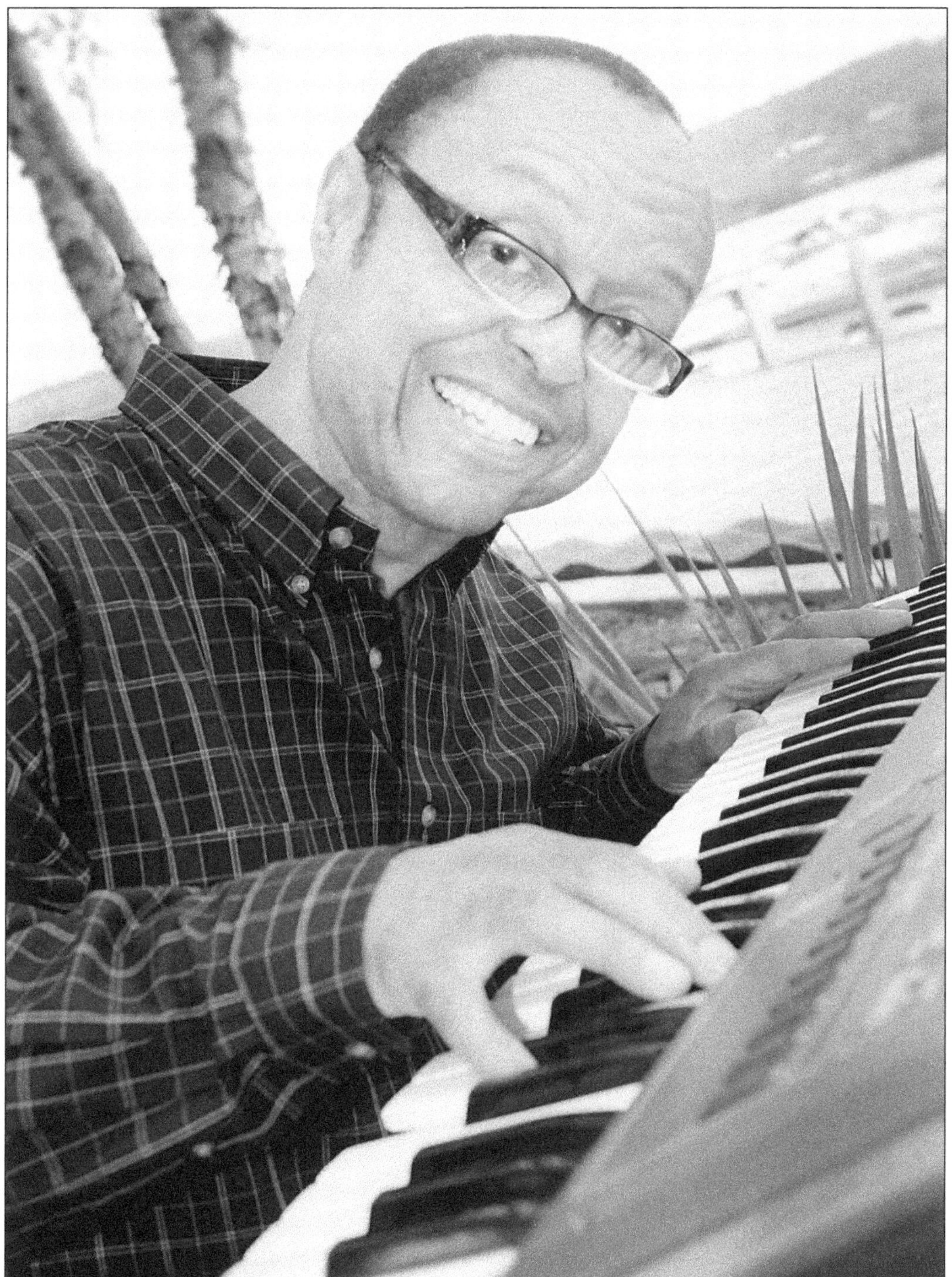

COLLINS JOHNSON, 2018. Organist Collins Johnson has worked as a classroom educator, in corporate America, and as an entrepreneur. He can be heard throughout the DMV performing on the Hammond organ. Johnson, a member of DC Legendary Musicians Inc., is pictured here in the Yards Park on the Capitol Riverfront in Washington, DC. (Photograph by Nathaniel Rhodes; courtesy of DC Legendary Musicians Inc.)

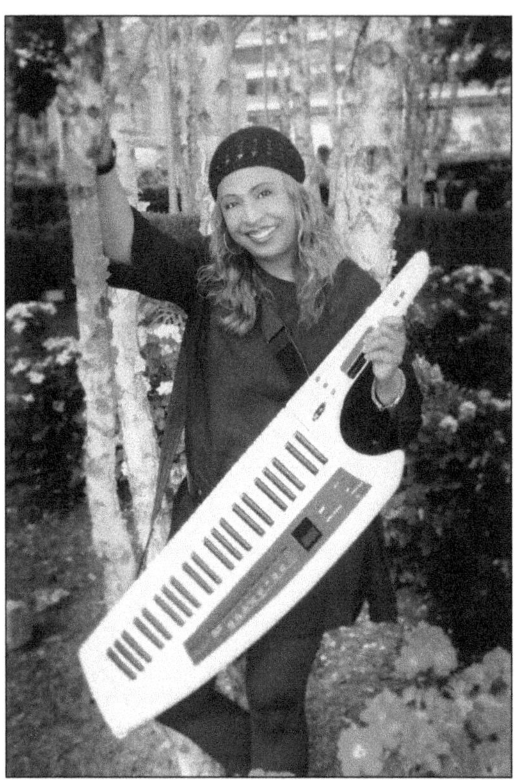

Kim Jordan, 2018. An accomplished pianist, composer, and arranger in her own right, Howard University alumna Kim Jordan served as the music director for Gil Scott-Heron for more than 20 years. As versatile as she is energetic, Jordan, an ordained minister, is also well versed in the music of the church. She is pictured here in the Yards Park on the Capitol Riverfront in Washington, DC. Jordan was interviewed for the 2017–2018 Washington, DC, Jazz Oral History Project. (Photograph by Nathaniel Rhodes; courtesy of DC Legendary Musicians Inc.)

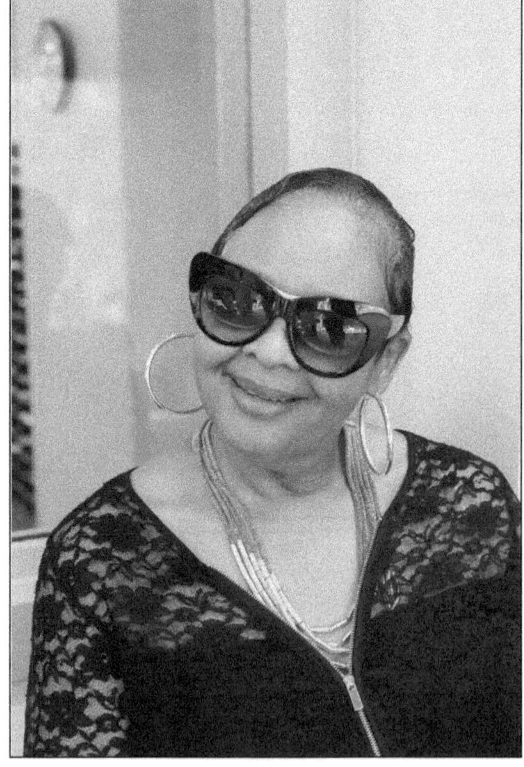

Ida Campbell, 2018. Ida Campbell was born in Guantanamo Bay, Cuba, and raised in Washington, DC. She has been singing all her life, and her Blues Nations Soul Band was formed in 2008. She recently added the Eclectic Soul Band to create a distinctive blues, R&B, and jazz sound. Campbell is the programmer responsible for WPFW Radio's Friday afternoon *Don't Forget the Blues* program. (Photograph by Lawrence A. Randall; courtesy of DC Legendary Musicians.)

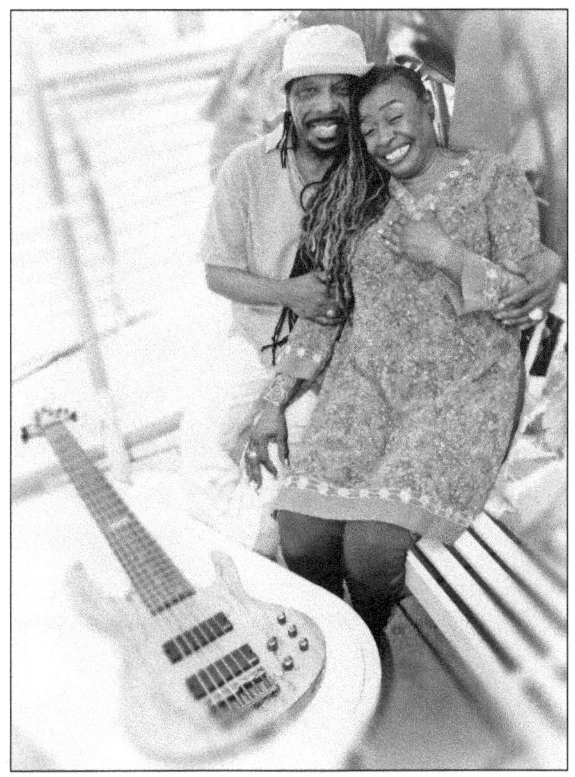

JAMES CUNNINGHAM AND LINDA EVANS, 2018. Guitarist James Cunningham and vocalist Linda Evans have thrilled audiences throughout the DMV with their special blend of various subgenres of great black music. They are pictured here in the Yards Park on the Capitol Riverfront in Washington, DC. Both are members of DC Legendary Musicians Inc. (Photograph by Nathaniel Rhodes; courtesy of DC Legendary Musicians Inc.)

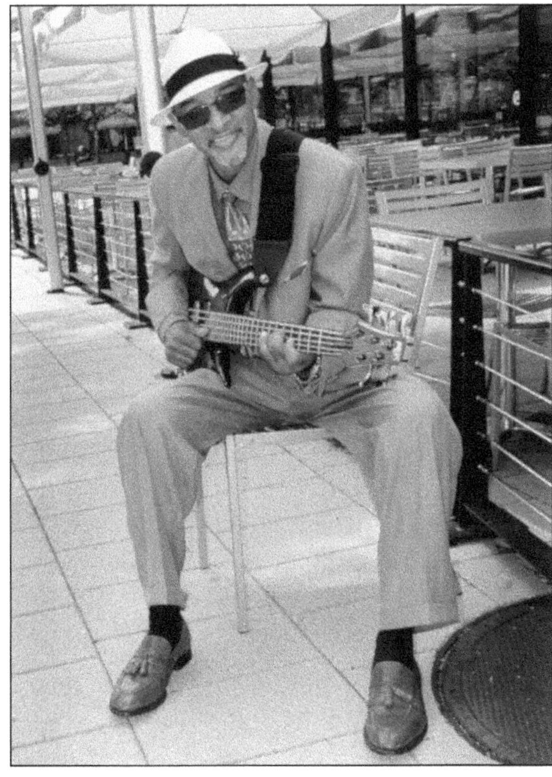

TONY FOSTER, 2018. Bass guitarist Tony Foster is pictured here at the Yards Park on the Capitol Riverfront in Washington, DC. Foster is a member of DC Legendary Musicians Inc. (Photograph by Nathaniel Rhodes; courtesy of DC Legendary Musicians Inc.)

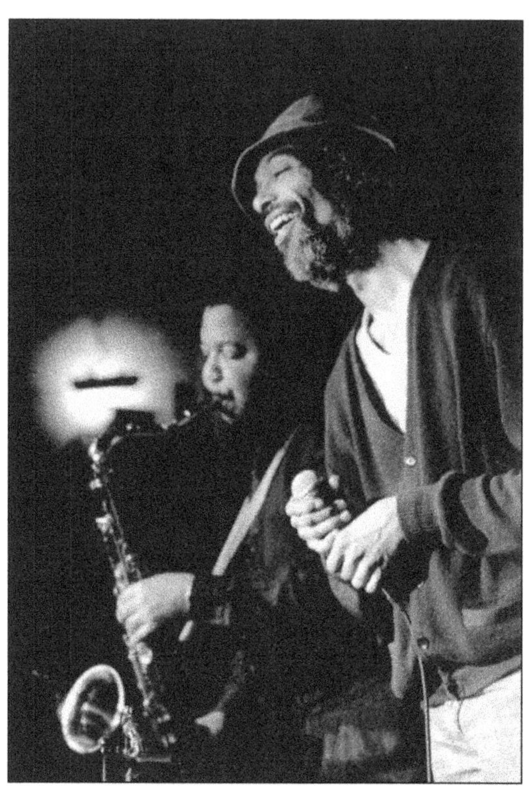

Gil Scott-Heron and Ron Holloway. Poet, spoken word artist, pianist, vocalist, former Federal City College faculty member, and "bluesologist" Gil Scott-Heron is pictured here with saxophonist Ron Holloway during a February 26, 1989, performance at the Blues Alley jazz and supper club. (Photograph by Michael Wilderman.)

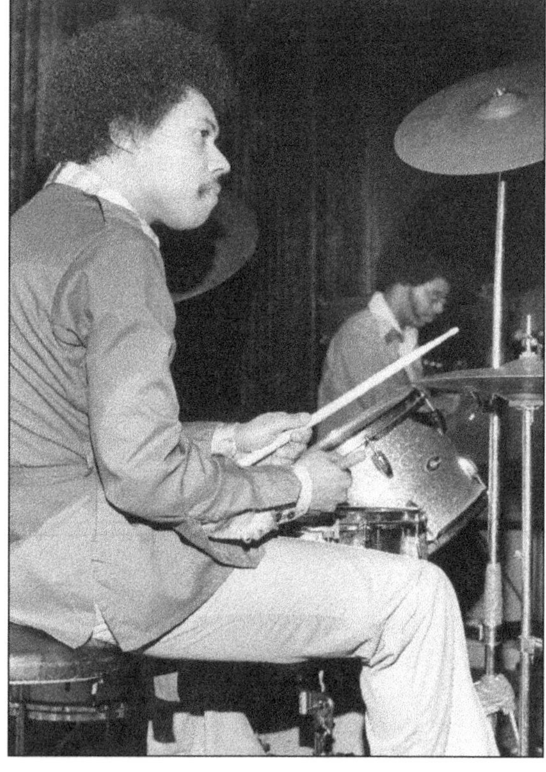

Howard Chichester on Drums. A native Washingtonian and product of District of Columbia Public Schools, Howard Chichester distinguished himself as a gifted percussionist early in life and performed at Howard University, Harold's Rogue and Jar, the Chevy Chase Club, Top O' the Foolery, and other local venues. Among his most memorable performances is a Left Bank Jazz Society concert with pianist Donny Hathaway, bassist Marshall Smith, and Ernie Douglas on vibes around 1965. Chichester was interviewed for the 2017–2018 Washington, DC, Jazz Oral History Project. (Courtesy of Howard Chichester.)

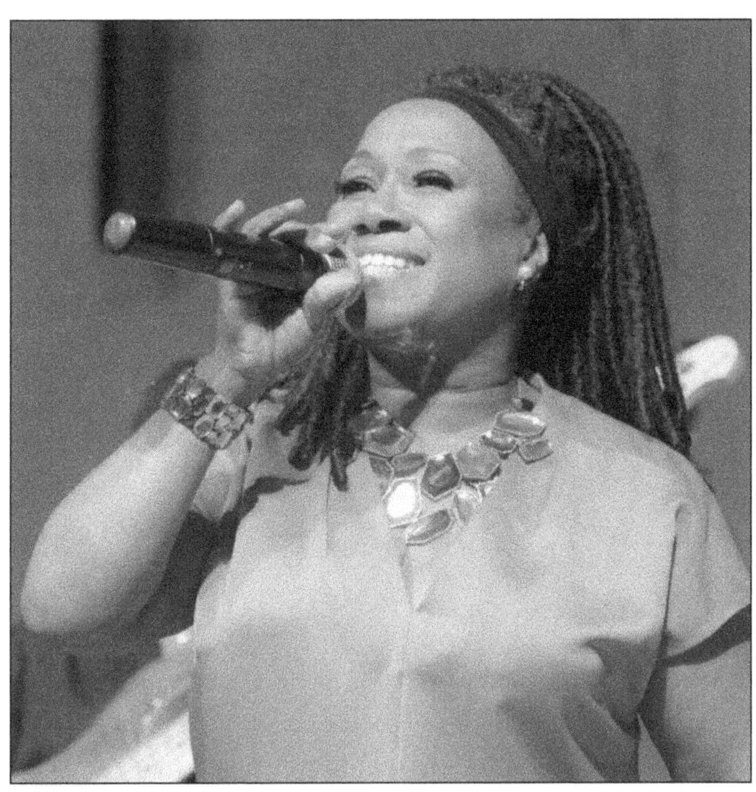

Shirleta Settles. The consummate entertainer, Shirleta Settles has won acclaim for her vocal performances and storytelling. A favorite with audiences at the Blue Monday Blues concerts at Washington, DC's Westminster Presbyterian Church, Settles has also performed at the Hamilton, the White House, and Wolf Trap, among other venues. (Photograph by Lawrence A. Randall.)

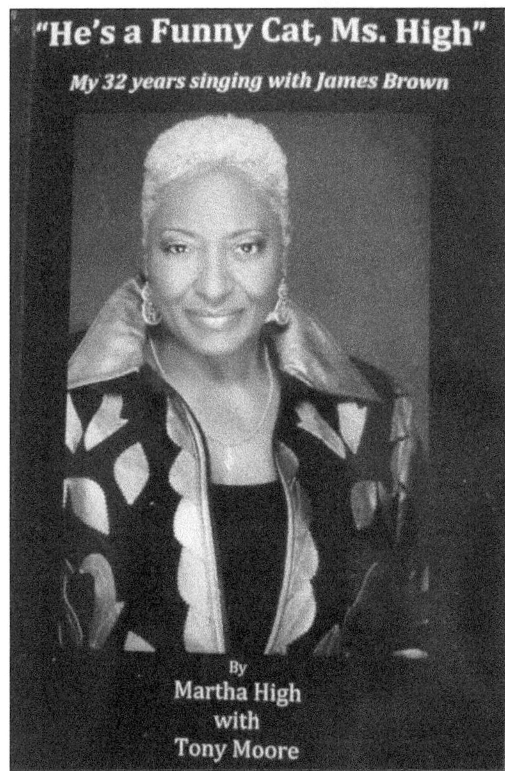

Martha High. Vocalist, Virginia native, and author Martha High attended Roosevelt High School in Washington, DC. She is a former member of the Jewels and was a longtime background singer for James Brown. Her book, *He's a Funny Cat, Ms. High: My 32 Years Singing with James Brown*, was published in 2017. (Courtesy of Martha High.)

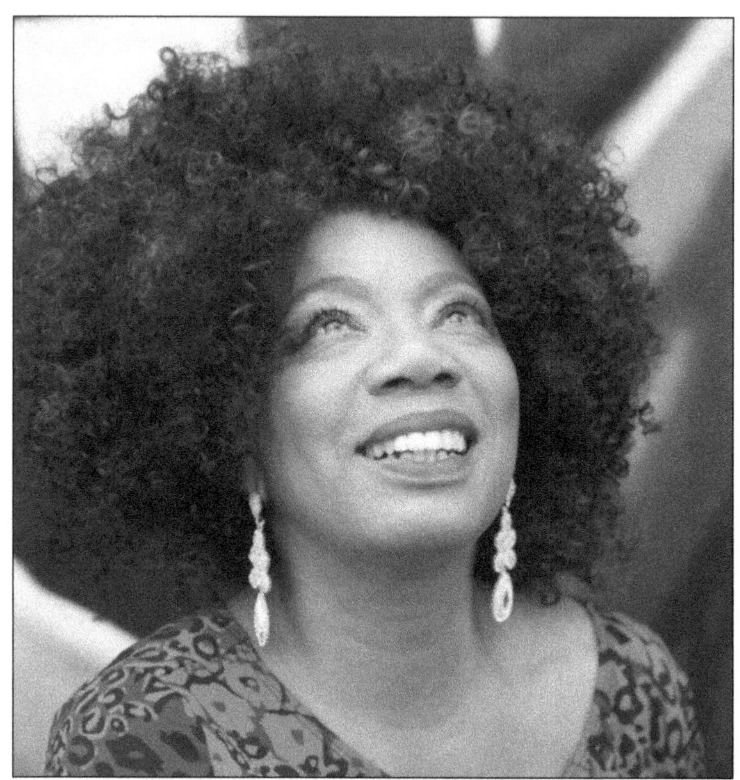

Coniece Washington. Vocalist Coniece Washington is at home performing both jazz and gospel. A New Jersey native and US Army veteran, Washington's performance credits include appearances at Twins Jazz, Mr. Henry's, and Jazz Night at Westminster Presbyterian Church. Washington was interviewed for the 2017–2018 Washington, DC, Jazz Oral History Project. (Courtesy of Coniece Washington.)

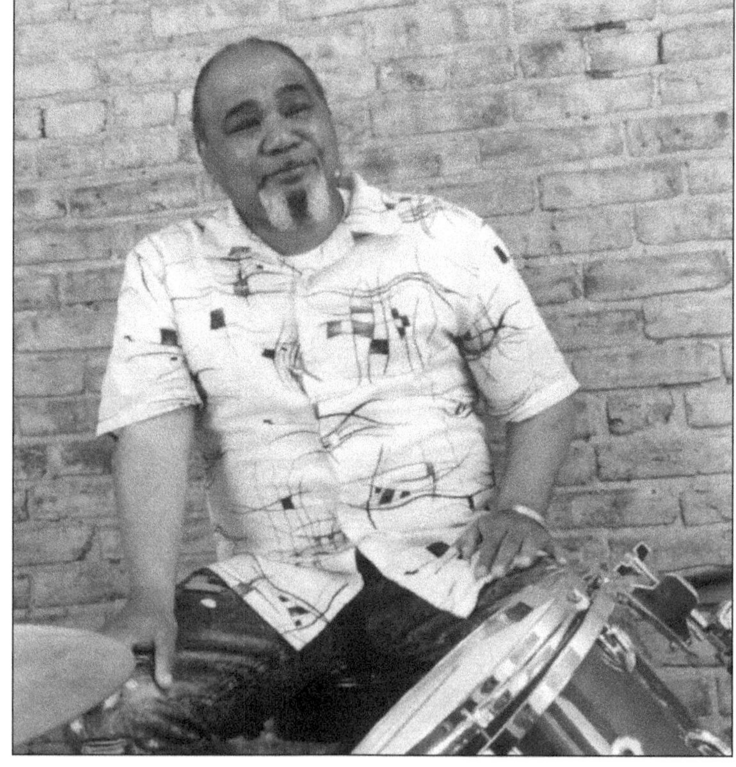

Donald Edwards, 2017. Drummer Donald "Big Foot" Edwards is pictured here in the Chinatown Gibson Guitar showroom following his May 2017 interview for the Washington, DC, Jazz Oral History Project. Edwards has performed at DC's Takoma Station Tavern and other area venues. (Photograph by Regennia N. Williams.)

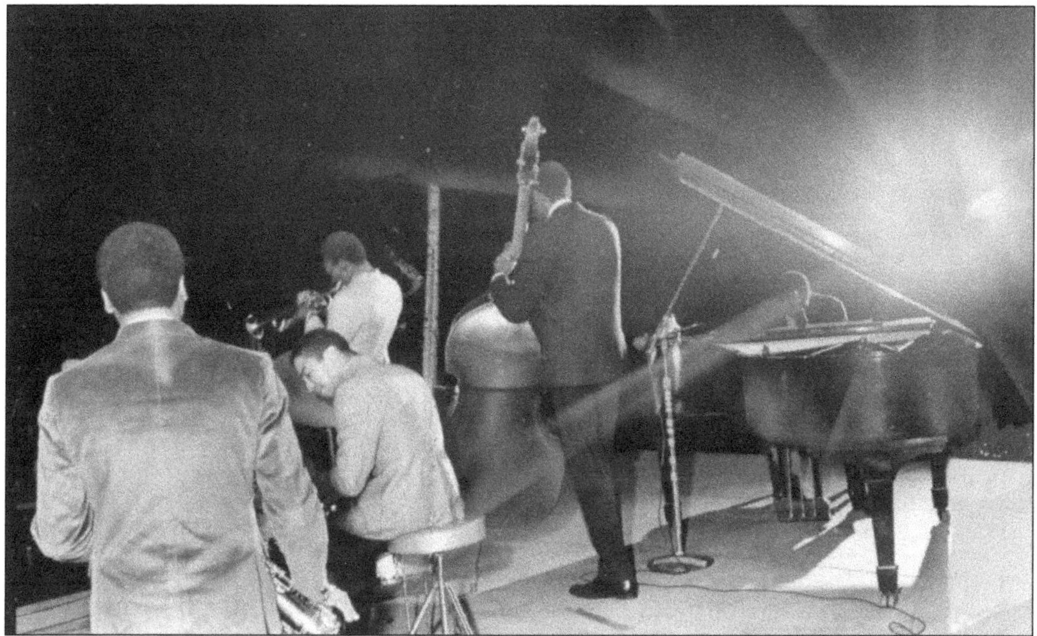

The Miles Davis Quintet. This image of the Miles Davis Quintet appeared in the *Washington Star* on August 29, 1978. The innovative trumpeter and award-winning performer was a close friend of pianist Shirley Horn, who maintained her Washington, DC, ties throughout her career. Davis performed as a sideman on Horn's 1991 album *You Won't Forget Me*. (Courtesy of DC Public Library, Washington Star Newspaper Collection.)

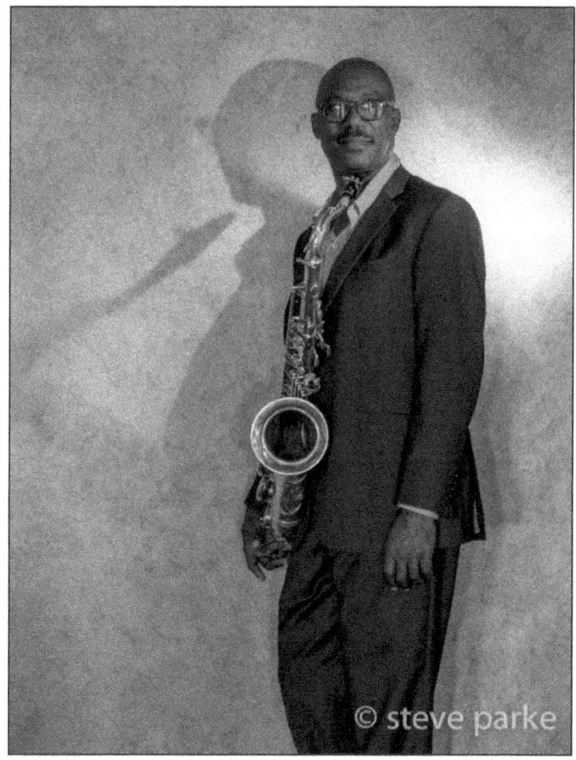

Paul Carr. Saxophonist Paul Carr is a native of Houston, Texas, and an alumnus of Howard University in Washington, DC. His work as a performing artist has taken him to concert venues in the Americas, the Caribbean, the Middle East, and Europe. A distinguished educator and an awarding-winning musician, Professor Carr is the founder and president of the Jazz Academy of Music, the director of the Jazz Ensemble at Gettysburg College, and the executive director and artistic director for the Mid-Atlantic Jazz Festival. In October 2018, Dr. Regennia N. Williams interviewed him for the DMV Jazz Oral History Project. (Courtesy of Paul Carr.)

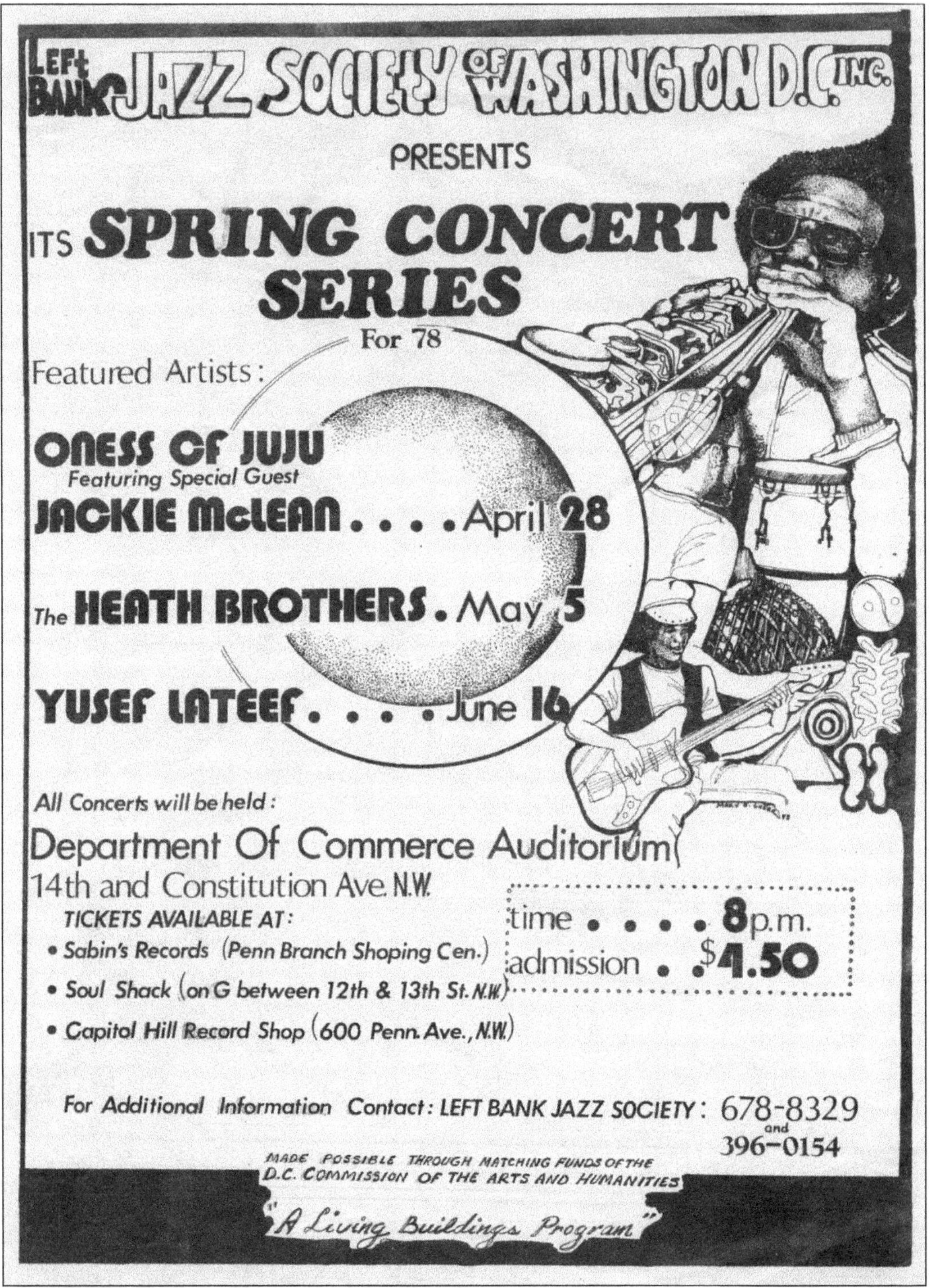

BROADSIDE FOR THE LEFT BANK JAZZ SOCIETY. Vernon Welsh and Benny Kearse organized the Baltimore-based Left Bank Jazz Society in 1964. For decades, it hosted performances and live recordings of locally and nationally known artists. (Courtesy of the Historical Society of Washington, DC.)

Five

No Limits

The Expansion of Jazz in the Academy and throughout the Global Community

With the official end of the Vietnam War and the black power, civil rights, and women's movements, Americans' struggles for security, power, and equality of opportunity did not disappear. They were, instead, transformed yet again, as black and Pan-African studies programs were institutionalized on the campuses of colleges and universities across the country and record numbers of citizens took advantage of enhanced opportunities to pursue postsecondary education. In this era, jazz underwent its own transformations, as many artists continued to travel and tour throughout the international community, and growing numbers of established and emerging artists moved more easily between the club and the conservatory, as new programs focusing on jazz history, theory, and performance were created.

Soon after Duke Ellington's passing in 1974, postsecondary jazz education programs came into their own. At Howard University, Dr. Fred Irby created the jazz studies program and founded the Howard University Jazz Ensemble. The University of the District of Columbia would, in time, become home to the Felix E. Grant Jazz Archives and the Calvin Jones Big Band. In nearby Maryland, the Peabody Conservatory of Johns Hopkins University and the music departments at Montgomery College and Morgan State employed many of the nation's distinguished artist-educators, while Wolf Trap in neighboring Virginia won the applause of music lovers for its excellent concerts of vocal and instrumental jazz.

While the above discussion focuses on the transformation of jazz education at the postsecondary level, it must also be noted that many of the students who eventually enrolled in the college and university programs named above began their studies with classroom teachers and bandleaders at the elementary and secondary levels—including those at the Duke Ellington School of the Arts. Alternatively, they could and did seek private instruction at the Levine School of Music and other institutions. Indeed, the last quarter of the 20th century was a key era in the history of jazz in the DMV.

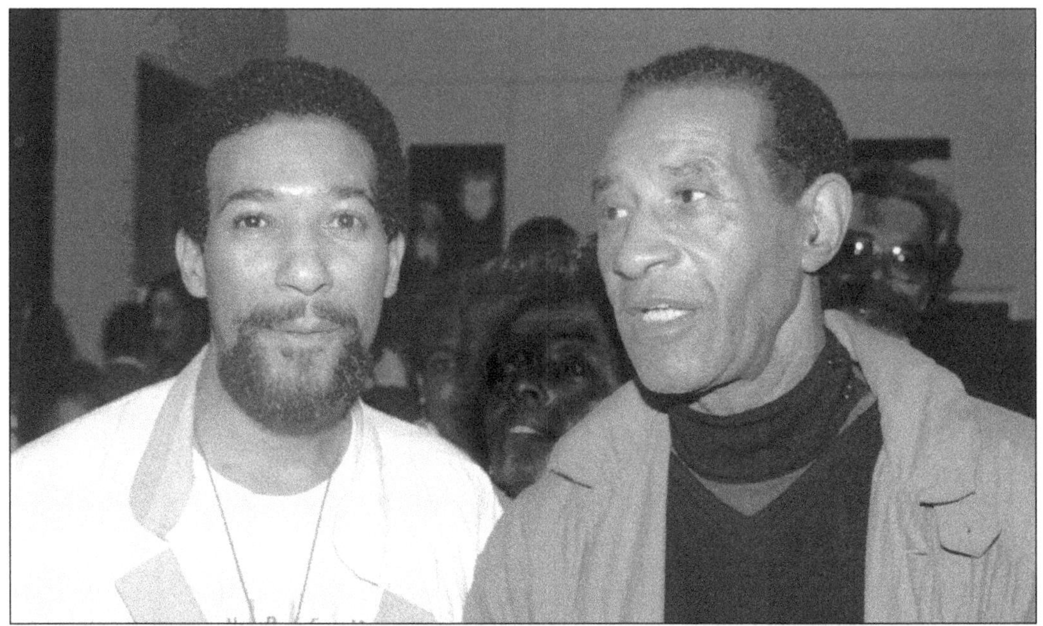

Nasar Abadey and Max Roach. Master drummer Nasar Abadey (left) is pictured with the legendary Max Roach, who was a great influence on Abadey. They were backstage at the Sacred Drums concert at the Duke Ellington School of the Arts in Washington, DC, on October 17, 1990. Abadey is a board member of DC Legendary Musicians Inc. (Photograph by Michael Wilderman.)

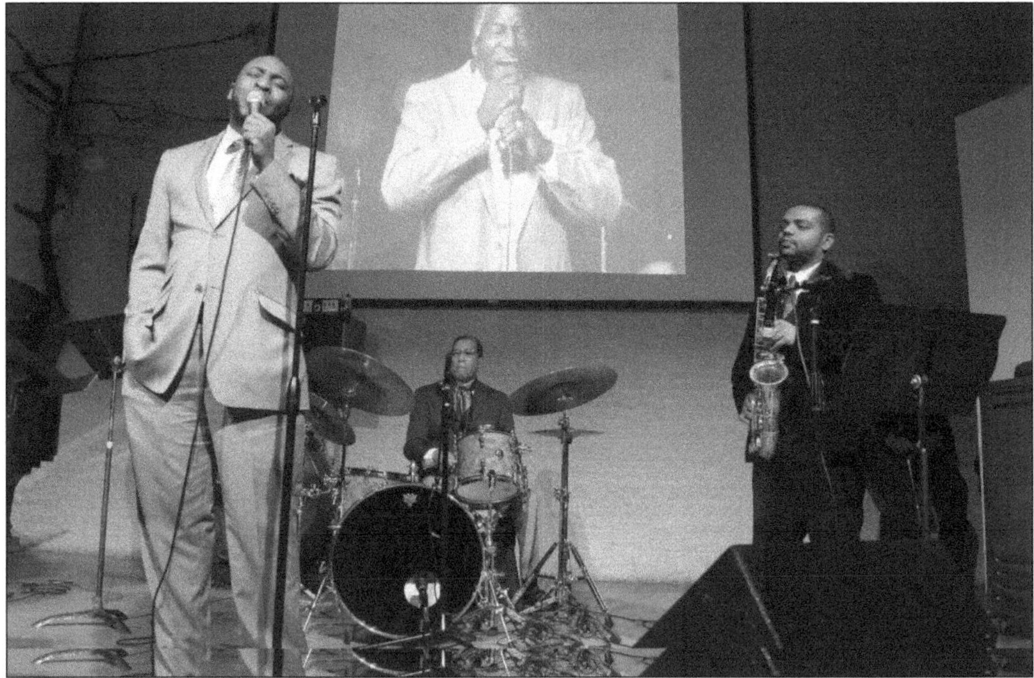

Aaron Myers, Nasar Abadey, and Herb Scott. Vocalist Aaron Myers, drummer Nasar Abadey, and saxophonist Herb Scott are pictured during a 2017 tribute to Joe Williams at Washington, DC's Westminster Presbyterian Church. Myers, Abadey, and Scott were all interviewed for the 2017–2018 Washington, DC, Jazz Oral History Project. (Photograph by Lawrence A. Randall.)

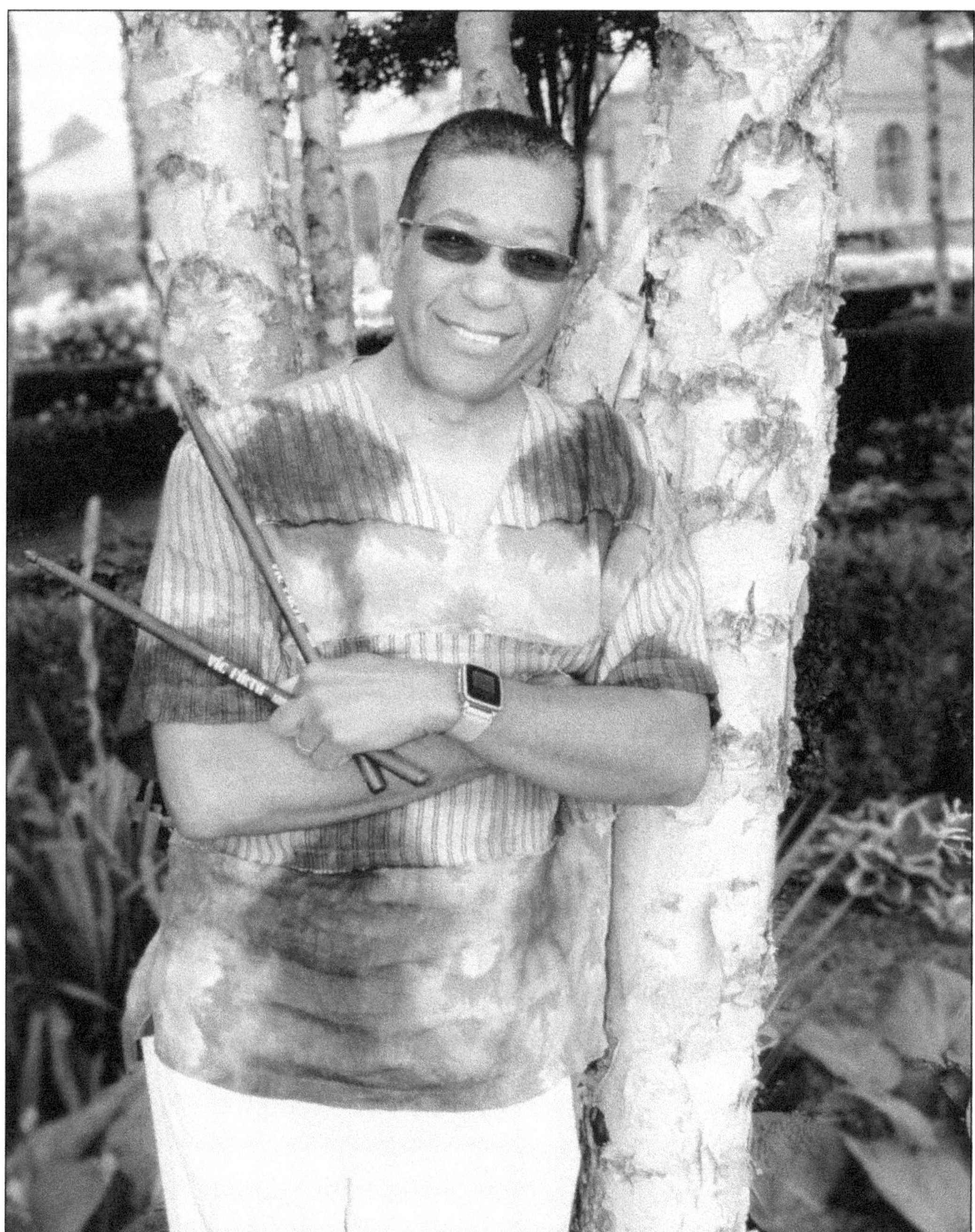

Nasar Abadey, 2018. Nasar Abadey, recipient of the 2018 DC Jazzfest Lifetime Achievement Award, is pictured in the Yards Park on the Capitol Riverfront in Washington, DC. Abadey is a member of DC Legendary Musicians Inc., and was interviewed for the 2017–2018 Washington, DC, Jazz Oral History Project. (Photograph by Nathaniel Rhodes; courtesy of DC Legendary Musicians Inc.)

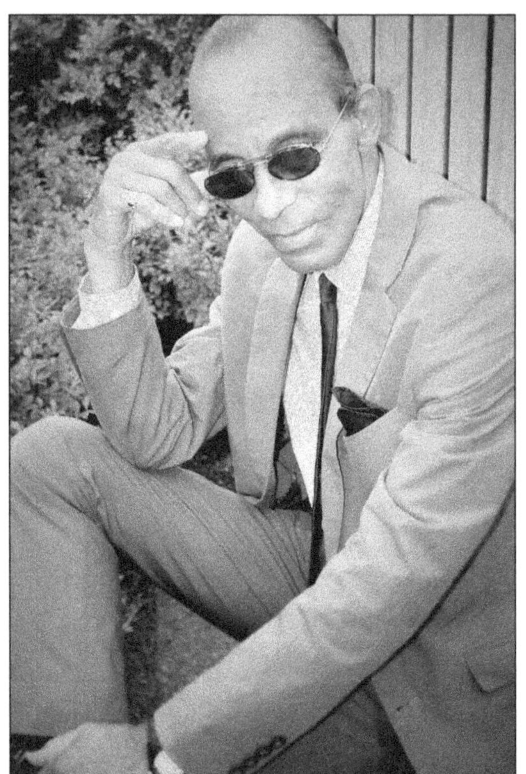

Jimi Smooth, 2018. Vocalist, dancer, and all-around entertainer Jimi Smooth is pictured here in the Yards Park on the Capitol Riverfront in Washington, DC. Smooth is a member of DC Legendary Musicians Inc. (Photograph by Nathaniel Rhodes; courtesy of DC Legendary Musicians Inc.)

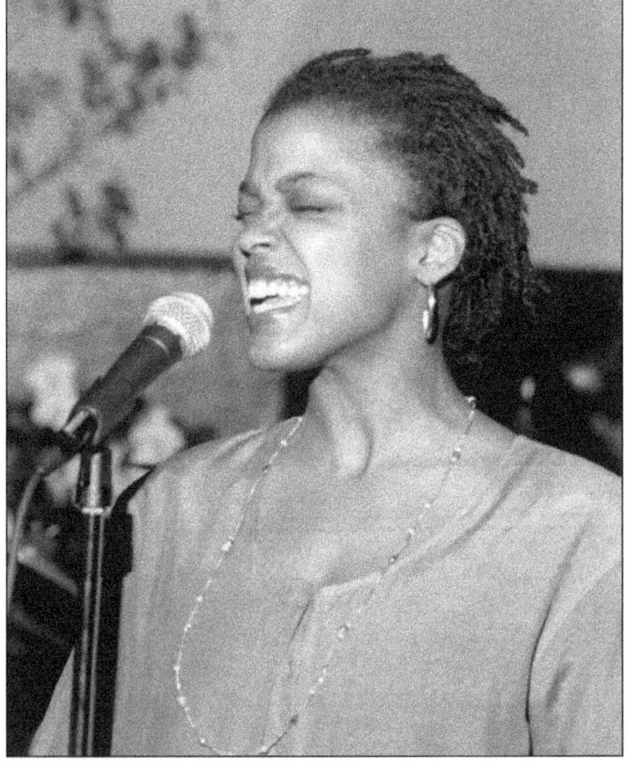

Sunny Sumter. Vocalist Sunny Sumter is shown here in a May 1, 1997, performance at the Smithsonian Institution. An alumna of Howard University and an award-winning performing artist and arts administrator, she currently serves as the executive director of the DC Jazz Festival. (Photograph by Michael Wilderman.)

Steve Novosel. Bassist and longtime Washingtonian Steve Novosel is a Pennsylvania native who came of age playing trumpet. By the 1960s, he was in Washington performing with the US Army Band and slowly gravitating toward the instrument that would make him a highly sought-after bassist. He is shown here in a Maryland recording studio on July 12, 1992. (Photograph by Michael Wilderman.)

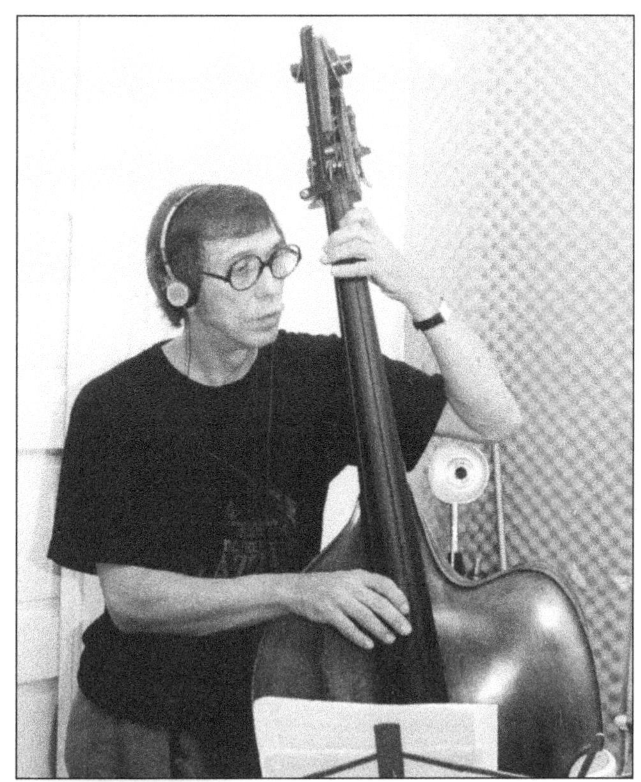

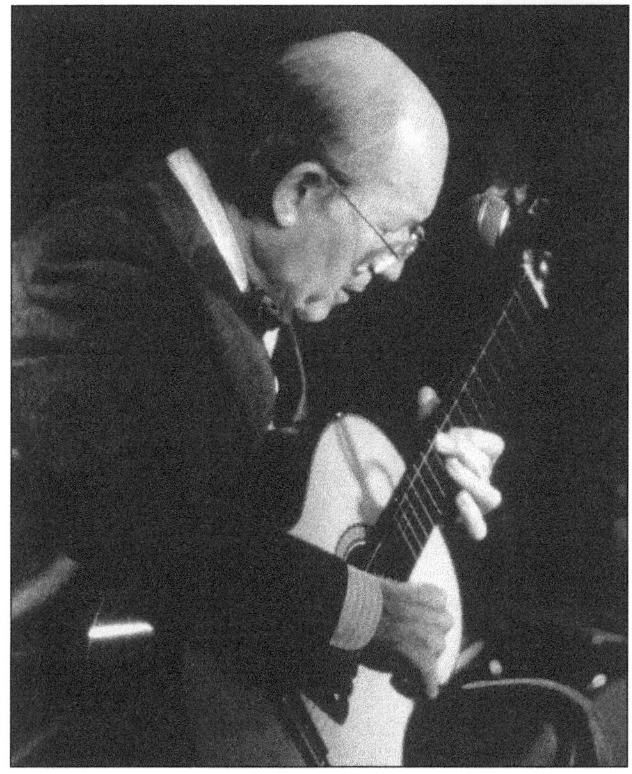

Charlie Byrd, 1991. Felix E. Grant introduced guitarist Charlie Byrd to Brazilian music. Because of the success of Byrd's 1962 album *Jazz Samba*—led by saxophonist Stan Getz and featuring Keter Betts on bass—Byrd is credited with popularizing bossa nova among American listeners. Byrd is shown here during a live recording at Blues Alley. (Photograph by Michael Wilderman.)

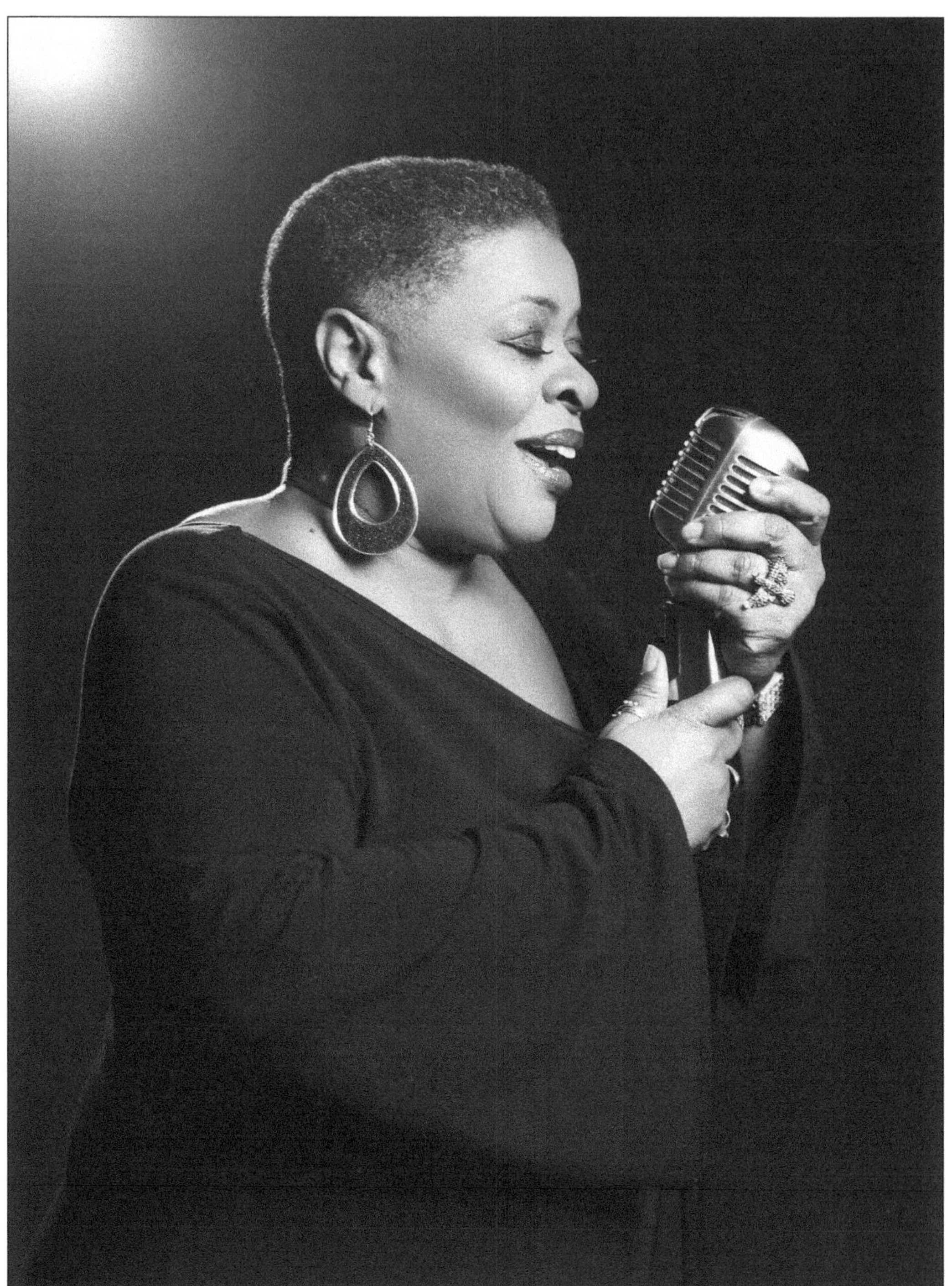

VOCALIST JANINE GILBERT-CARTER. Vocalist Janine Gilbert-Carter has performed locally, nationally, and internationally. Her first compact disc recording, *In the Moment*, was released in 2003, and that collection contained both gospel and jazz selections. By 2018, she had seven recordings to her credit. She was interviewed for the 2017–2018 Washington, DC, Jazz Oral History Project. (Courtesy of Janine Gilbert-Carter.)

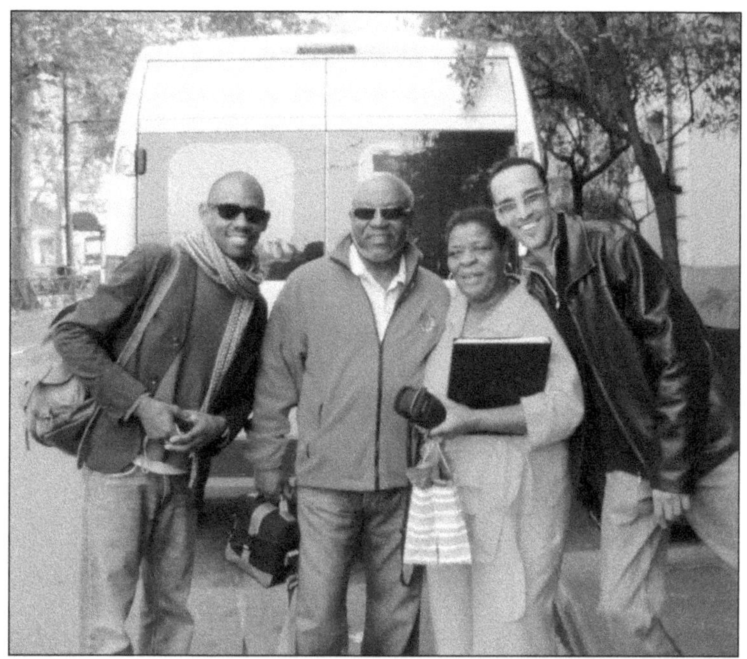

Janine Gilbert-Carter and Band in Italy. Janine Gilbert-Carter currently resides in Maryland, but her international engagements have taken her to Israel, Russia, and Italy. She is seen here with (from left to right) saxophonist Brian Settles, bassist Wes "Sugar" Biles, and drummer Jeffrey J. "Left Hand" Neal. (Courtesy of Janine Gilbert-Carter.)

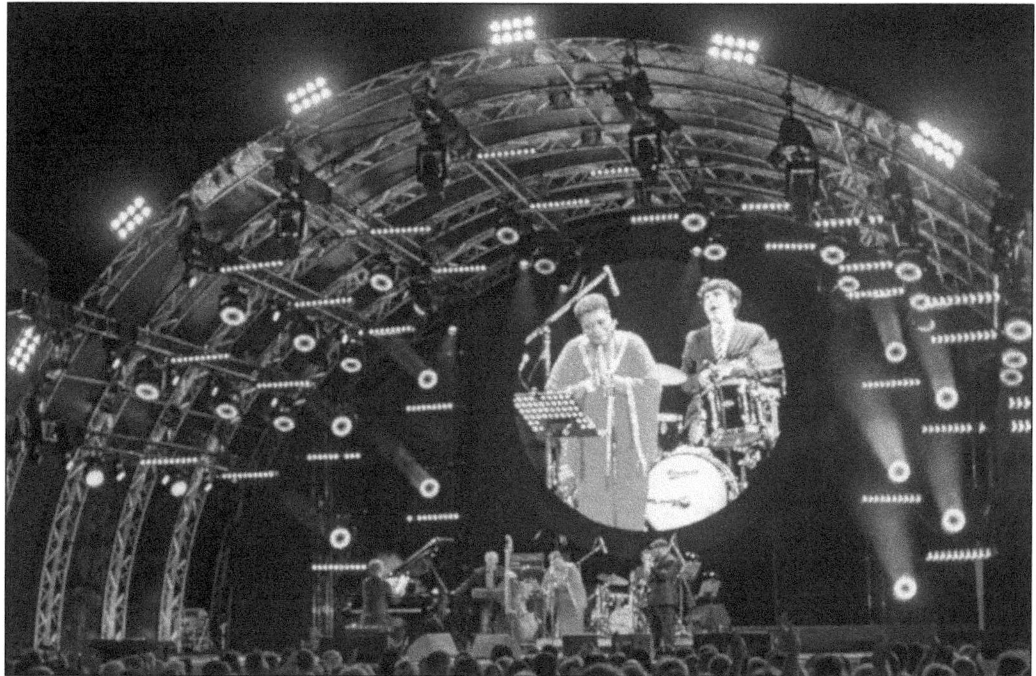

Janine Gilbert-Carter and Band on Stage in Russia. Whether performing in an intimate setting like DC Blues Alley, before large audiences during Maryland's Mid-Atlantic Jazz Festival, or internationally in Russia, Gilbert-Carter welcomes the opportunity to share her gifts with music lovers. Her favorite songs include "Here's to Life" and "Stormy Monday Blues." (Courtesy of Janine Gilbert-Carter.)

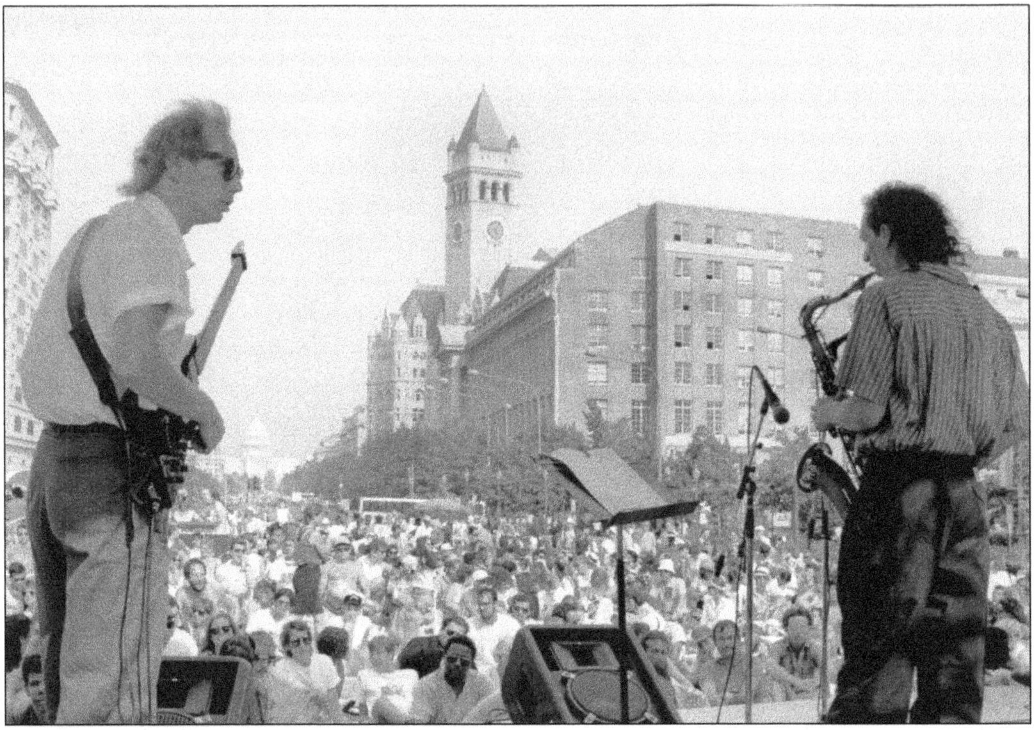

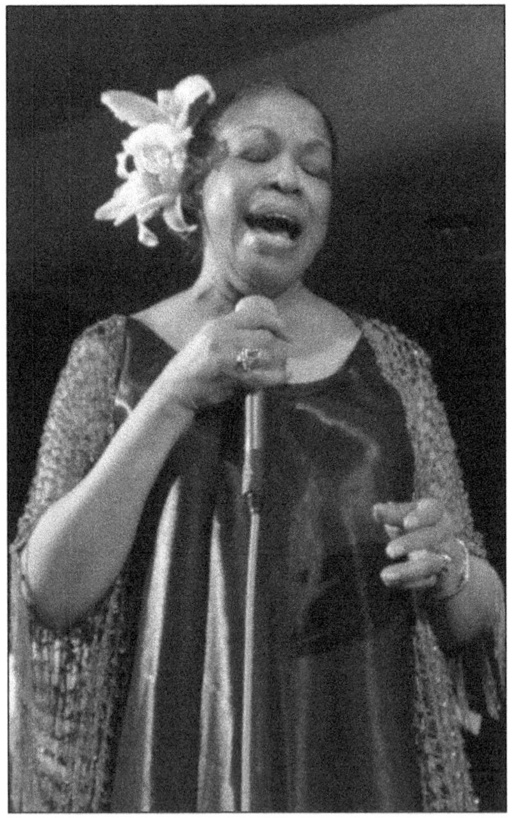

Paul Bollenback. Guitarist Paul Bollenback (left) counts among his musical influences the sounds of India, where he spent part of his childhood; rock and roll, and jazz. Bollenback recorded with some of the top artists and served on the faculty of American University. He is shown here on July 4, 1988, at the DC Free Jazz Festival, which was produced annually by District Curators at Freedom Plaza on Pennsylvania Avenue. (Photograph by Michael Wilderman.)

Ronnie Wells Elliston. Vocalist Ronnie Elliston and her husband, pianist Ron Elliston, were the cofounders of the East Coast Jazz Festival, which is now known as the Mid-Atlantic Jazz Festival. The Ronnie Wells and Ron Elliston Collection, which is housed in the Felix E. Grant Jazz Archives at the University of the District of Columbia, is comprised of materials from both the East Coast Jazz Festival and the Elliston Music Studio for Jazz Studies. (Courtesy of Janine Gilbert-Carter.)

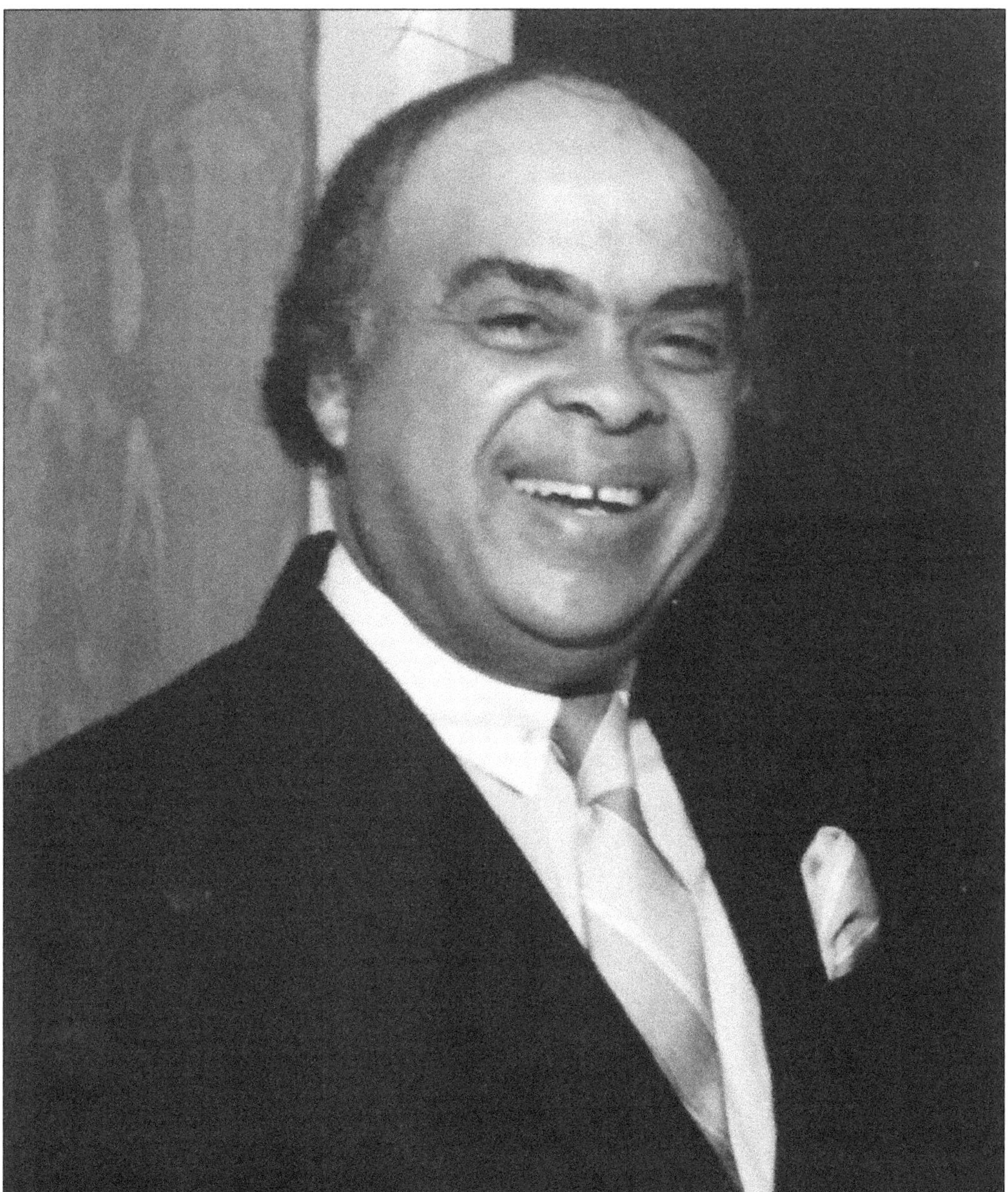

Robert "Bobby" Nicholas Felder. Florida native Bobby Felder is an alumnus of Fisk University, a US Air Force veteran, and a respected educator, composer, arranger, bandleader, and recording artist. Having taught for many years at Federal City College and its successor, the University of the District of Columbia, he played an active role in establishing both the instrumental music program and the Felix E. Grant Jazz Archives. He has performed and/or recorded with Keter Betts, Buck Hill, the Capital All Stars, and many other DC artists. As the director of jazz services at Peoples Congregational Church, he recorded several CDs for Bobby Felder and Friends. In September 2018, he celebrated the release of his latest CD with a performance at Washington's Westminster Presbyterian Church. Professor Felder is shown here in a 1988 University of the District of Columbia Department of Music photograph. (Courtesy of the Felix E. Grant Jazz Archives, University of the District of Columbia.)

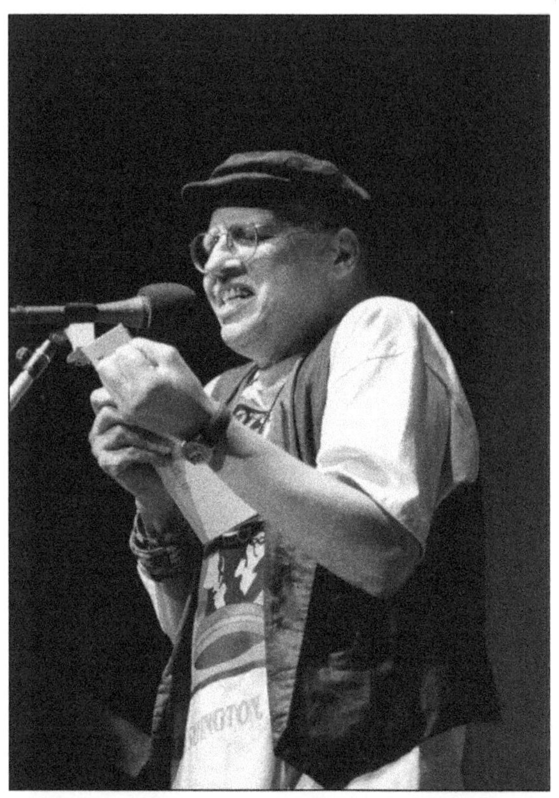

GASTON NEAL AT THE LINCOLN THEATRE, 1997. Activist poet Gaston Neal combined his performance poetry with jazz music in ways that enlightened his listening audiences. In 1966, he founded the New School for Afro-American Thought, which he directed until 1971. (Photograph by Michael Wilderman.)

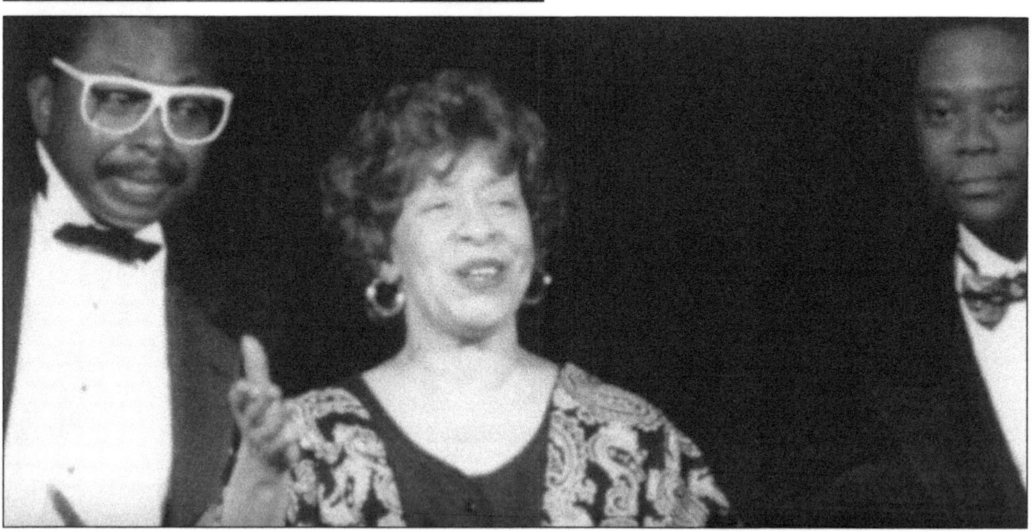

CHARLES ABLES, SHIRLEY HORN, AND STEVE WILLIAMS. Native Washingtonian Shirley Horn began to display her musical gifts very early in life, and she often reminisced about having discovered the joys of playing the piano in her grandmother's home at age four, as well as her private lessons and studying piano and composition in the Howard University Junior School of Music. Trained as a classical pianist, she fell in love with jazz in her teen years and formed her first trio in the 1950s. She released her first recording, *Embers and Ashes*, on the Stereo-Craft label in 1961. Horn is pictured here with bassist Charles Ables (left) and drummer Steve Williams. (Courtesy of the Library of Congress.)

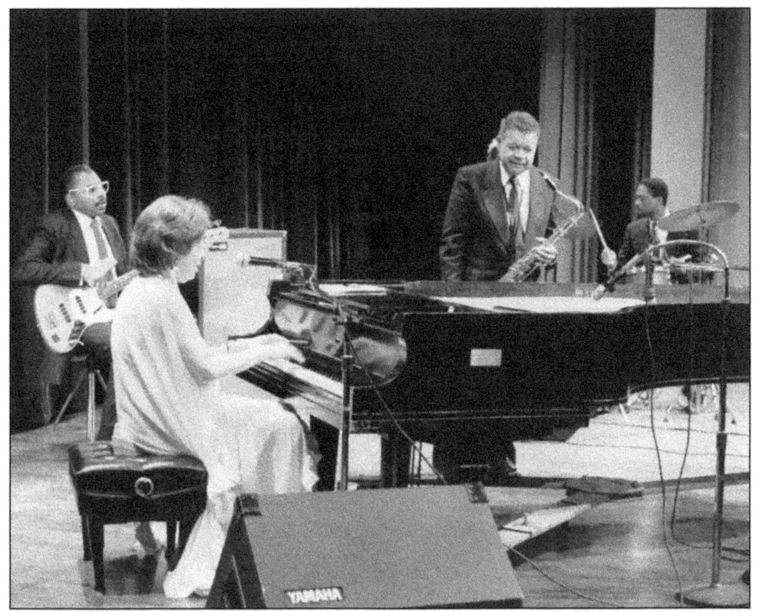

THE SHIRLEY HORN TRIO WITH BUCK HILL, DUKE ELLINGTON SCHOOL OF THE ARTS, 1989. Pianist Shirley Horn is pictured here with fellow Washingtonian and saxophonist Roger Wendell "Buck" Hill and longtime members of the Shirley Horn Trio, drummer Steve Williams and bassist Charles Ables. (Photograph by Michael Wilderman.)

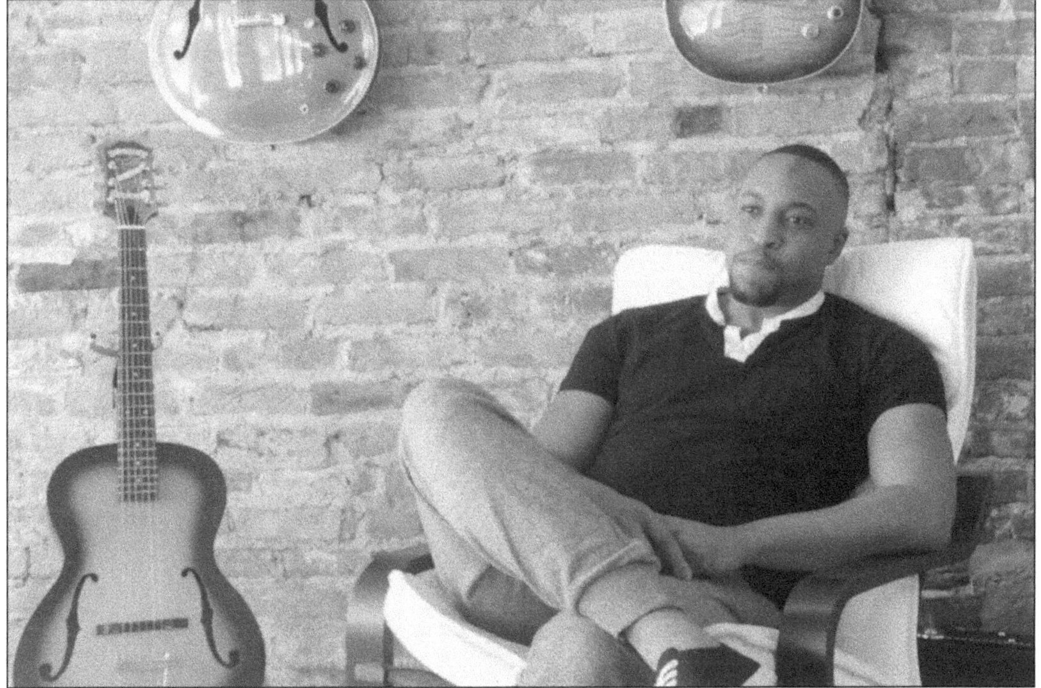

AARON MYERS, FOUNDER, CAPITOL HILL JAZZ FOUNDATION. Aaron Myers is a pianist, vocalist, recording artist, US Army veteran, arts advocate, and activist. His professional credits include stand-up comedy and performing and teaching gospel music in Los Angeles and, after relocating to Washington, DC, teaching and performing in the Capital Jazz Festival and the DC Jazz Festival. He currently serves as the board chair for the Capitol Hill Jazz Foundation. Myers was interviewed for the 2017–2018 Washington, DC, Jazz Oral History Project. (Photograph by Lawrence A. Randall.)

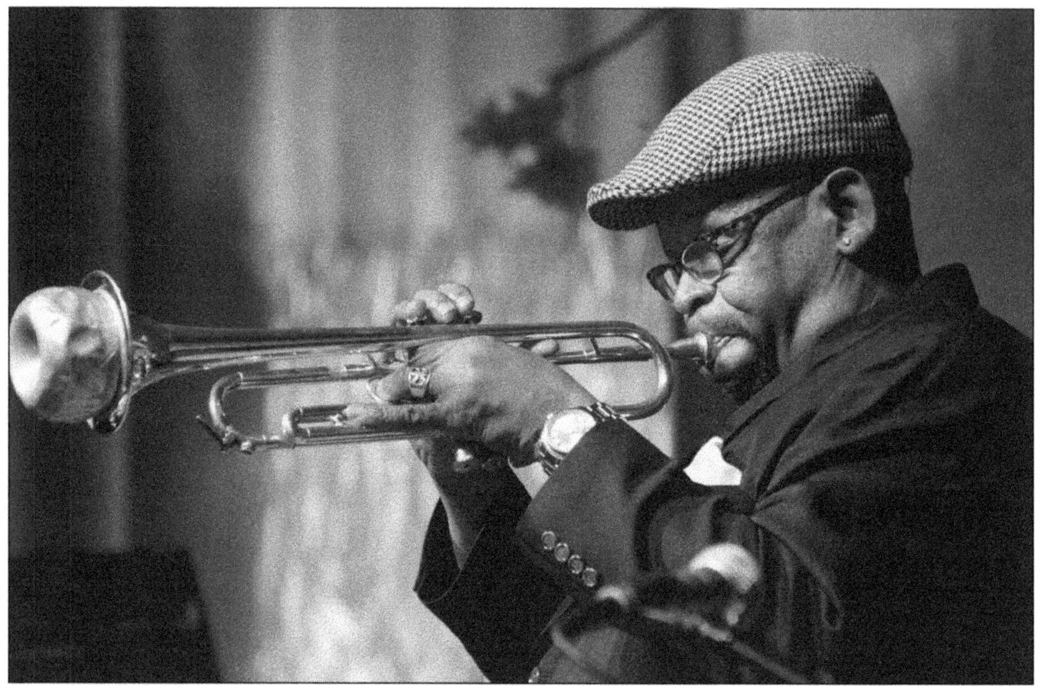

DeAndrey Howard. Howard, a multi-instrumentalist, building contractor, and business partner (with Dr. Alice Johnson), operates Washington, DC's Alice's Jazz and Cultural Society, which promotes, in Howard's words "real jazz"—à la Duke Ellington and John Coltrane—to intergenerational performers and audiences. (Photograph by Lawrence A. Randall.)

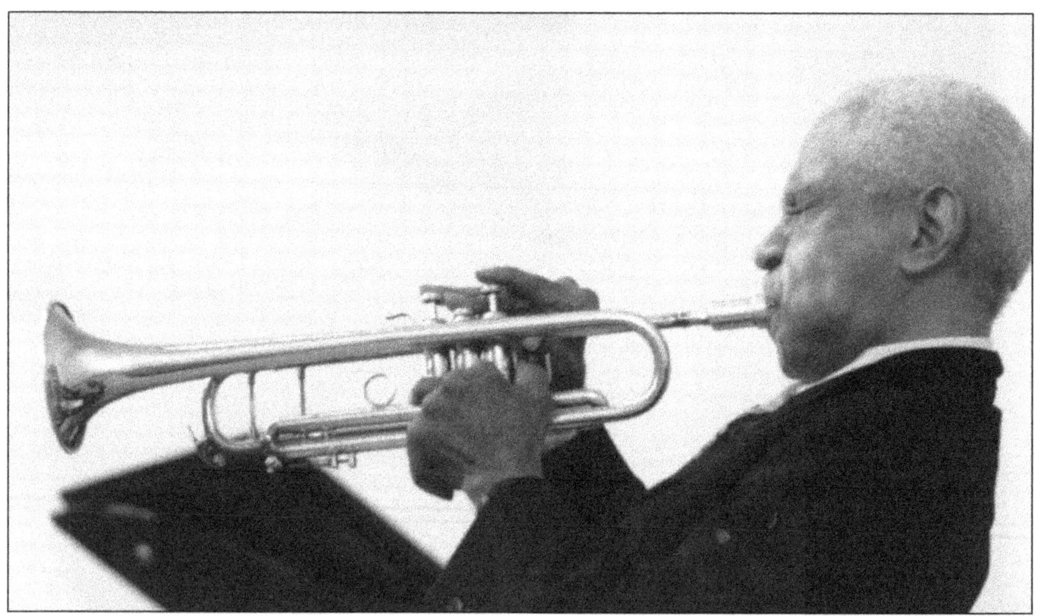

Webster Young, Kennedy Center, 1994. An accomplished trumpeter and cornet player, Webster Young, who grew up in Washington, DC, enjoyed a successful career as a performing artist and served on the music faculty at the University of the District of Columbia. (Photograph by Michael Wilderman.)

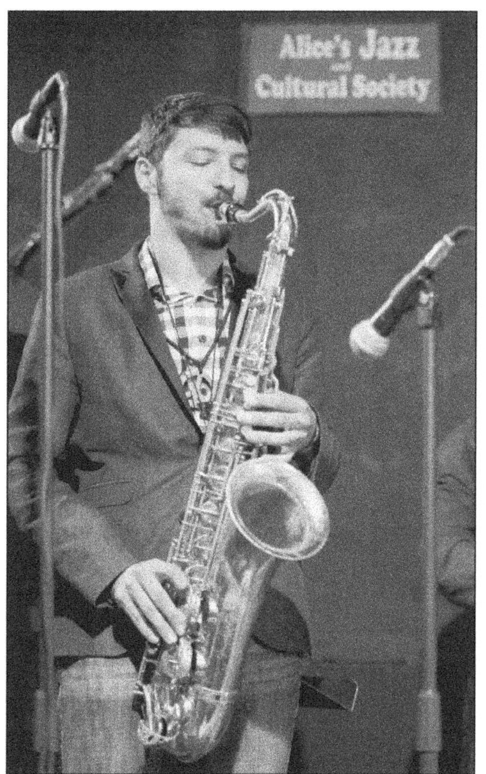

Elijah Jamal Balbed. Howard University alumnus Elijah Jamal Balbed is a versatile and sought-after saxophonist whose local performances include shows at Alice's Jazz and Cultural Society, Blues Alley, Westminster Presbyterian Church, the Kennedy Center, and many other venues. Balbed has also traveled and performed across the length and breadth of the United States and around the world, including work with the Jazz at Lincoln Center initiative in Doha, Qatar. Adept at performing everything from straight-ahead jazz to JoGo, Balbed can be heard on recordings with the Chuck Brown Band, Mark Meadows, and others. (Photograph by Lawrence A. Randall.)

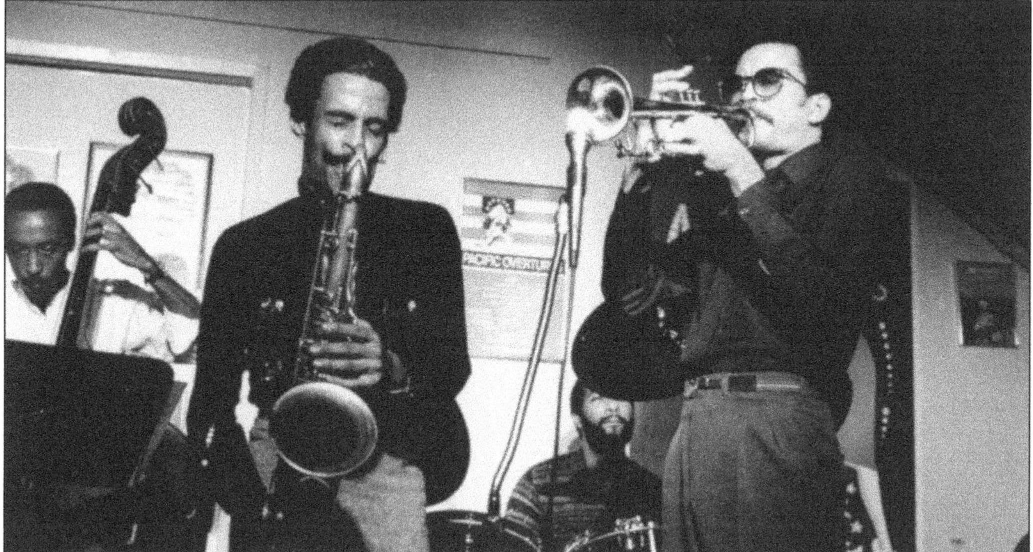

Malachi Thompson, DC Space, 1983. Jazz trumpeter Malachi Thompson explored the roots of African American culture in his 1993 recording *Lift Every Voice*. Thompson is shown here with Carter Jefferson (saxophone), James King (bass), and Nasar Abadey (drums). From 1977 to 1991, DC Space was a popular venue with those who performed and listened to alternative jazz, punk, and other new musical styles. It was located at Seventh and E Streets. In 2015, cofounder Bill Warrell compared DC Space to CapitalBop, stating that smaller venues are critical since they support creative experimentation by new artists. (Photograph by Michael Wilderman.)

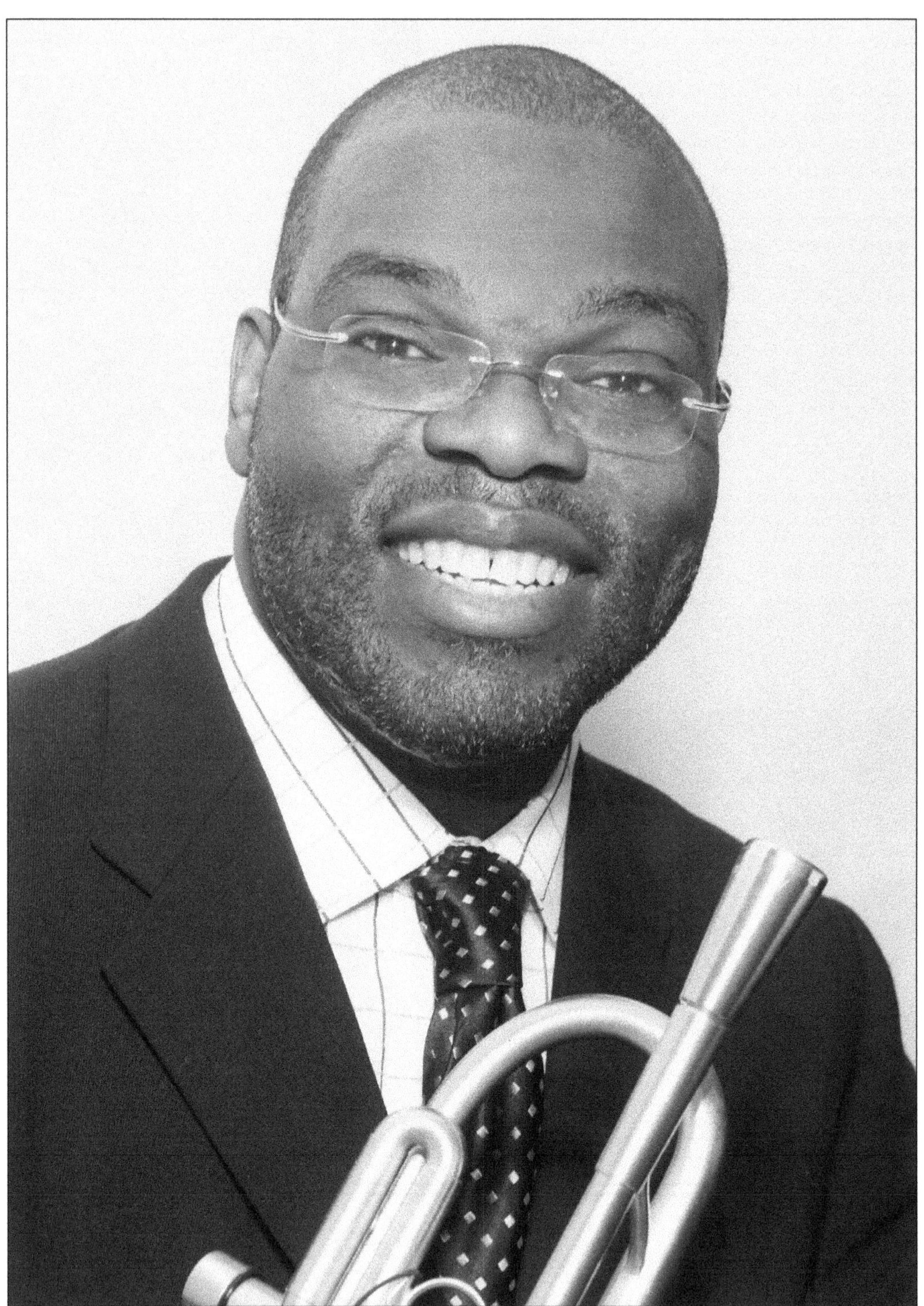

Alvin Trask. Louisiana native and Howard University alumnus Alvin Trask studied with the renowned Dr. Fred Irby. He currently chairs the performing arts department at Montgomery College in Rockville, Maryland. (Courtesy of Alvin Trask.)

LAWRENCE WHEATLEY, 1992. Pianist Lawrence Wheatley was a native Washingtonian and a fixture on the District of Columbia's jazz scene for decades, performing at Bohemian Caverns, One Step Down, and other local jazz venues. He attended the city's Armstrong Technical High School but left before graduating to pursue a career as a professional musician. (Photograph by Michael Wilderman.)

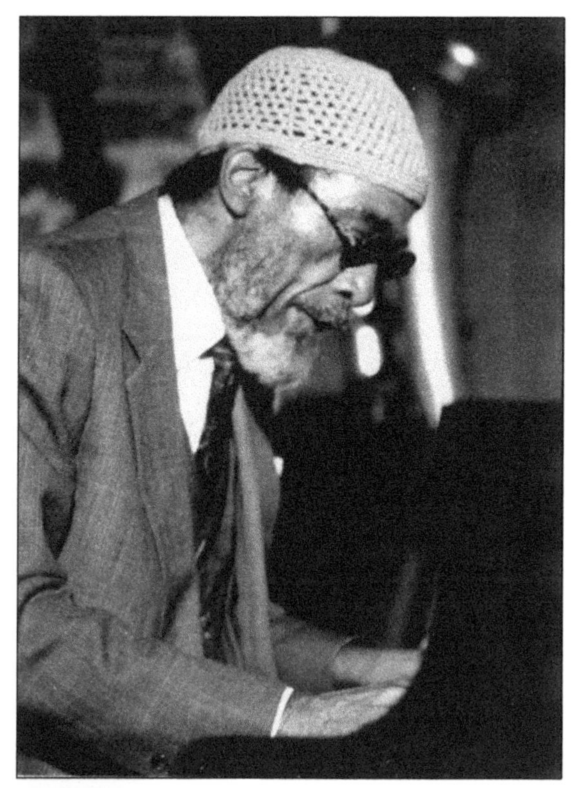

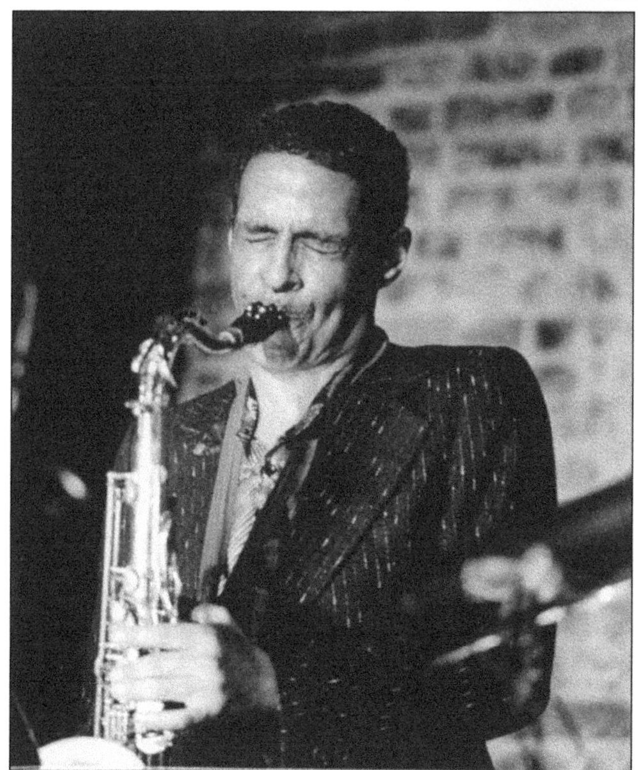

CARTER JEFFERSON. Saxophonist Carter Jefferson performs at Blues Alley in 1993. A native Washingtonian, Jefferson was one of the original El Corols. (Photograph by Michael Wilderman.)

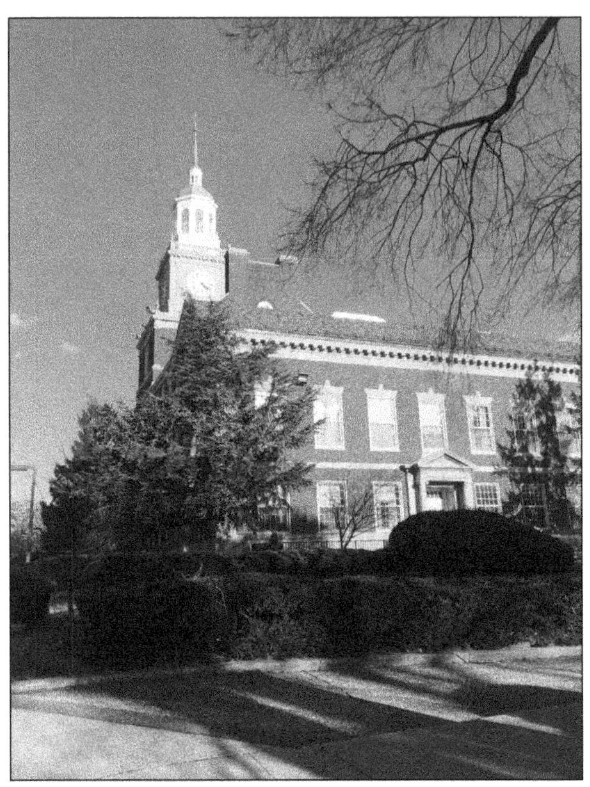

Founders Library, Howard University, 2016. Established in 1939 on the campus of Howard University in Washington, DC, the Founders Library is home to extensive collections of books and manuscript materials related to African American history and culture. Several images in this book are from the *Pittsburgh Courier's* Washington Bureau Collection, which is housed in the library's Moorland-Spingarn Research Center. (Photograph by Regennia N. Williams.)

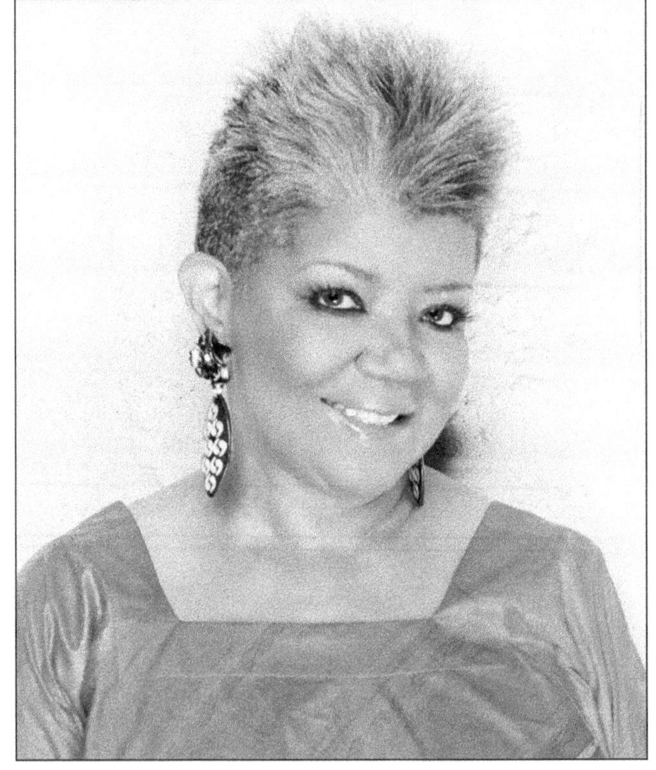

Lavenia Nesmith. Vocalist Lavenia Nesmith has won the applause of audiences at both the local and national levels for her performances of a wide range of works, including jazz and gospel. A native Washingtonian, she attended Howard University. She launched her recording career with the *Introducing Lavenia Nesmith* album in 2013. Equally at home in intimate clubs, church sanctuaries, and at outdoor events, she has performed at Bohemian Caverns, Blues Alley, the White House, the Mid-Atlantic Jazz Festival, and the DC Jazz Festival, among other venues and programs. She was one of the original members of the El Corols. Nesmith was interviewed for the 2017–2018 Washington, DC, Jazz Oral History Project. (Courtesy of Lavenia Nesmith.)

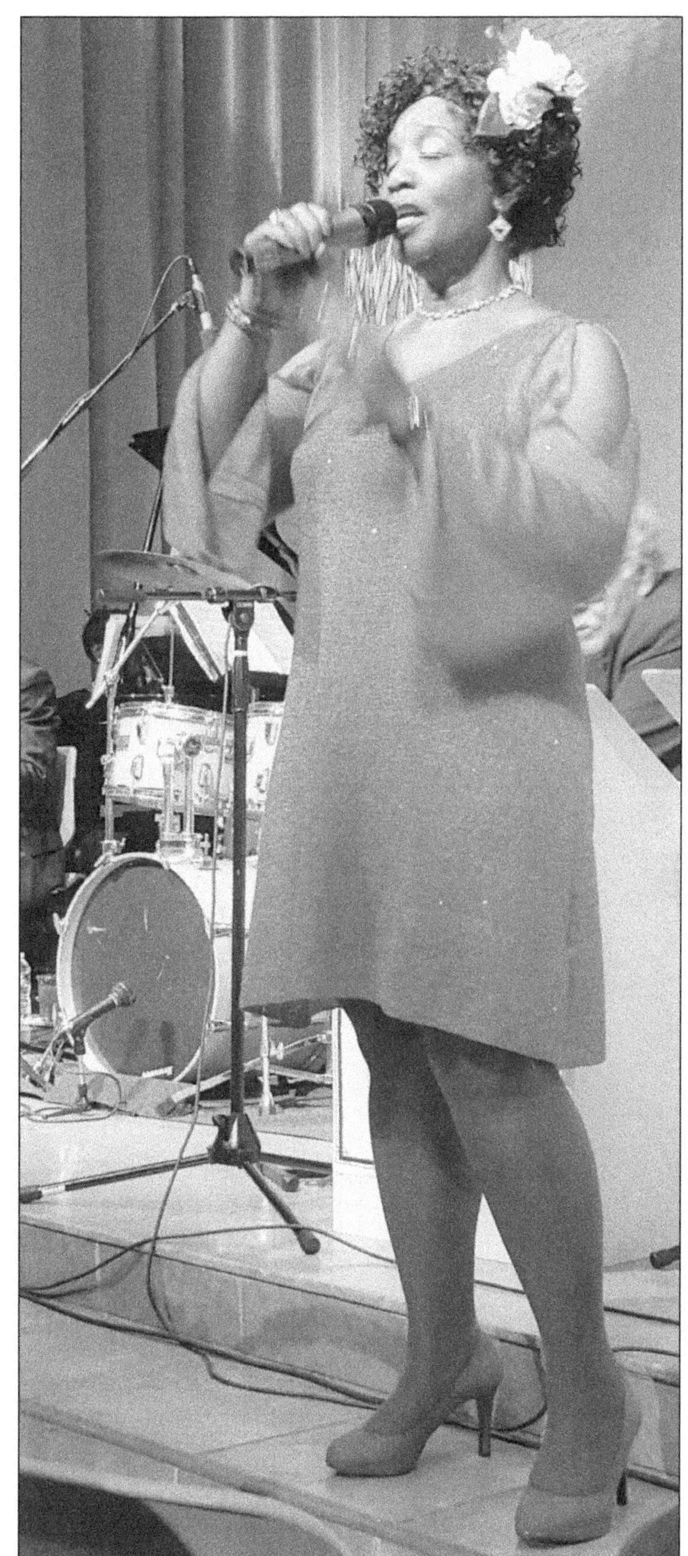

Denyse Pearson-Williams. Jazz vocalist and longtime DMV resident Denyse Pearson-Williams (1952–2017) was a popular performing artist, respected teacher-coach, and active member of the governing board for DC Legendary Musicians Inc. She performed at the Kennedy Center and numerous other venues throughout the Washington, DC, metropolitan area. (Courtesy of Sandra Butler-Truesdale.)

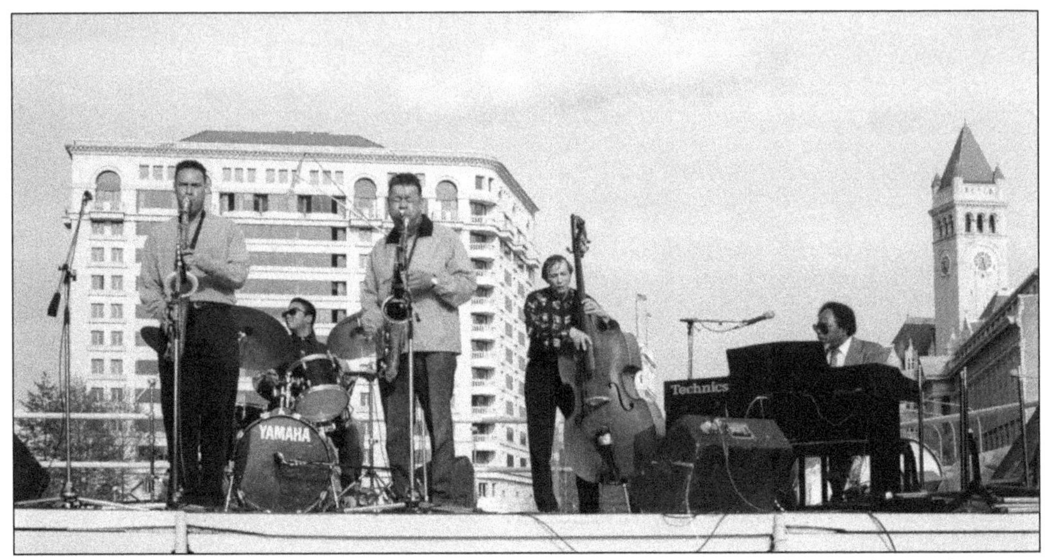

Ellington Birthday Tribute on Western Plaza. Saxophonist Joshua Redman, drummer Warren Shadd, saxophonist Buck Hill, bassist Steve Novosel, and pianist Sir Roland Hanna honor native son Duke Ellington, who was born in Washington, DC, on April 29, 1899. (Photograph by Michael Wilderman.)

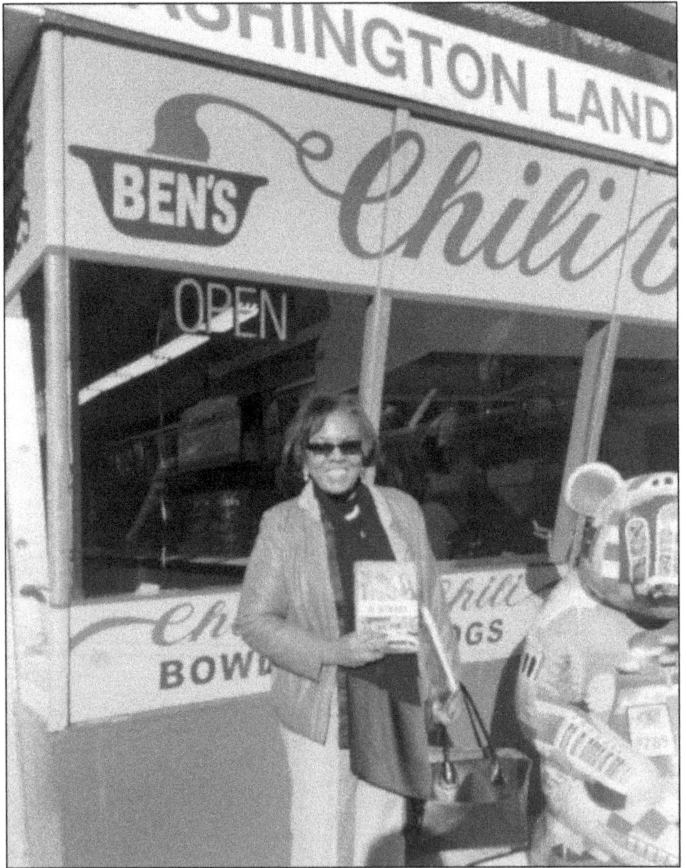

The Original Ben's Chili Bowl, 2016. Regennia N. Williams, holding a copy of Blair Ruble's *U Street: A Biography*, is shown outside the original Ben's Chili Bowl restaurant on U Street. Founded by Howard University alumnus Ben Ali, the restaurant has been a fixture in the community for more than 50 years. Located in a building that once housed the Jungle Inn, where Jelly Roll Morton performed in late 1939, this Washington landmark was the December 7, 2016, site of the first planning meeting for *Washington, DC, Jazz*. (Photograph by Sandra Butler-Truesdale; courtesy of Regennia N. Williams.)

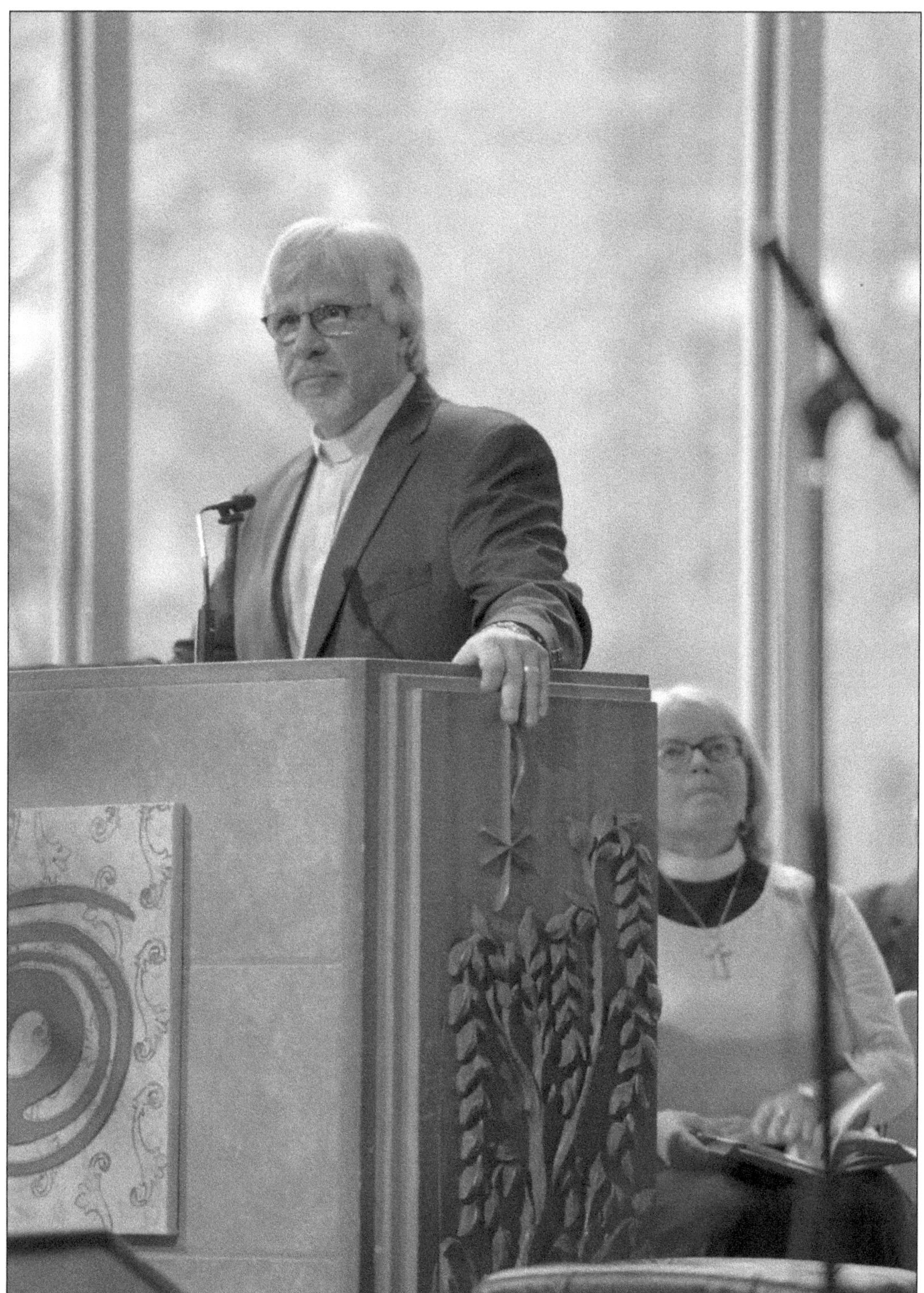

The Rev. Brian Hamilton. The Rev. Brian Hamilton and his wife, the Rev. Ruth Hamilton (right), are both pastors at Westminster Presbyterian Church, home of Washington's Jazz Night and Blue Monday Blues series. (Photograph by Lawrence A. Randall.)

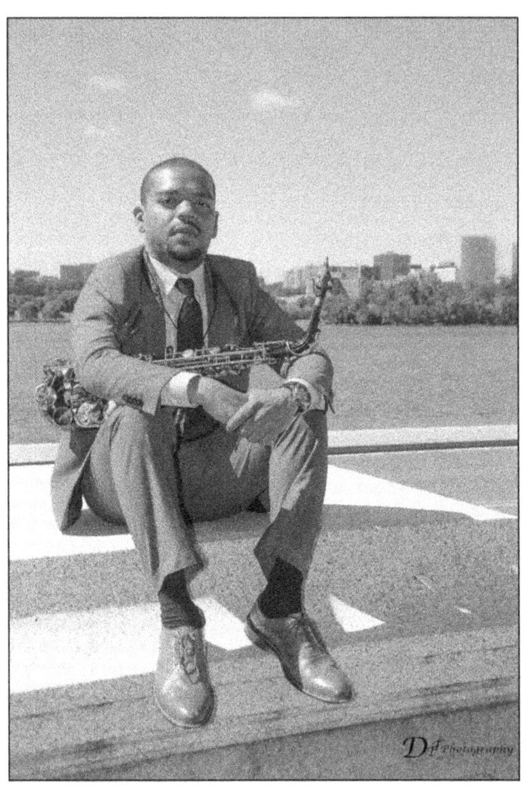

Herbert James Scott. Saxophonist Herbert James Scott is both a jazz artist and activist. A familiar face at Mr. Henry's restaurant and club in Washington, he is a DC native and alumnus of the Levine School of Music, the Duke Ellington School of the Arts, and Michigan State University. Scott was interviewed for the 2017–2018 Washington, DC, Jazz Oral History Project. (Courtesy of Herbert Scott.)

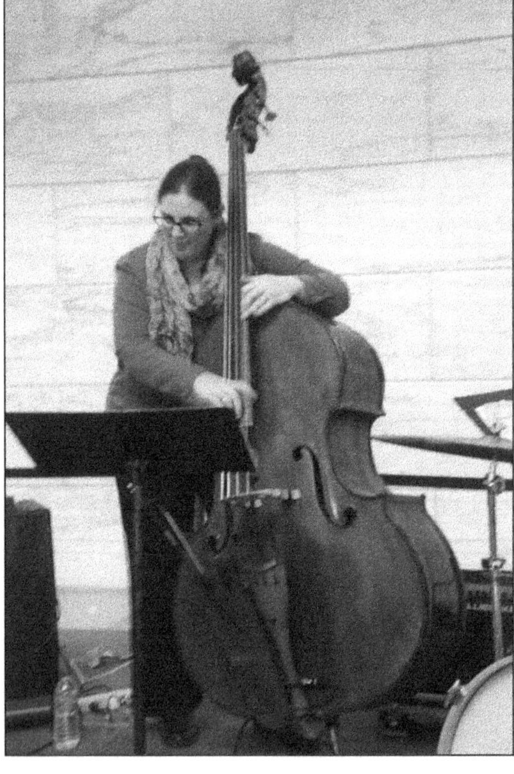

Amy Shook. Bassist Amy Shook is a three-time alumna of the University of Idaho, a composer, singer-songwriter, music educator, recording artist, and coleader (with her husband, Pat) of the Shook/Russo Trio. She has performed at the John F. Kennedy Center for the Performing Arts, the Smithsonian National Museum of American History, the Cleveland Playhouse, and numerous other venues. (Courtesy of Smithsonian Jazz.)

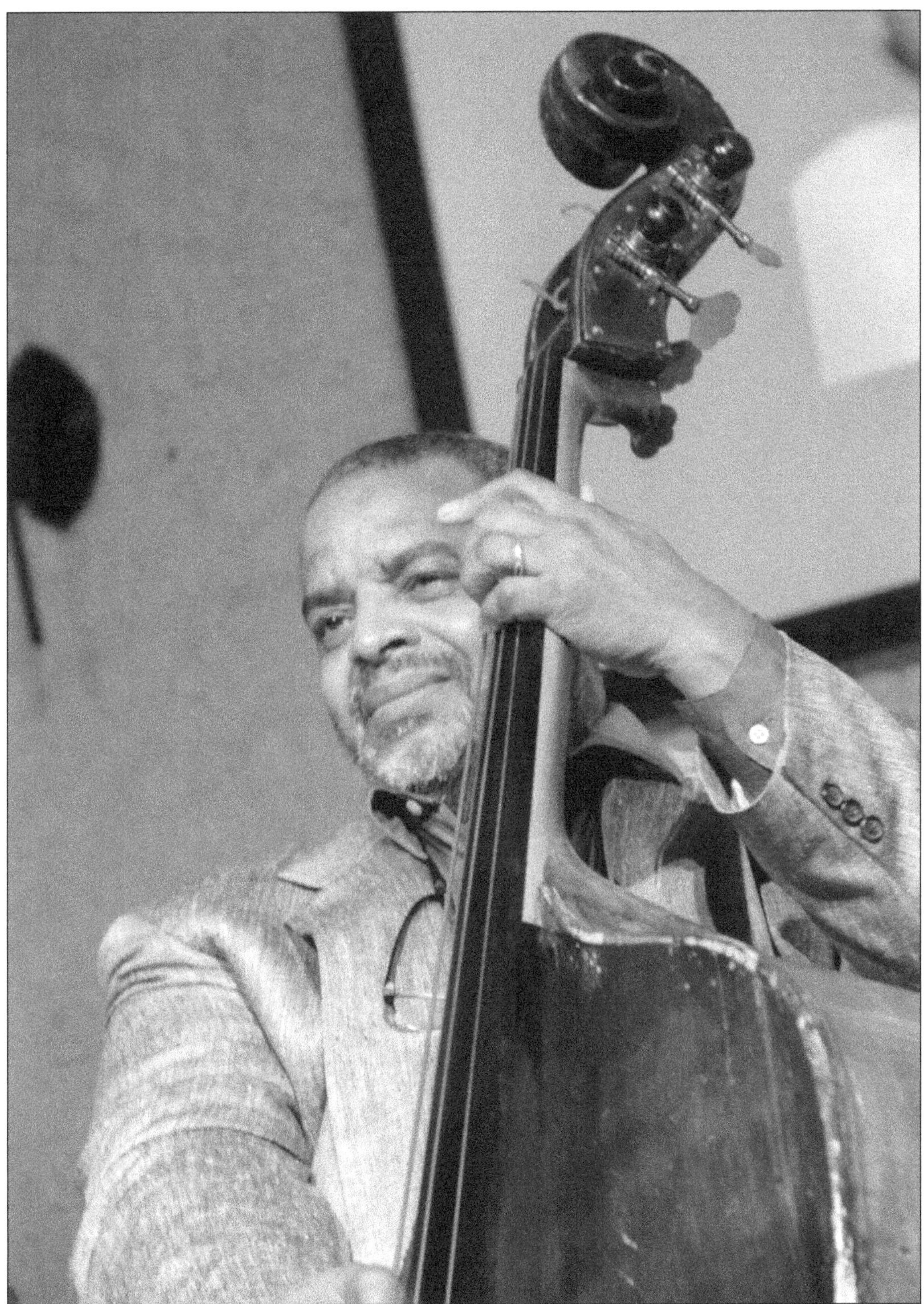

Cheyney Thomas. Howard University alumnus Cheyney Thomas is a sought-after solo bassist and music educator. His is also the founder and director of the Prince George's County (Maryland) Youth Jazz Ensemble. (Photograph by Lawrence A. Randall.)

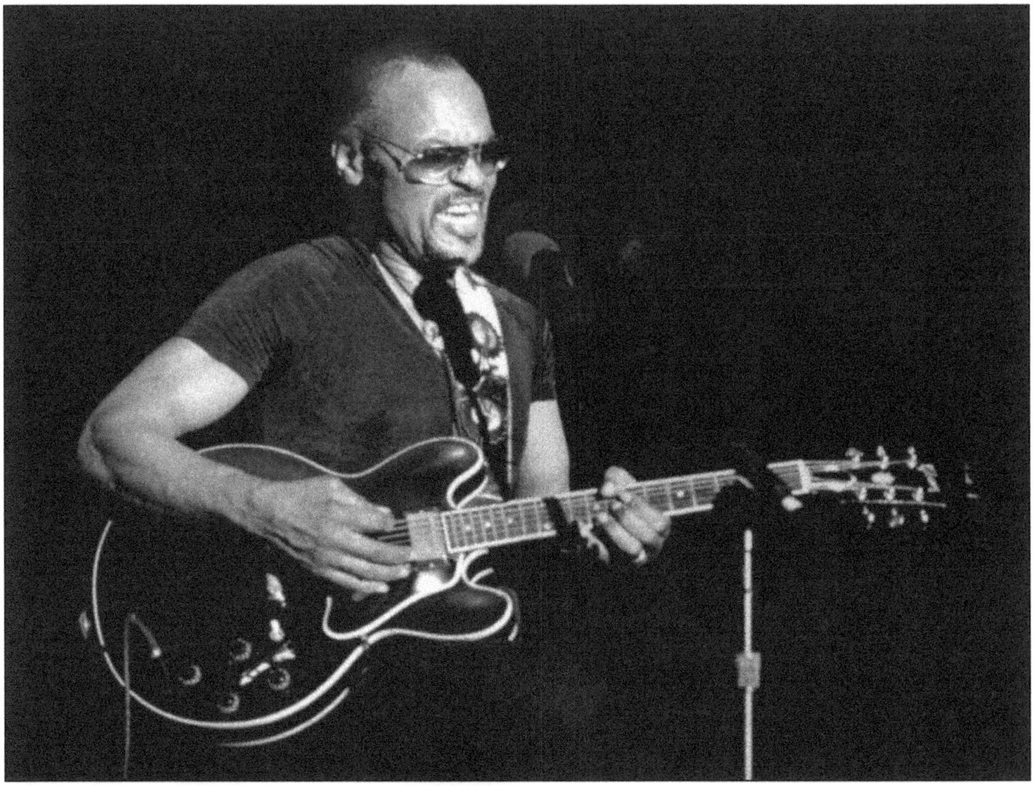

Chuck Brown at the Carter Barron. Guitarist Chuck Brown, Washington's "Godfather of Go-Go Music," is shown here during an August 3, 1979, performance with the Chuck Brown Jazz Band at the Carter Barron Amphitheatre. (Photograph by Michael Wilderman.)

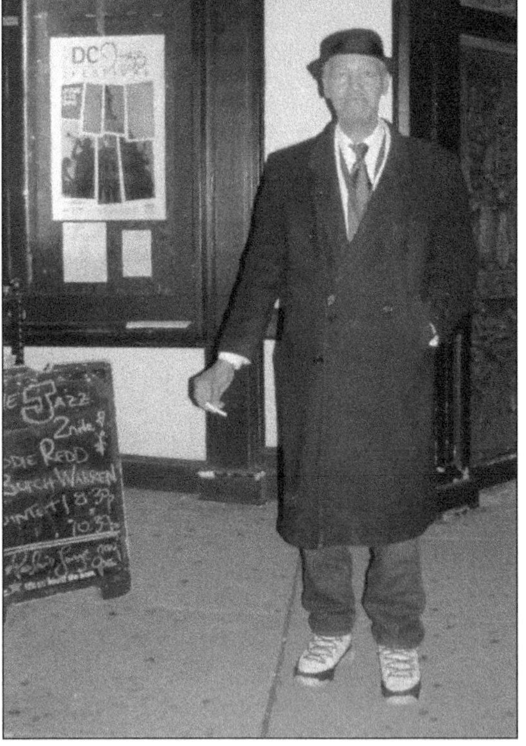

Butch Warren. Native Washingtonian Edward Rudolph "Butch" Warren Jr. was a celebrated bassist, especially for the work he produced in the 1950s and 1960s. For a time, he served as the house bassist for Blue Note Records and toured with Thelonious Monk. After struggling for many years with mental illness and homelessness, he recorded his first album as a leader, *Butch's Blues*, in 2008. He is pictured here outside Bohemian Caverns on February 11, 2011. (Photograph by Michael Wilderman.)

Andrew White. Native Washingtonian, composer, conductor, publisher, and multi-instrumentalist Andrew White is best known for his work as a saxophonist, electric bassist, and oboist. As a child, he moved with his family to Tennessee but returned to DC to complete his baccalaureate studies at Howard University. He also studied at the Paris Conservatory of Music. He has performed with a number of internationally known artists, including Stevie Wonder, the Fifth Dimension, and the American Ballet Theatre. He is shown here at the July 5, 1986, District Curators–produced DC Free Festival on Freedom Plaza. (Photograph by Michael Wilderman.)

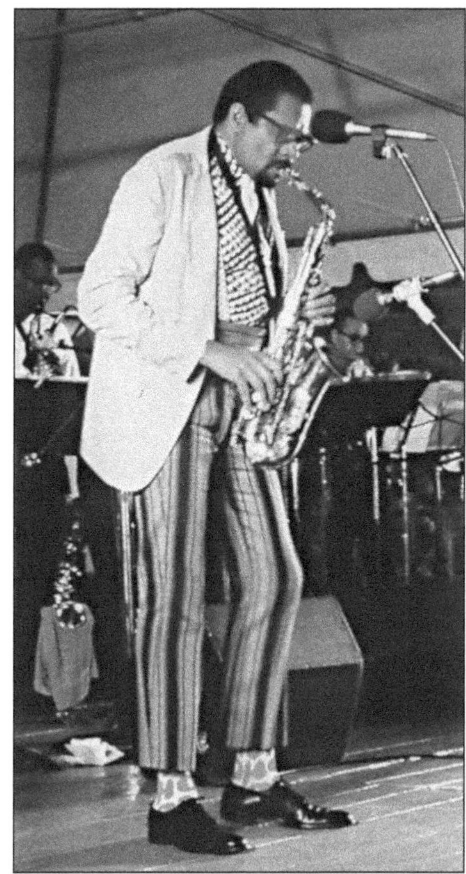

HR-57 Cultural Center. Bassist Ben Williams shares the stage with saxophonist Hamiet Bluiett, percussionist Chief Bey, guitarist Ed Cherry, and drummer Nashiet Waits. (Photograph by Michael Wilderman.)

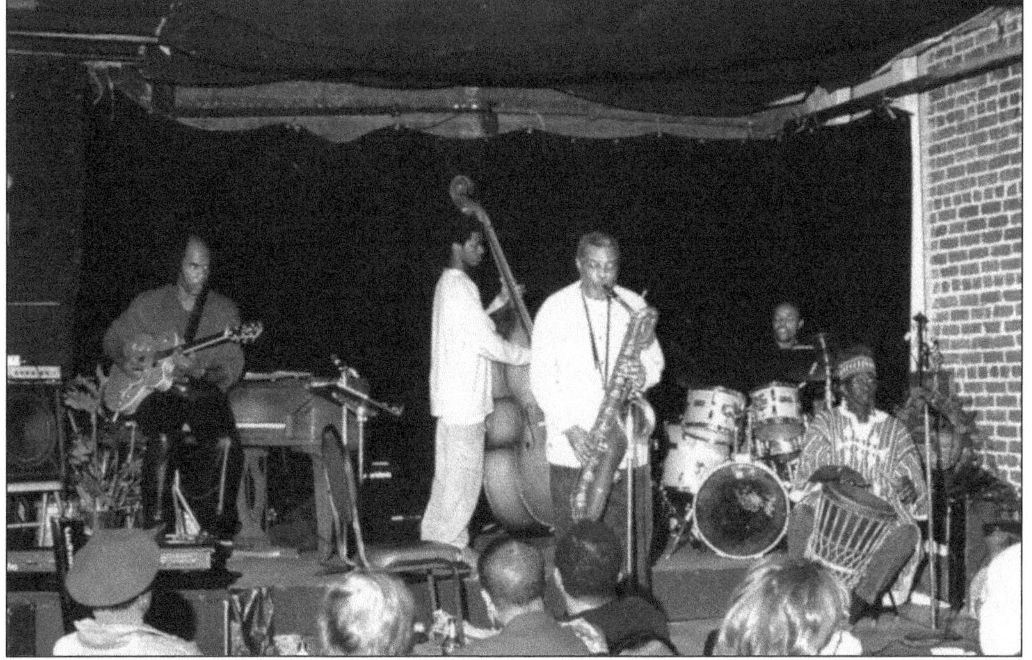

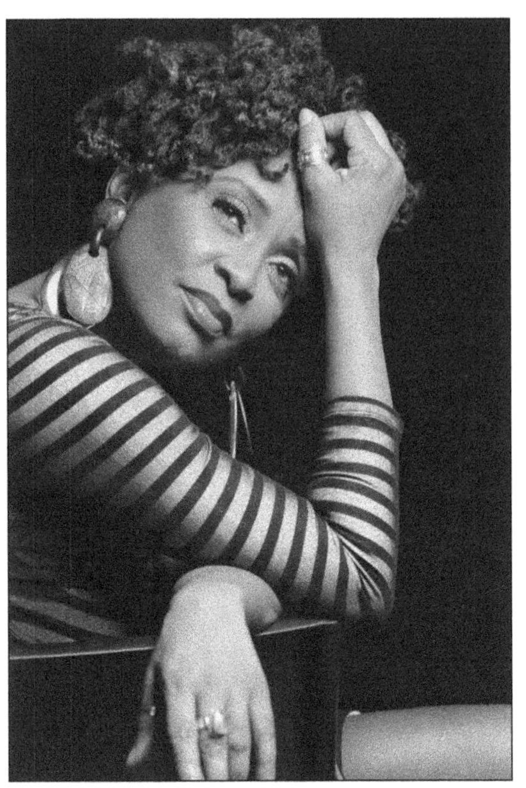

Lori Williams. Vocalist and music educator Lori Williams believes that artists should make connections across genres. At home with jazz and the choral music repertoire for church and school choirs, she calls Dianne Reeves her muse. Williams has recorded nationally and internationally, and usually completes three or four tours per year. Recently, Russian colleagues dubbed her the "Jazz Ambassador." Williams was interviewed for the 2017–2018 Washington, DC, Jazz Oral History Project. (Courtesy of Lori Williams.)

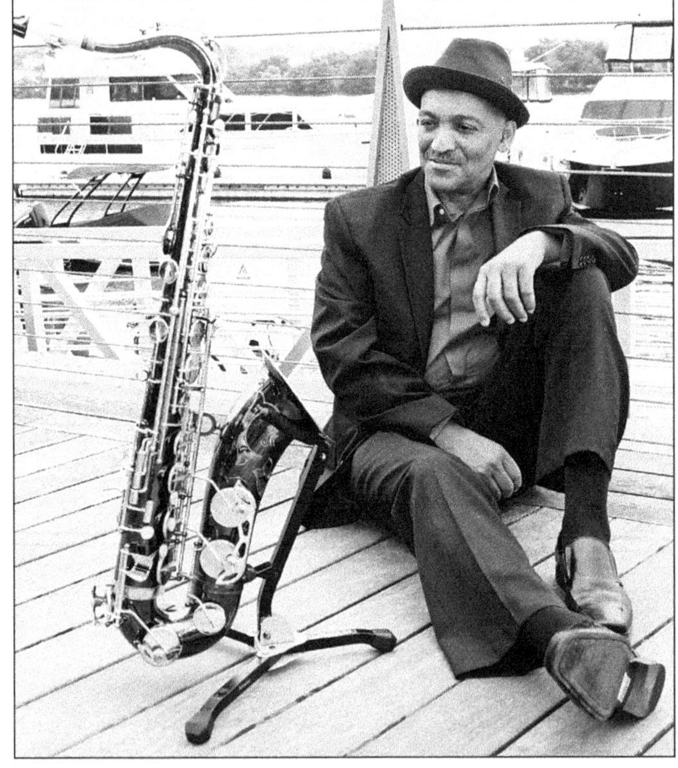

Lenny Harris, 2018. Saxophonist and vocalist Lenny Harris grew up in Maryland and has performed R&B, jazz, and rock music in a variety of settings with such artists as Lloyd Price, Miki Howard, Chante Moore, Chuck Brown, and others. His musical mentors included Al Johnson of the Unifics, and Louis Satterfield and Don Myrick of the Phenix Horns, the main horn section for Earth, Wind & Fire and Phil Collins. Harris is the founder of New World Order, a nine-piece band. Harris is pictured here in the Yards Park on the Capitol Riverfront in Washington, DC. (Photograph by Nathaniel Rhodes; courtesy of DC Legendary Musicians Inc.)

Marty Lamar. Pianist Marty Lamar is the minister of music at Washington's historic Metropolitan African Methodist Episcopal Church. He also serves on the Theatre Arts faculty at Howard University. (Courtesy of Marty Lamar.)

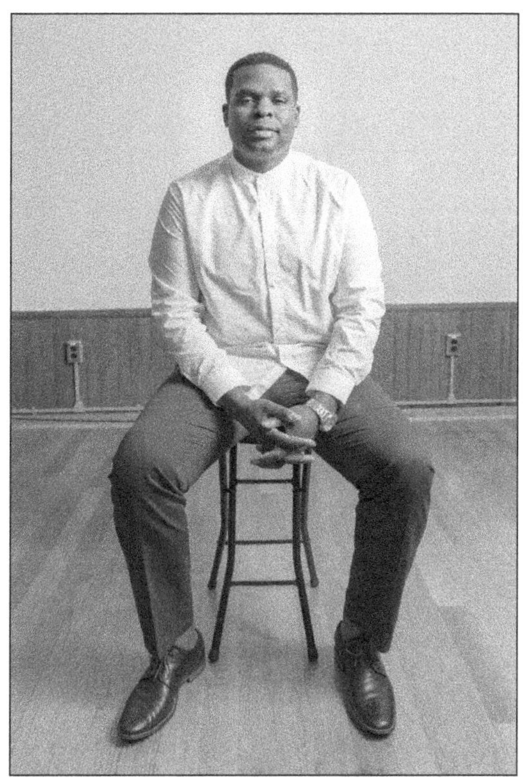

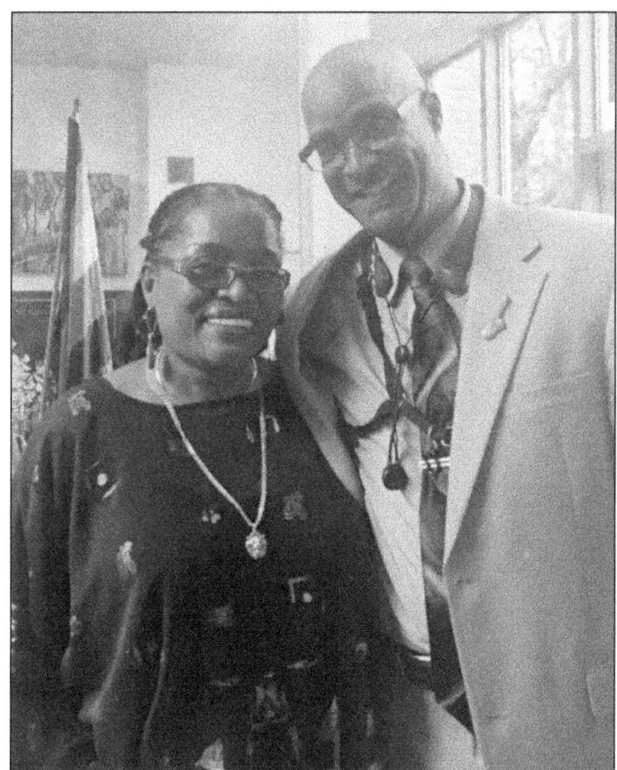

Esther Williams and Davey Yarborough. The husband and wife duo of vocalist Esther Williams and saxophonist Davey Yarborough are popular jazz educators and the founders and directors of DC's Jazz Arts Institute. (Photograph by Regennia N. Williams.)

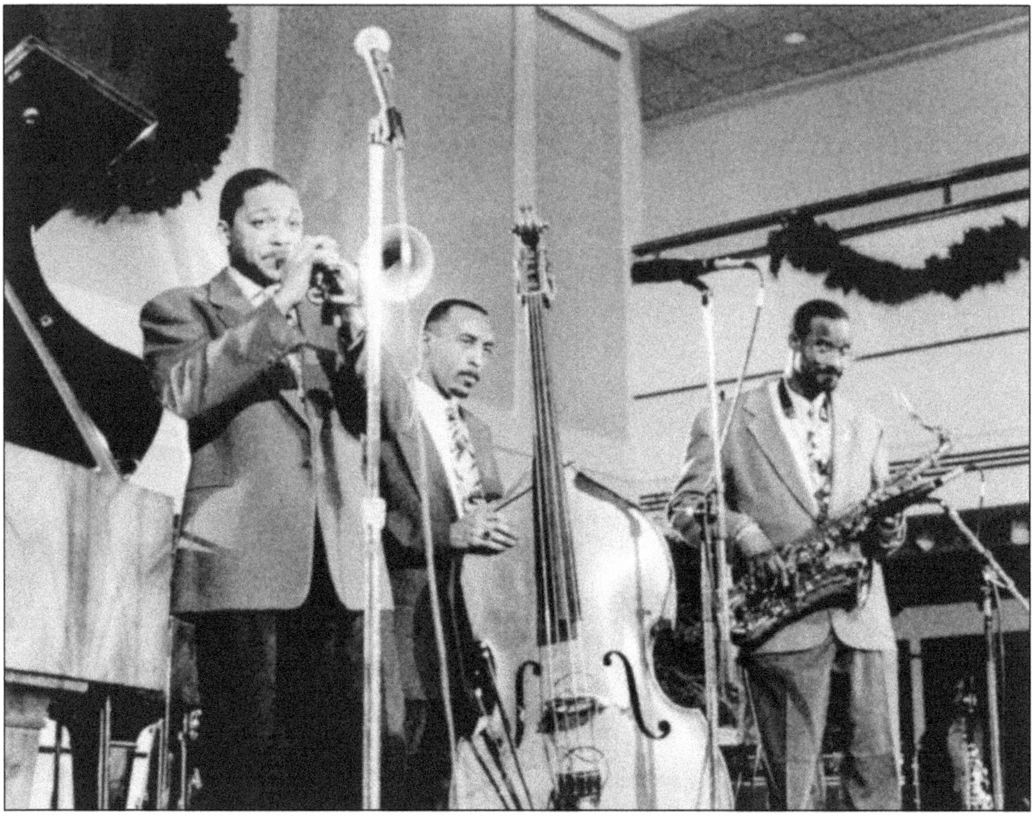

CARTER JEFFERSON TRIBUTE. Saxophonist Davey Yarborough performs here with trumpeter Wynton Marsalis and bassist James King at the Austrian Embassy during a December 7, 1993, tribute to the late saxophonist Carter Jefferson. (Photograph by Michael Wilderman.)

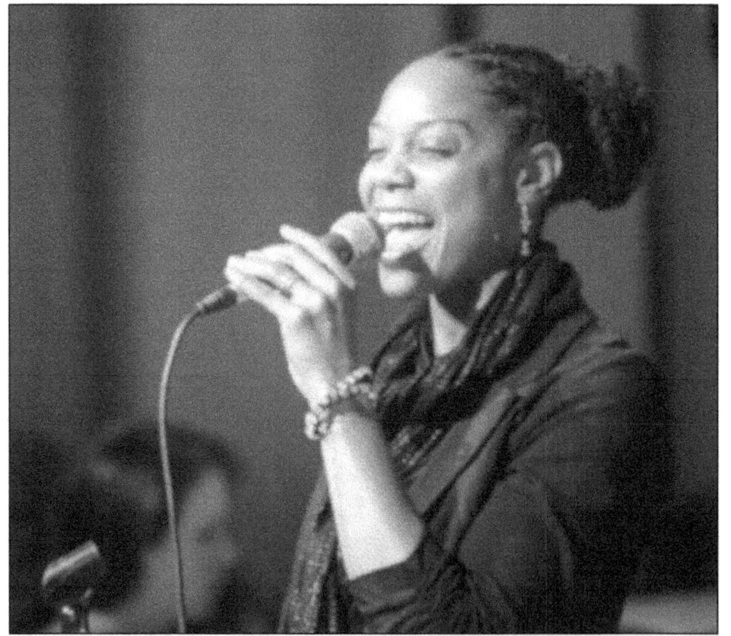

JESSICA BOYKIN-SETTLES. Jazz vocalist Jessica Boykin-Settles is both a Howard University alumna and lecturer. She teaches private lessons and jazz theory, arranging, and improvisation. Boykin-Settles conducted Howard University's female vocal jazz ensemble SAASy. She also conducts workshops and other activities that highlight the role of women in jazz. (Courtesy of Jessica Boykin-Settles.)

Six

DC Music and the Mass Media

Radio Programmers and Jazz Journalists

Since the early decades of the 20th century, the recording industry and print and broadcast media have played a crucial role in both promoting and documenting the history of jazz. From Duke Ellington's legendary broadcasts from New York's Cotton Club and the "race records" of the 1920s and 1930s through Felix E. Grant's tenure at WMAL Radio and Ellen Carter's work during the 21st century's "Jazz and Justice" era at WPFW Radio, Washington and Washingtonians have played a central role in broadcasting the music and sharing its message with the world, sometimes by way of the Washington Bureau of the *Pittsburgh Courier*, one of the most widely circulated African American newspapers; the mainstream *Washington Post*; and other publications.

In addition to the files of these media outlets, students of jazz history can also find evidence related to the influence of jazz journalists in some rather unexpected places, since many of these same journalists also helped inspire some of the region's top jazz festivals. This was certainly true of the work of WPFW's Elmore "Fish" Middleton, who inspired vocalist Ronnie Wells Elliston and pianist Ron Elliston, the husband and wife duo who cofounded the East Coast Jazz Festival.

There is, in fact, no shortage of excellent jazz-related and mass media–related archival material in the nation's capital. The images in the photographic collection of William P. Gottlieb, a longtime contributor to *Downbeat* magazine and the *Washington Post*, are now in the public domain and available in digital file formats via the Library of Congress website, and the Felix E. Grant Jazz Archives are available at the University of the District of Columbia. The Smithsonian Institution is home to the Scurlock Studio Collection, which includes images that once graced the entertainment pages of such well-known African American publications as the *Chicago Defender* and *Ebony* magazine.

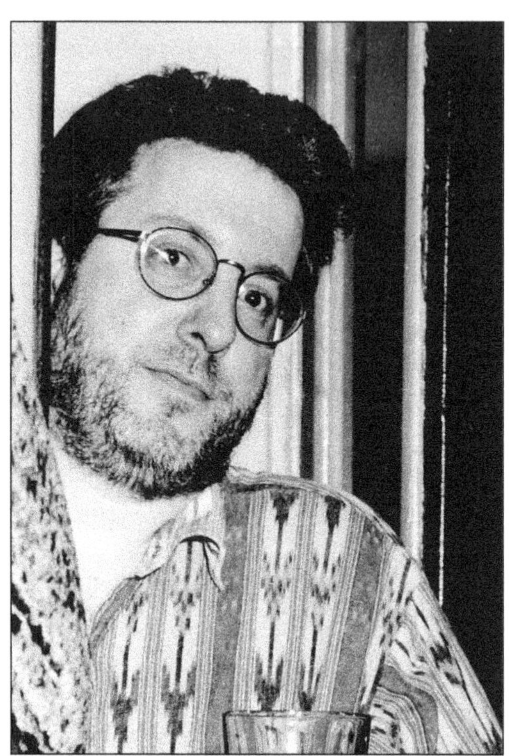

Larry Apelbaum. Larry Apelbaum, senior music specialist at the Library of Congress, is a jazz journalist, photographer, and programmer at WPFW Radio in Washington, DC. (Photograph by Michael Wilderman.)

The DC World Jazz Festival, 1989. Nap Turner (standing left, at microphone), the longtime host of the *Don't Forget the Blues* program on WPFW Radio, is pictured here at the DC World Jazz Festival. Also shown at this July 4, 1989, District Curators and WPFW production are Harold Summey, David Jernigan, Carl Turner, Paul Milesi, William F. Glaser, and Bruce Swaim. (Photograph by Michael Wilderman.)

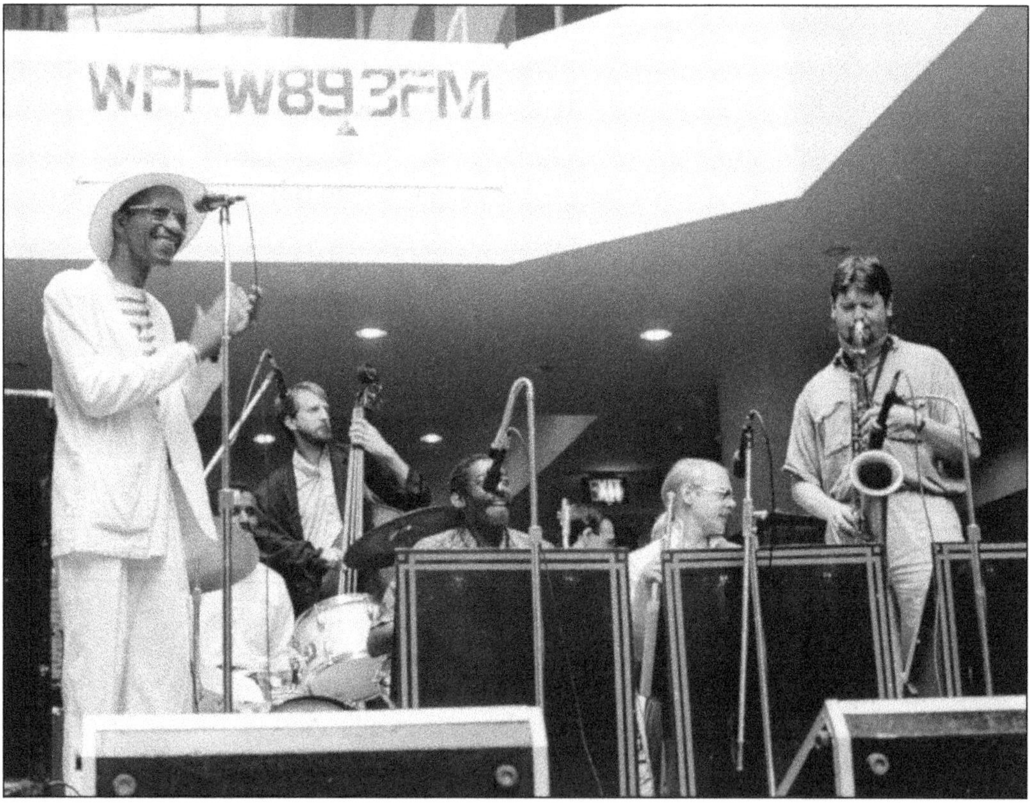

Keanna Faircloth. The host of *Evening Jazz* on WPFW 89.3 FM, Keanna Faircloth has worked as a radio programmer for more than 13 years. Faircloth, a native Washingtonian, studied piano and performed and toured in Europe twice with a children's gospel choir and performed with the DC Youth Ensemble. A graduate of the Benjamin Banneker High School, Faircloth completed her undergraduate work at Howard University, where she performed with SAASy, a women's jazz ensemble. While at Howard, her mentors included Professors Connaitre Miller, Arthur Dawkins, and James Weldon Norris. She was interviewed for the 2017–2018 Washington, DC, Jazz Oral History Project. (Courtesy of Keanna Faircloth.)

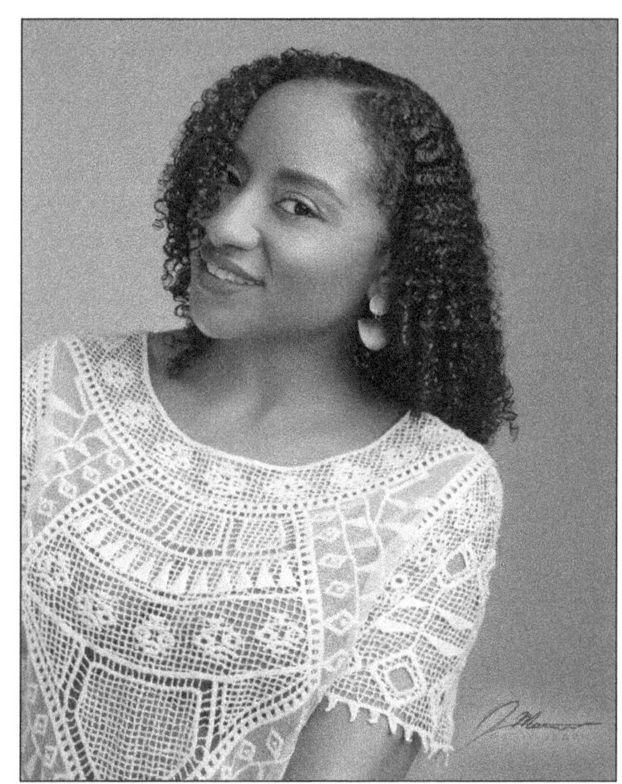

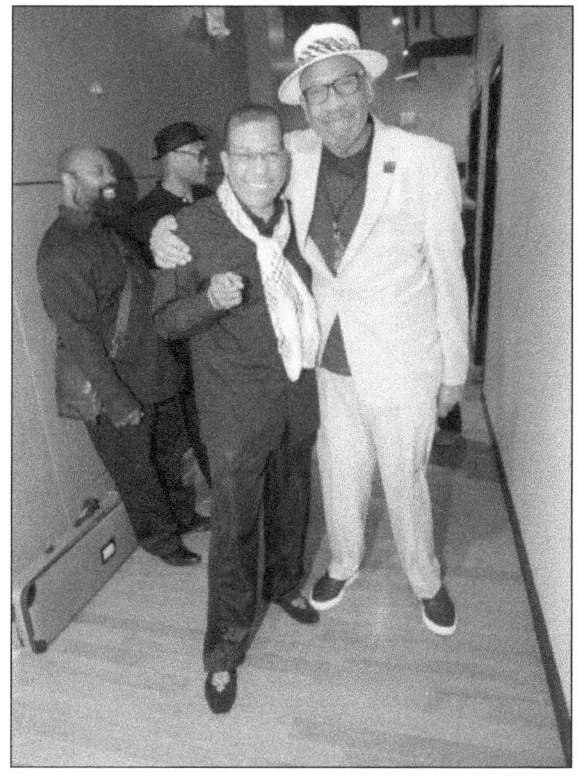

Willard Jenkins and Nasar Abadey, 2018. In addition to serving as the artistic director for the DC Jazzfest, Willard Jenkins (right) is a successful educator, jazz journalist, author, blogger, and radio personality. He hosts the *Late Night Jazz: Ancient Futures* program on WPFW, Washington's "Jazz and Justice" station. Jenkins is pictured here with Nasar Abadey, recipient of the 2018 DC Jazzfest Lifetime Achievement Award. (Photograph by Lawrence A. Randall.)

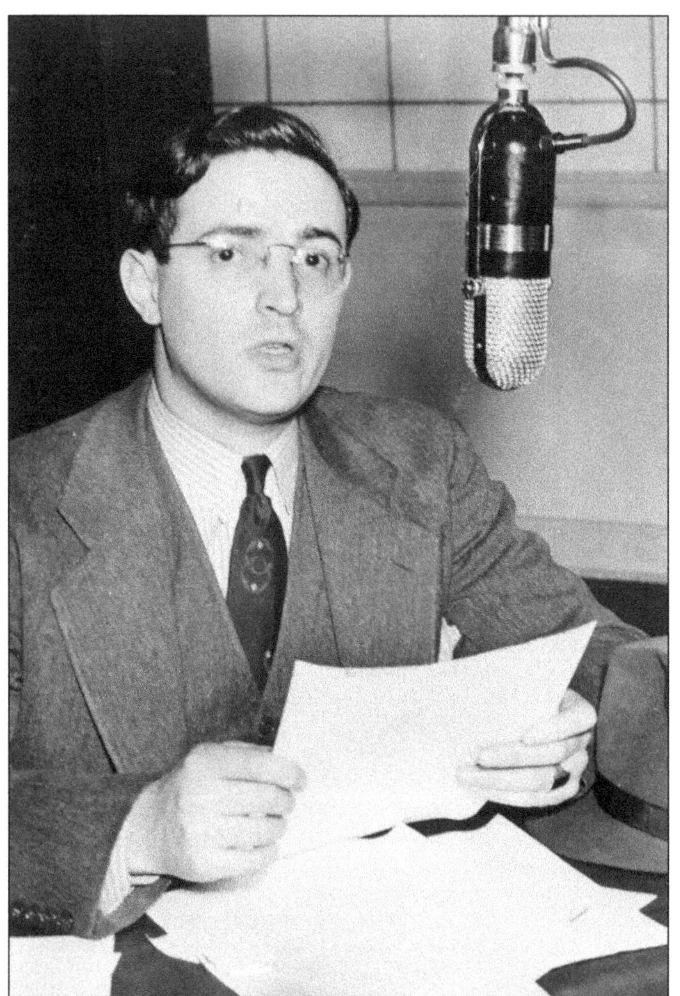

William P. Gottlieb. Photojournalist William P. Gottlieb contributed photographs and related stories to the *Washington Post*, *Downbeat* magazine, and other publications. During his active years, he amassed an incredible collection of prints and negatives, which, after being purchased by the Library of Congress in 1995, entered the public domain in 2010. (Courtesy of the William P. Gottlieb / Ira and Leonore S. Gershwin Fund Collection, Music Division, Library of Congress.)

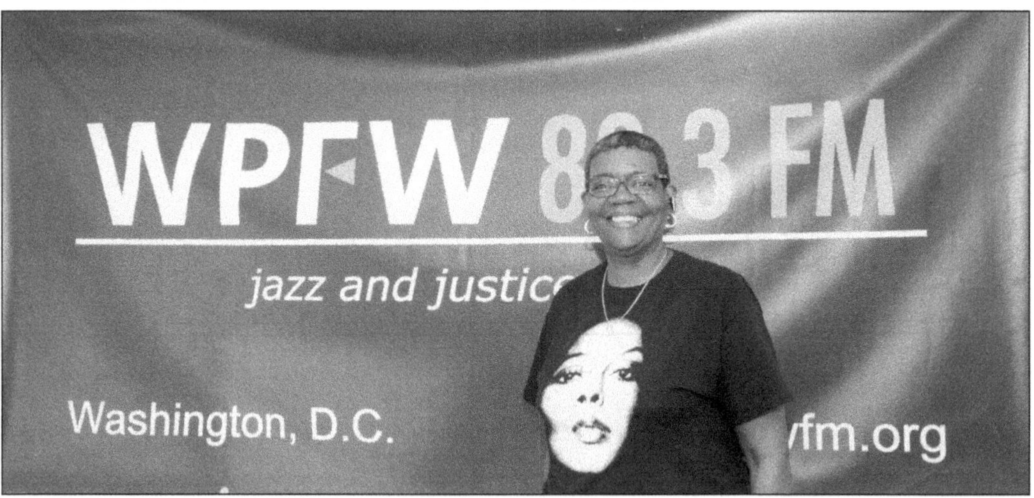

Robyn Holden, 2018. As a veteran programmer at WPFW, Robyn Holden hosts *Robyn's Place* on Friday evenings. (Photograph by Lawrence A. Randall.)

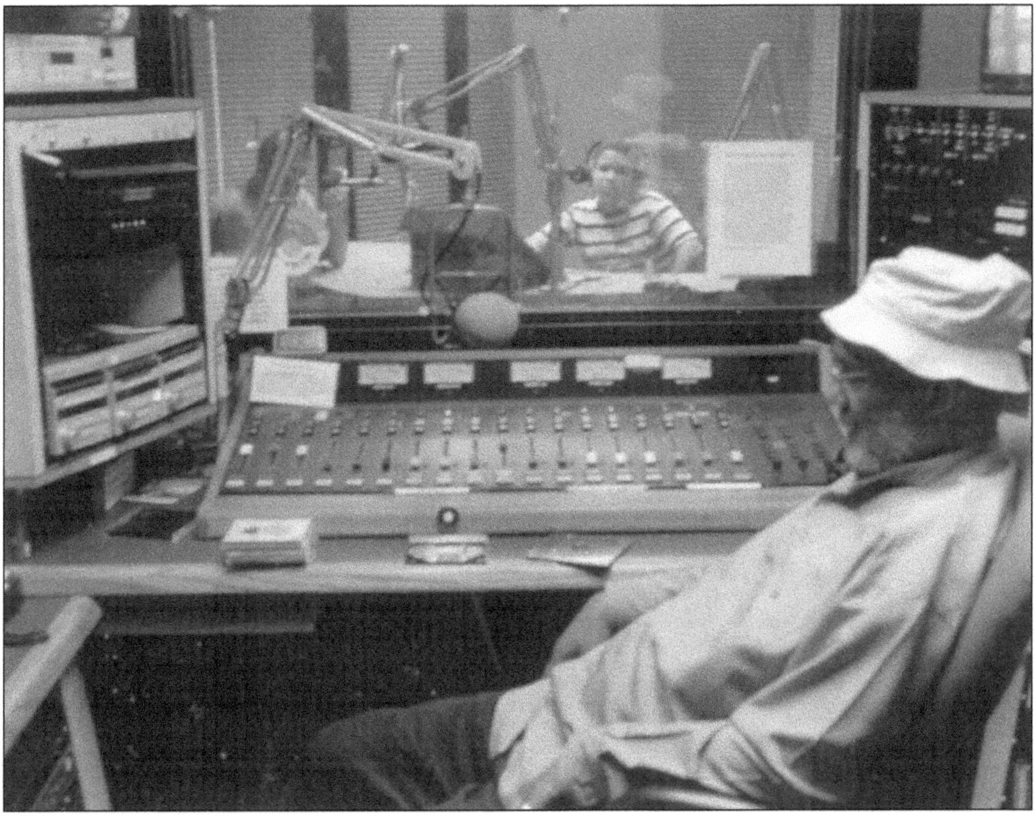

Kush Abadey and Jamal Muhammad. A young Kush Abadey, who is now a world-class drummer based in New York, is shown here in the studios of WPFW with the late Jamal Muhammad (1934–2012). A native Washingtonian, Muhammad was born Phillip White in 1934 and changed his name in adulthood when he joined the Nation of Islam. Muhammad was a jazz programmer at WPFW for more than 25 years. (Courtesy Sandra Butler-Truesdale.)

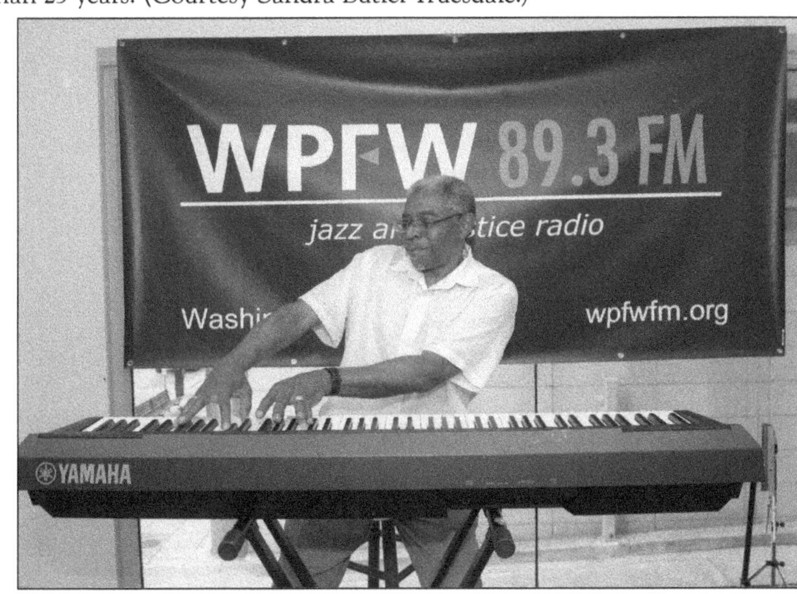

Jerry Paris, 2018. Keyboard artist Jerry Paris is the general manager of WPFW. (Photograph by Lawrence A. Randall.)

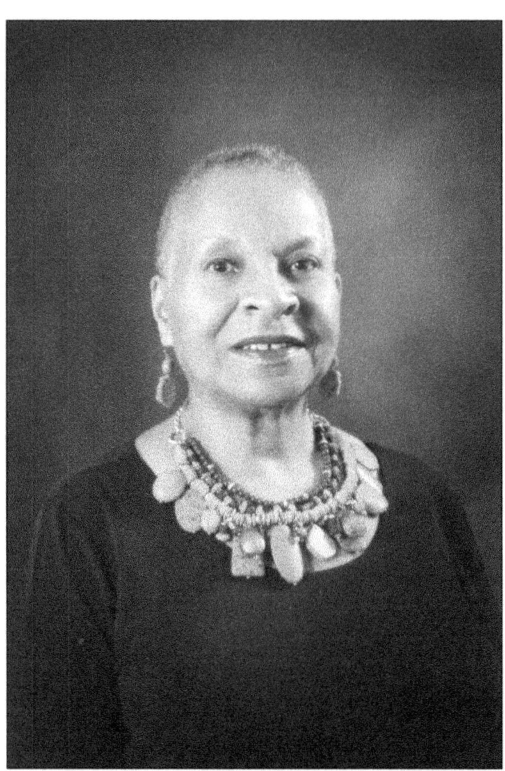

Ellen Williams Carter. An alumna of Boston University and Howard University Law School, Ellen Williams Carter hosts *Morning Brew, the Jazz Notes Edition* on WPFW, where she has served as a jazz programmer for more than 30 years. (Courtesy of Ellen Carter.)

Felix E. Grant and Cab Calloway. Host Felix E. Grant (left) is pictured here with conductor and vocalist Cab Calloway, the "King of Hi-De-Ho," in the studio of radio station WWDC . (Courtesy of the Felix E. Grant Jazz Archives, University of the District of Columbia.)

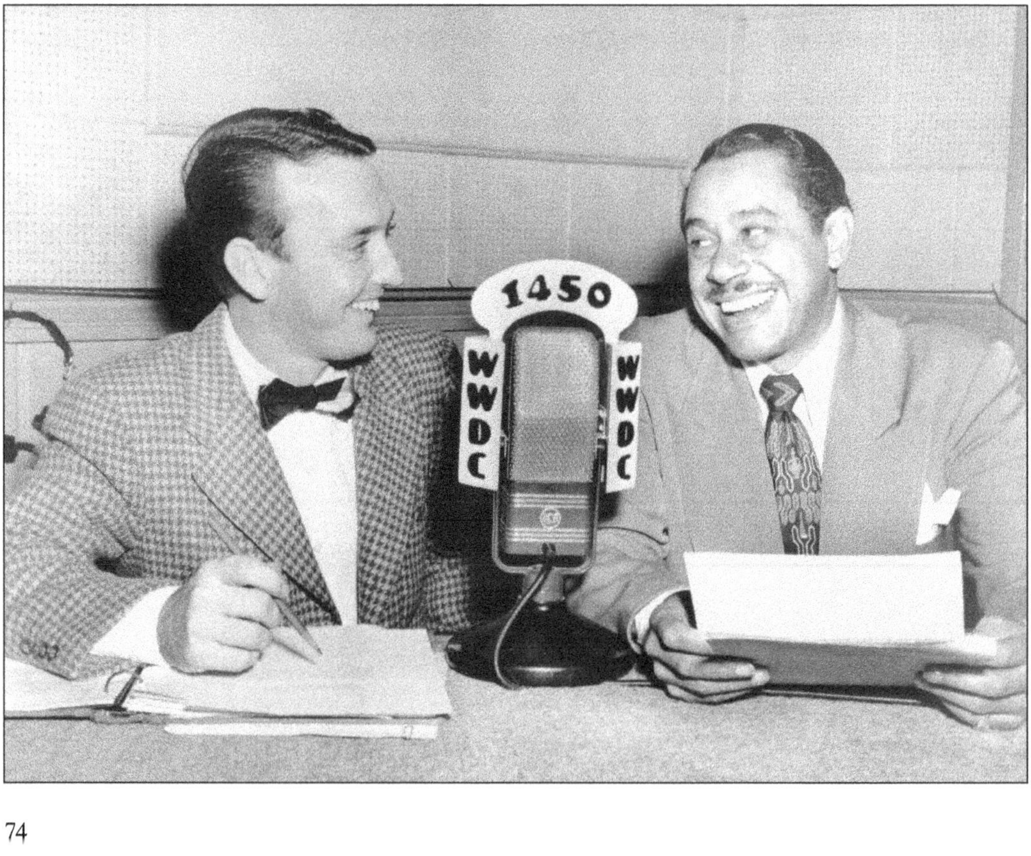

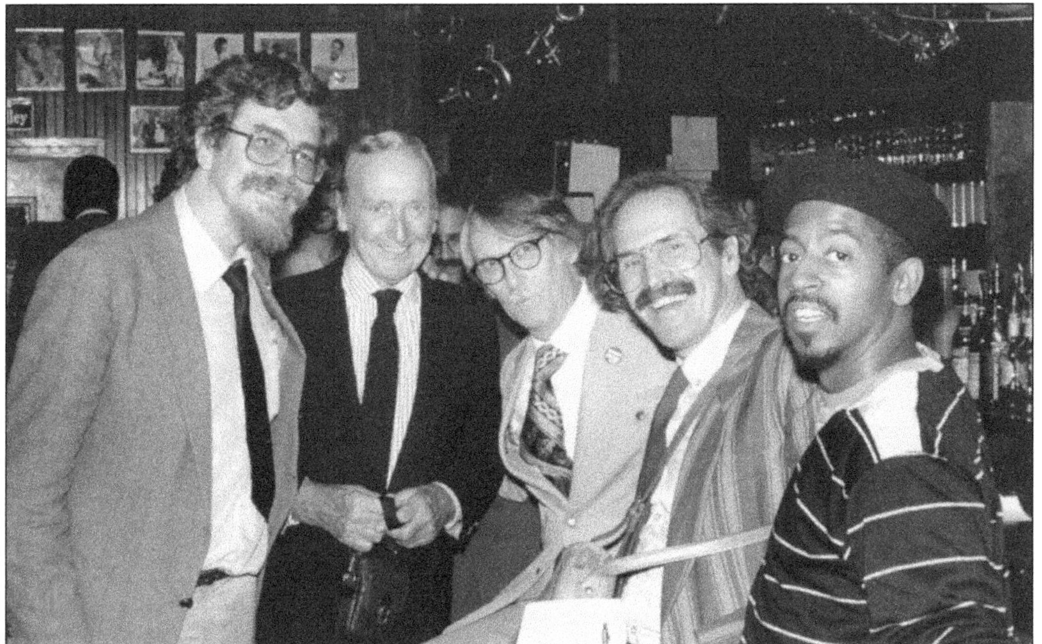

Jazz Journalists and Programmers at Blues Alley. Legendary radio host Felix E. Grant (second from left) is shown here with fellow jazz aficionados, including (from left to right) Rusty Hassan (jazz programmer at WPFW), W. Royal Stokes, Alexey Batashev, and Bill Brower, on October 24, 1988. (Photograph by Michael Wilderman.)

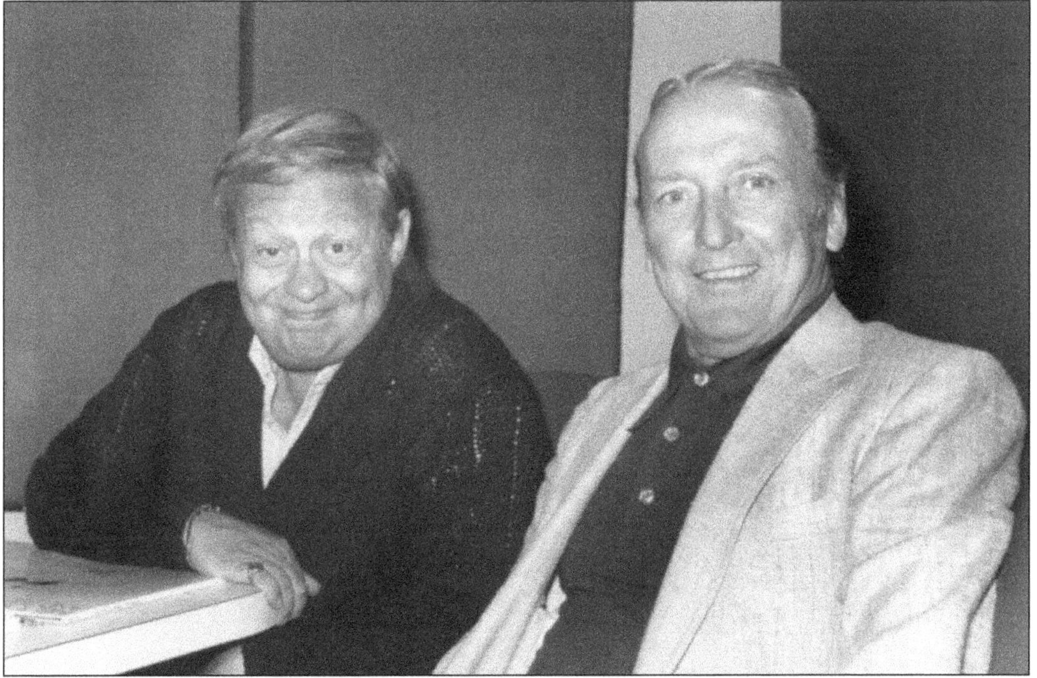

Felix E. Grant with Mel Torme. Pictured here with DC radio host Felix E. Grant is vocalist Mel Torme (left), who was celebrated for his vocal artistry and scatting ability. (Courtesy of the Felix E. Grant Jazz Archives, University of the District of Columbia.)

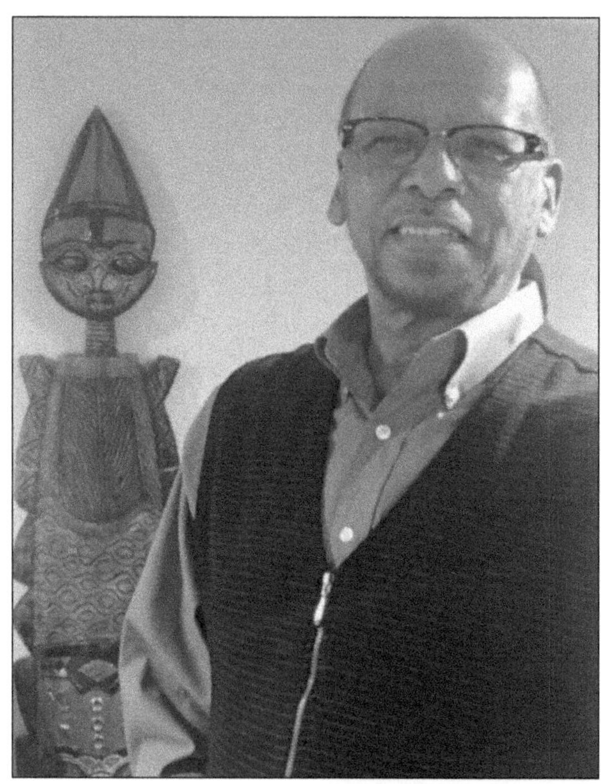

Brother Ah. A world traveler and multi-instrumentalist, Robert Northern III (Brother Ah) has been influenced greatly by the arts of Africa and other parts of the world. In addition to sharing his oral history narrative with Regennia N. Williams for the 2017–2018 Washington, DC, Oral History Project, Brother Ah was interviewed by Rusty Hassan for the 2017 Washington, DC, Jazzfest Oral History Project. (Photograph by Regennia N. Williams.)

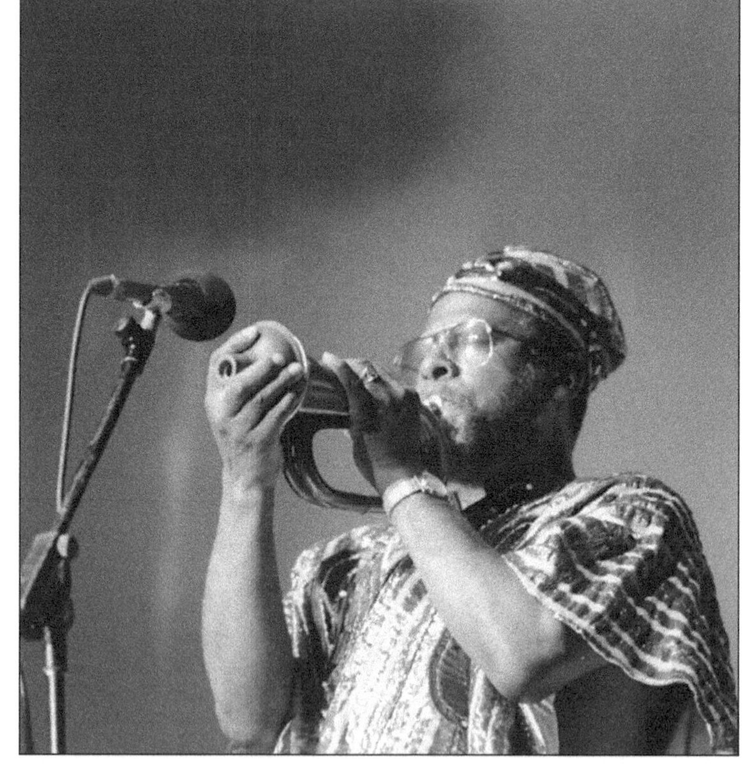

Brother Ah Playing Bugle, Lincoln Theatre. Brother Ah, born in 1934 in North Carolina and a current DC resident, is a jazz programmer at WPFW and a multi-instrumentalist whose credits include work with Miles Davis, John Coltrane, Dizzy Gillespie, Sun Ra, and Thelonious Monk, among others. Manufactured Recordings recently released Brother Ah's three-album set *Divine Music*. He is shown performing at the Lincoln Theatre on July 5, 1997. (Photograph by Michael Wilderman.)

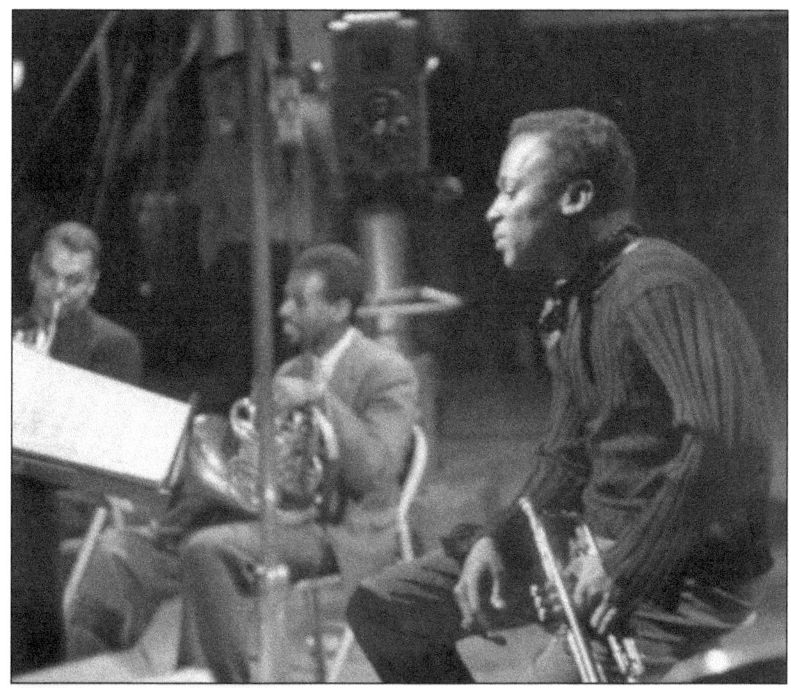

Brother Ah with Miles Davis. Very early in his career, Robert "Brother Ah" Northern III (center) distinguished himself as a gifted French horn player and an effective educator at the postsecondary level. His experiences include work at Dartmouth College and Brown University. Today, he is a popular radio programmer at WPFW. (Courtesy of Brother Ah.)

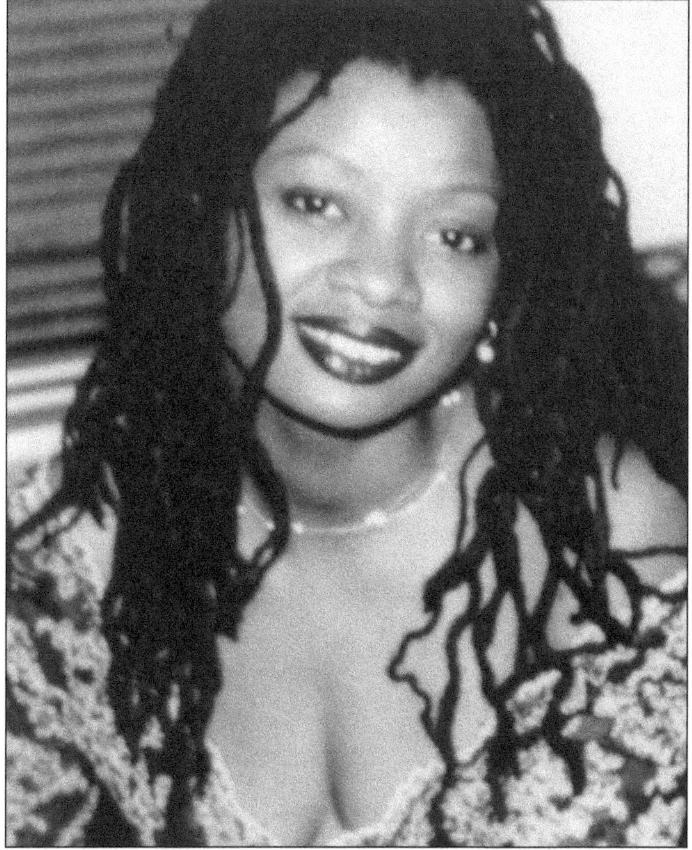

Katea Stitt. Georgetown University alumna Katea Stitt has worked as a performing arts producer and manager, and served as coordinator and oral historian for the Smithsonian Institution's Jazz Oral History Program. The founder of Anyanwu Management, her clients have included Ntozake Shange, Lester Bowie, Sweet Honey in the Rock, Washington Performing Arts Society, District Curators, the Duke Ellington Jazz Festival, and others. As a tour manager, she has worked throughout the United States and in Europe, Asia, and Africa. A longtime jazz programmer at WPFW, Stitt has served as the station's interim program director since 2013. She is the daughter of jazz saxophonist Sonny Stitt. (Courtesy of Katea Stitt.)

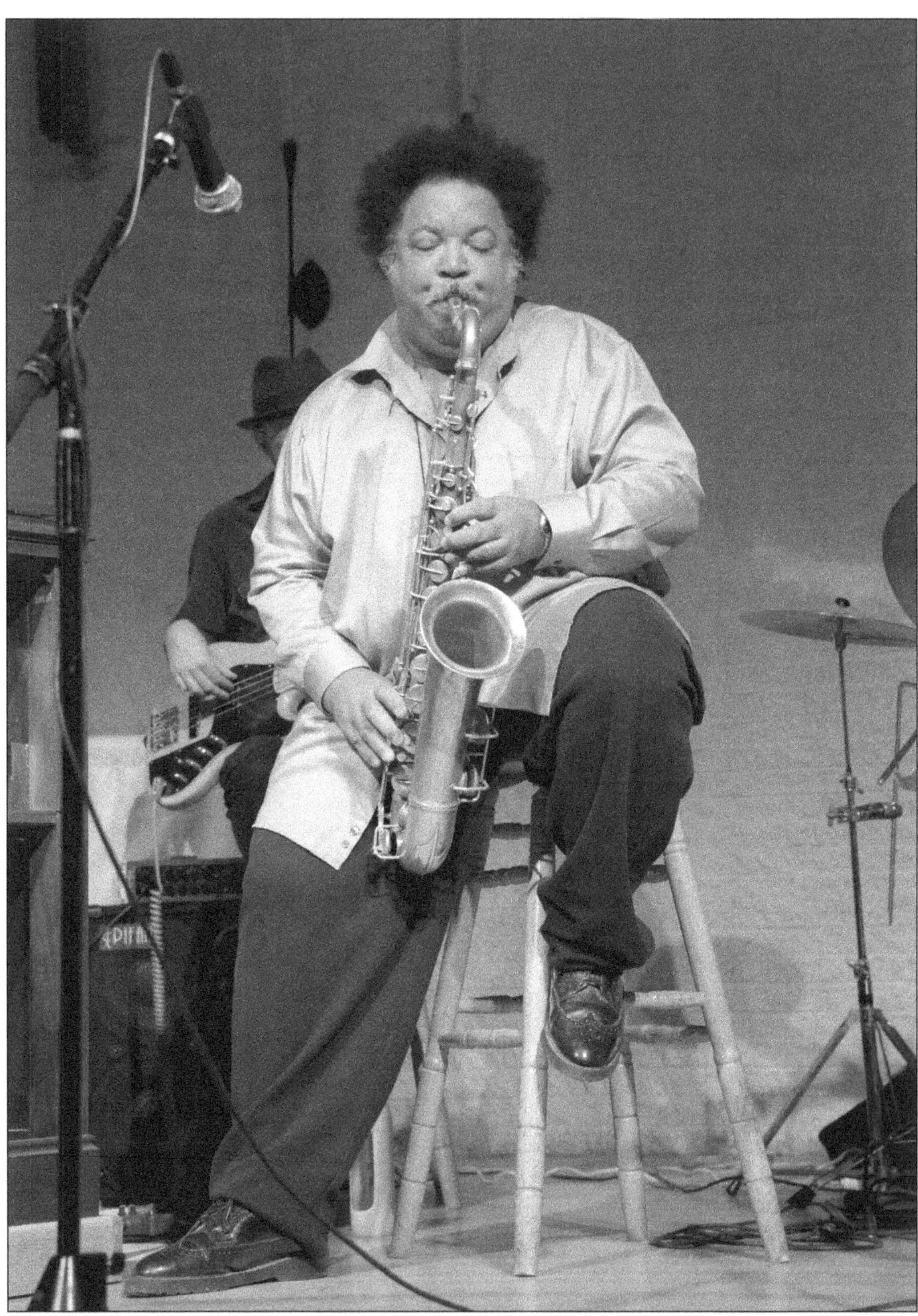

Ron Holloway. Saxophonist Ron Holloway (born 1953 in Washington, DC) performs at Jazz Night at Westminster Presbyterian Church. Holloway was interviewed for the 2017–2018 Washington, DC, Jazz Oral History Project. (Photograph by Lawrence A. Randall.)

Seven

Place Matters

Jazz Clubs and Other Arts Venues, Then and Now

James K. Zimmerman, senior producer of public programs for the Smithsonian Institution's National Museum of American History and an accomplished jazz vocalist, once described Washington, DC's Mr. Y's Gold Room as "a great gathering place for heritage keepers." There is, in fact, abundant evidence in the area's libraries and archival collections to suggest that, beyond providing food, drink, and musical entertainment, many jazz venues were also sites for intergenerational cultural communion.

In addition to Mr. Y's, Zimmerman's list of favorite clubs includes One Step Down, Pig Foot, and Takoma Station, where numerous jam sessions were held. Among the unforgettable "heritage keepers" were pianist Eddie Hayter, vocalist Gail Dixon, and bassist Clarence Seay. The messages in their music were not lost on those who were wise enough to listen.

A 2017 *Washington Post* article by Michael J. West reminded readers that while Mr. Y's, One Step Down, and several other clubs from the late 20th century were no longer open for business, Twins Jazz, established by twin sisters Kelly and Maze Tesfaye, was (and is) still going strong on U Street. Both Twins Jazz and Blues Alley are among the "great gathering place[s] for heritage keepers" in DC's 21st-century jazz community, and they are not alone.

As the organizer of and master of ceremonies for the popular Jazz Night concerts at Westminster Presbyterian Church on Fridays, Dick Smith has become a fixture on the DC jazz scene. For nearly 20 years, Jazz Night has helped change where and how audiences experience jazz. In order to create the most comprehensive list of performance spaces where jazz is likely to be heard, one must now include the meeting rooms and auditoriums of DC's libraries and scores of other venues. It can therefore be argued that, like the old grey mare of a traditional folk song, the old jazz club just "ain't what [it] used to be."

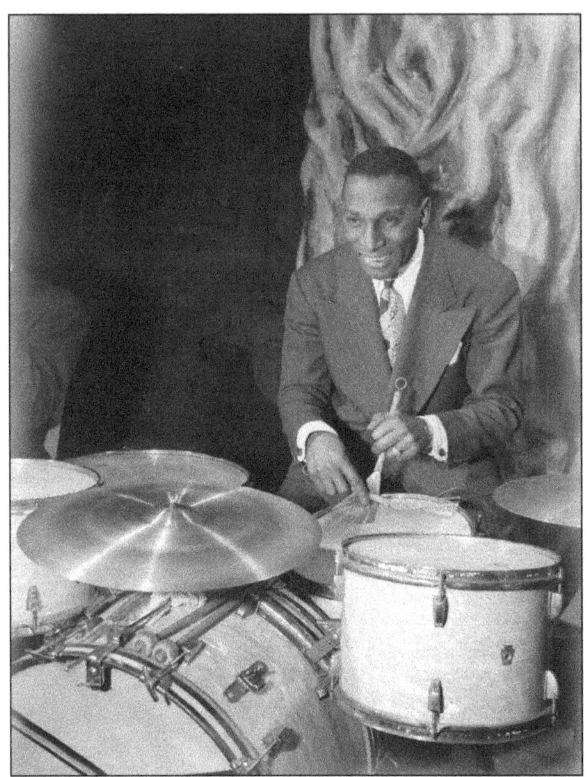

Cozy Cole at Ole South. Jazz drummer William R. "Cozy" Cole is shown here performing at Washington, DC's Ole South. During his long and successful career as a percussionist, Cole performed on Broadway in the musical *Carmen Jones* as well as numerous concert and/or recording dates with Jelly Roll Morton, Cab Calloway, and Louis Armstrong, among others. In 1953, he joined Gene Krupa in forming the Krupa and Cole Drum School in New York. (Courtesy of the William P. Gottlieb / Ira and Leonore S. Gershwin Fund Collection, Music Division, Library of Congress.)

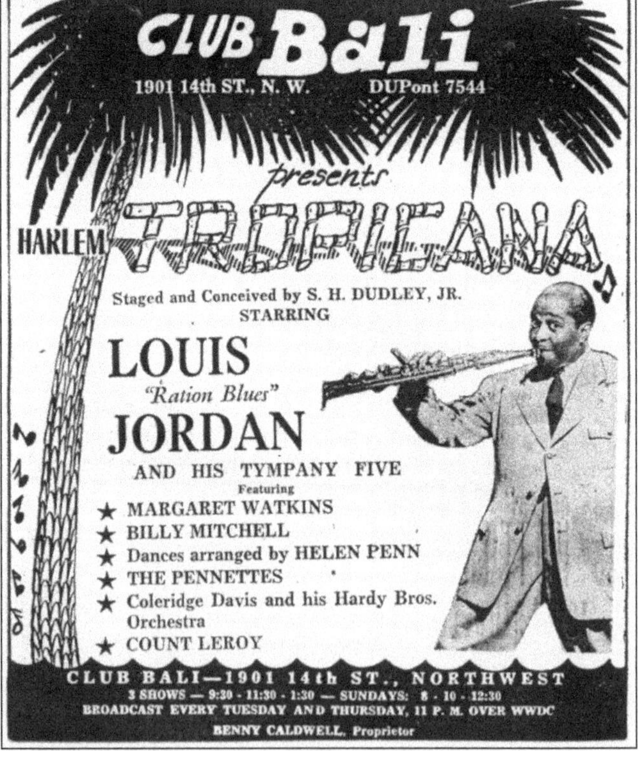

Club Bali Advertisement for Performance by Louis Jordan. Opened in the era of World War II by Benjamin Caldwell, Club Bali was a popular venue that featured live entertainment by the top jazz musicians and dancers. It was located at the intersection of Fourteenth and T Streets, in the Greater U Street entertainment community. (Courtesy of the Historical Society of Washington, DC.)

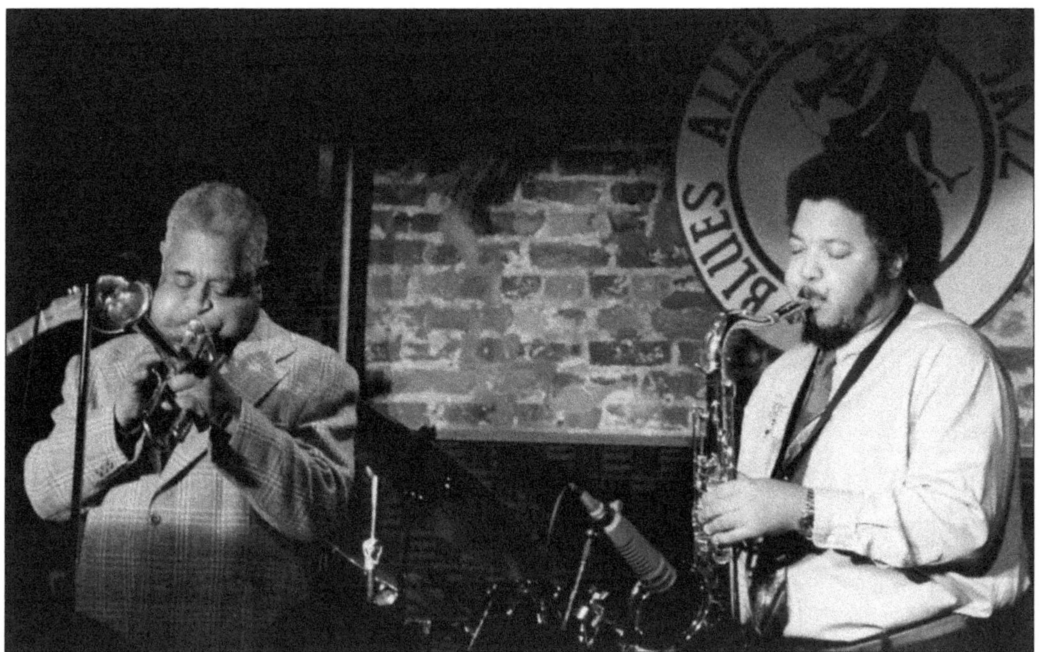

RON HOLLOWAY AND DIZZY GILLESPIE AT BLUES ALLEY. Trumpeter Dizzy Gillespie enjoyed a popular following in Washington, DC, and throughout the world. Gillespie, who is renowned for his pioneering work in bebop and early experiments that fused Afro-Cuban rhythms with American jazz, is pictured here in a performance at the Blues Alley jazz club. A veteran saxophonist and native Washingtonian, Holloway has toured and recorded with many of the leading lights in jazz, including Dizzy Gillespie, and is adept at performing blues, funk, and other musical genres. (Photograph by Michael Wilderman.)

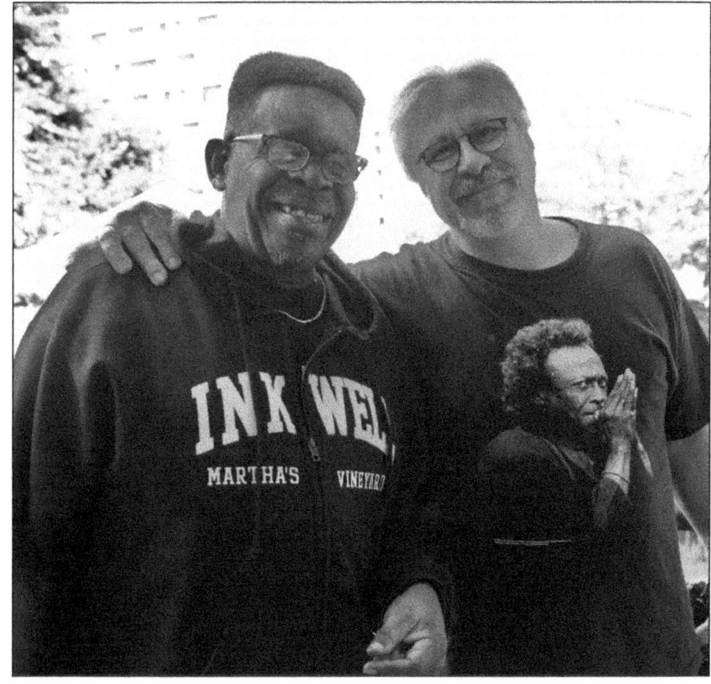

DEANDREY HOWARD AND REV. BRIAN HAMILTON. DeAndrey Howard, proprietor of Alice's Jazz and Cultural Society, is shown here with the Rev. Brian Hamilton, co-pastor of the Westminster Presbyterian Church, home of the Jazz Night and Blue Monday Blues concert series. (Photograph by Lawrence A. Randall.)

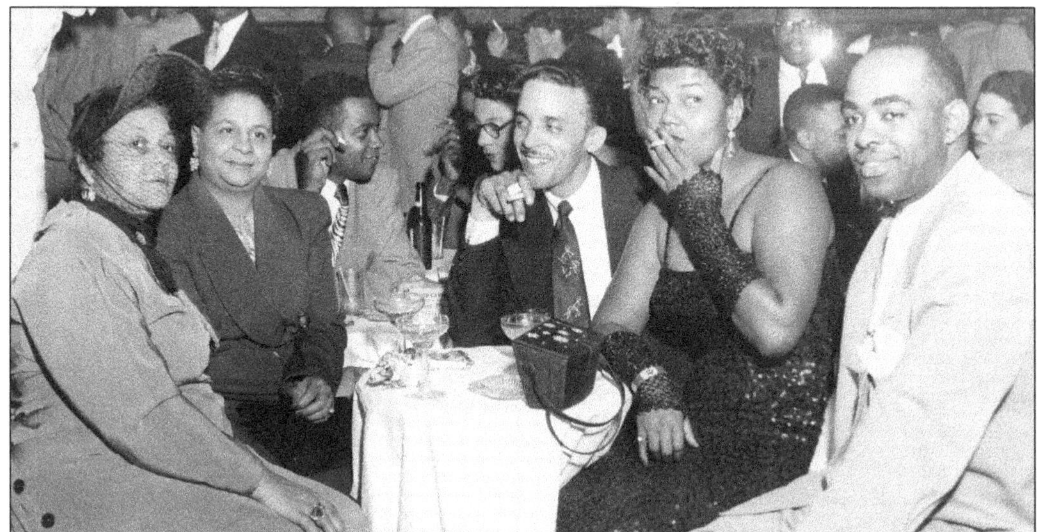

Pearl Bailey at the Crystal Caverns. Newport News, Virginia, native Pearl Bailey (second from right), one of Black Broadway's brightest stars, was a popular attraction at Washington, DC's Crystal Caverns, the U Street jazz nightclub that was later renamed the Bohemian Caverns. (Courtesy of the Pittsburgh Courier Collection–Washington Bureau, Moorland-Spingarn Special Collections, Howard University.)

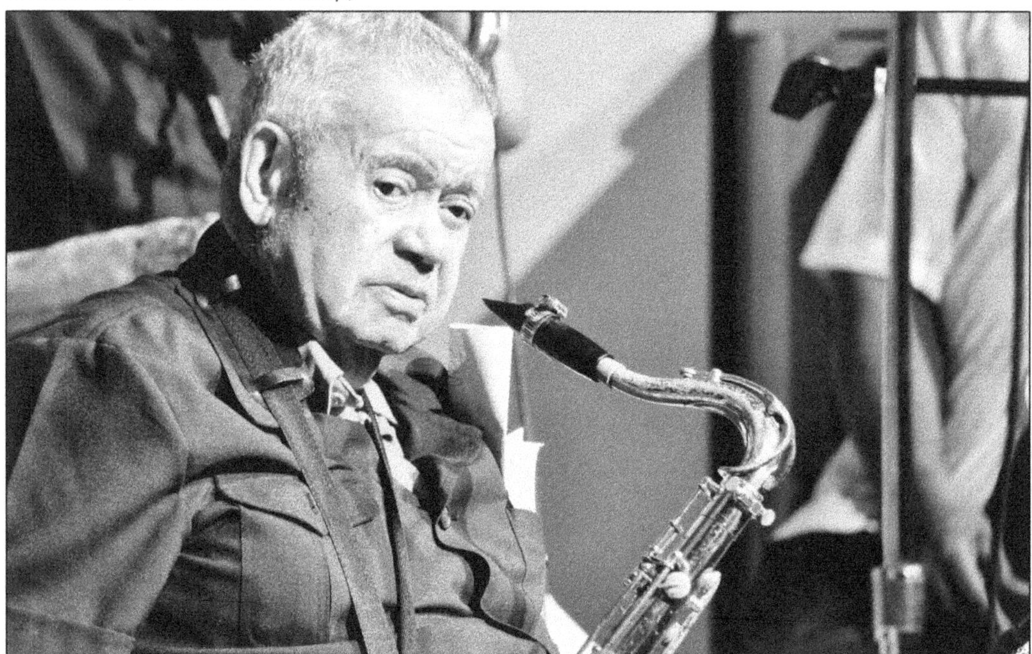

Buck Hill. Rather than take his talents on the road, saxophonist Roger Wendell "Buck" Hill chose to remain in DC with his wife, Helen, and their children, working for many years for the US Postal Service and earning the moniker "Wailin' Mailman" for his saxophone prowess. Hill, who passed away in 2017, can be heard on more than a dozen albums. His funeral service—complete with a post-eulogy jam session—was held on Sunday, March 26, 2017, at Westminster Presbyterian Church, home to Washington's popular Jazz Night concerts since 1999. (Photograph by Lawrence A. Randall.)

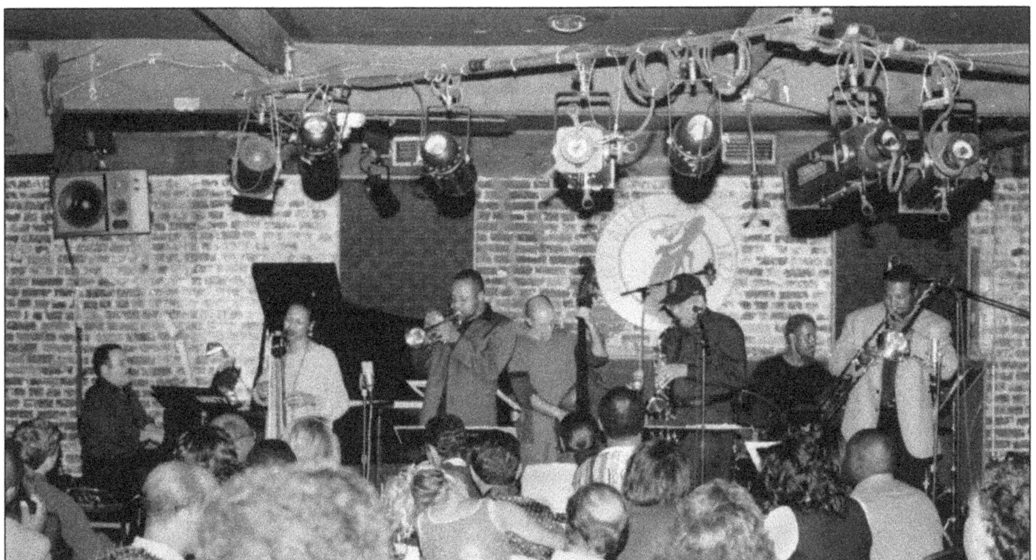

Byron Morris and Unity at Blues Alley, 1986. Saxophonist Byron Morris is the product of a musical family. After receiving his elementary and secondary education and early musical training in Virginia, he studied engineering at Alabama's Tuskegee Institute but never abandoned his love for music. He enjoys both live performances and studio work as well as lecturing and conducting music workshops. (Photograph by Michael Wilderman.)

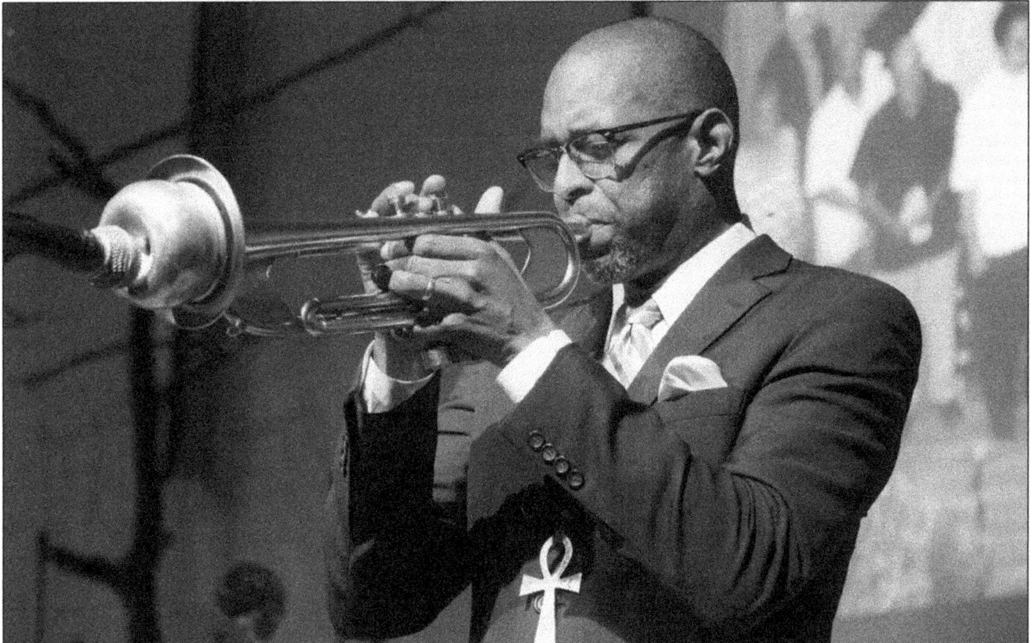

Michael Thomas, Trumpeter. An alumnus of Grambling State University, trumpeter Michael Thomas has distinguished himself as a solo artist and leader of the DC-based Michael Thomas Quintet. His performance credits include work with Andrew White, Betty Carter, Jimmy Heath, Larry Willis, Shirley Scott, Slide Hampton, Buck Hill, Webster Young, Gary Bartz, Joe Williams, and others. He is the founder of JazHead Entertainment LLC, the exclusive distributor for the recordings of the Michael Thomas Quintet. (Photograph by Lawrence A. Randall.)

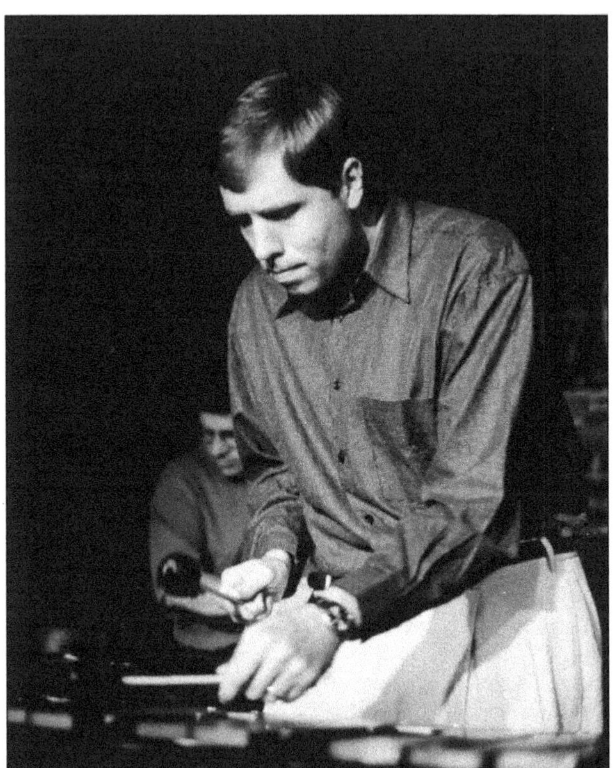

Chuck Redd Blues Alley. Drummer and vibraphonist Chuck Redd is pictured here at Blues Alley in DC's Georgetown community, which has hosted performances by some of the world's top jazz artists since its founding in 1965. (Photograph by Michael Wilderman.)

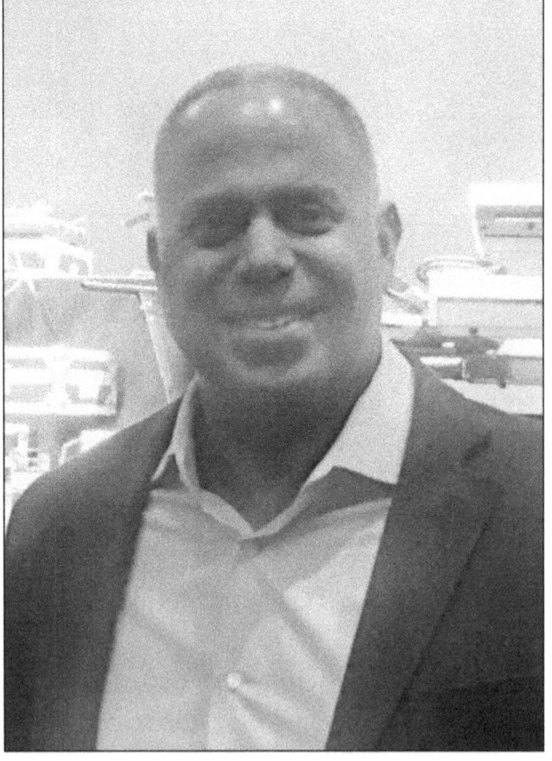

Chip Ellis at the Howard Theatre. Developer Chip Ellis, one of the narrators for the 2017–2018 Washington, DC, Jazz Oral History Project, partnered with Blue Note Entertainment to form Howard Theatre Entertainment, which in recent years served as the operator of the newly renovated Howard Theatre, after it reopened in 2012. (Photograph by Regennia N. Williams.)

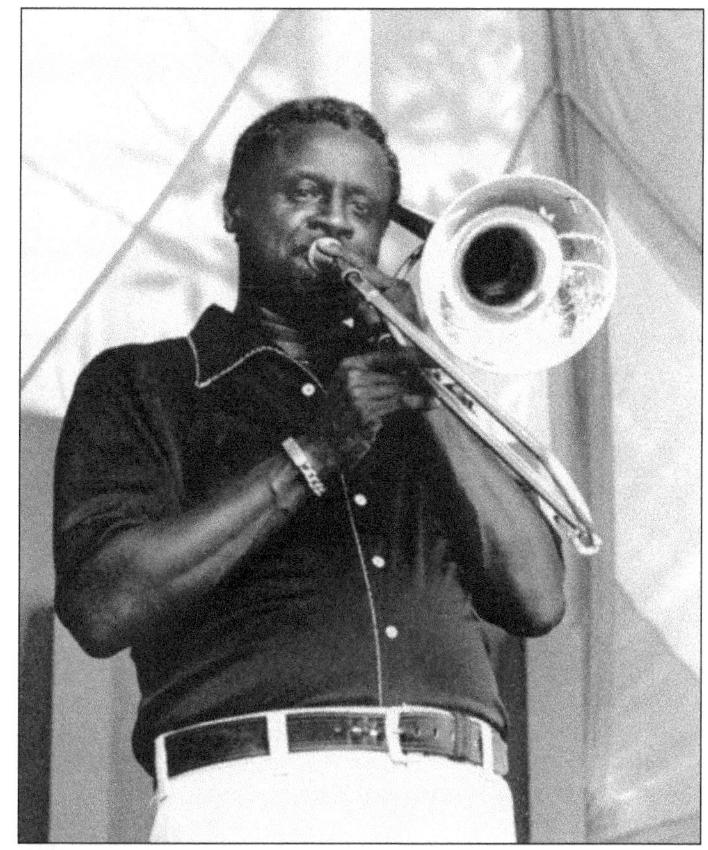

Calvin Jones at Wolf Trap. Composer, arranger, and multi-instrumentalist Calvin Jones was a longtime faculty member at the University of the District of Columbia, director of the jazz studies program from 1976 until his death in 2004, and progenitor of the school's annual big band festival. He also worked with Ray Charles, Duke Ellington, Count Basie, and others. He is pictured here at Wolf Trap on June 21, 1981. (Photograph by Michael Wilderman.)

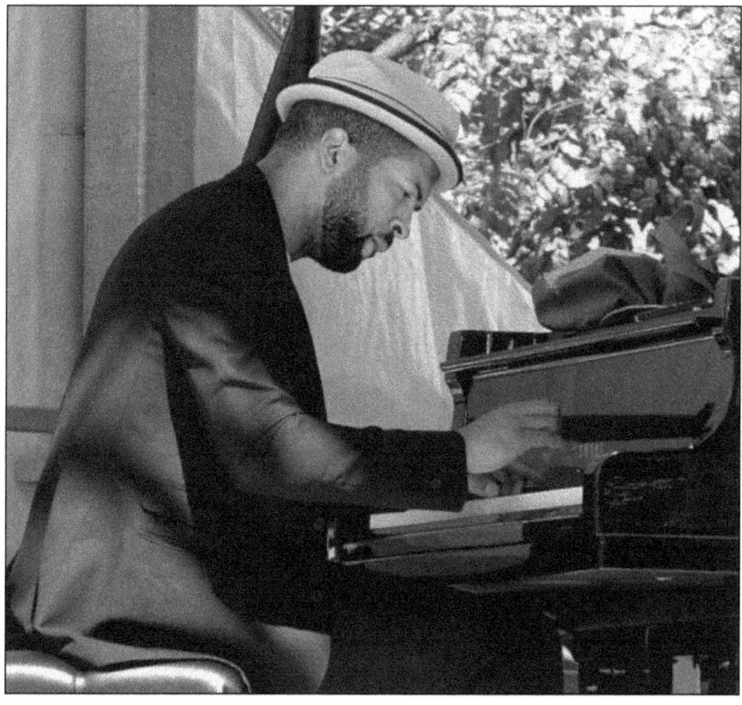

Jason Moran. Pianist Jason Moran is an award-winning composer, recording artist, and educator. An alumnus of the Kennedy Center's Betty Carter's Jazz Ahead project for rising stars on the jazz scene, Moran was named a MacArthur Fellow in 2010. He was appointed Kennedy Center artistic advisor for jazz in 2011 and artistic director for jazz in 2014. He is shown here at the Rosslyn Jazz Festival in Virginia on September 11, 2010. (Photograph by Michael Wilderman.)

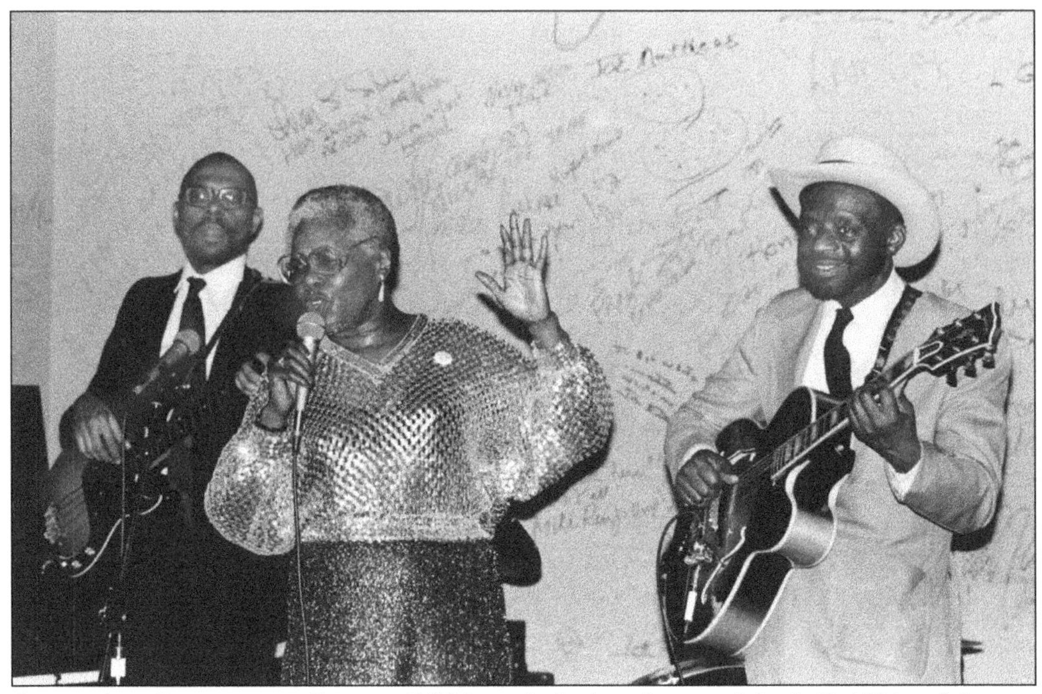

CHARLIE'S IN GEORGETOWN. Guitarist Bill Harris (in hat) performs on March 23, 1984, with bassist, saxophonist/reedist, and musicologist Andrew White and jazz and blues vocalist Mary Jefferson at Charlie's in Georgetown. Harris, who studied classical guitar at the Washington Junior College of Music, composed rhythm and blues works for the Clovers in the 1950s and opened the Pigfoot club in 1975. Jefferson, a Washington native, was, according to her 2002 *Washington Post* obituary, "dubbed Ambassador of the Blues by the DC Commission of the Arts and Humanities in 1988." (Photograph by Michael Wilderman.)

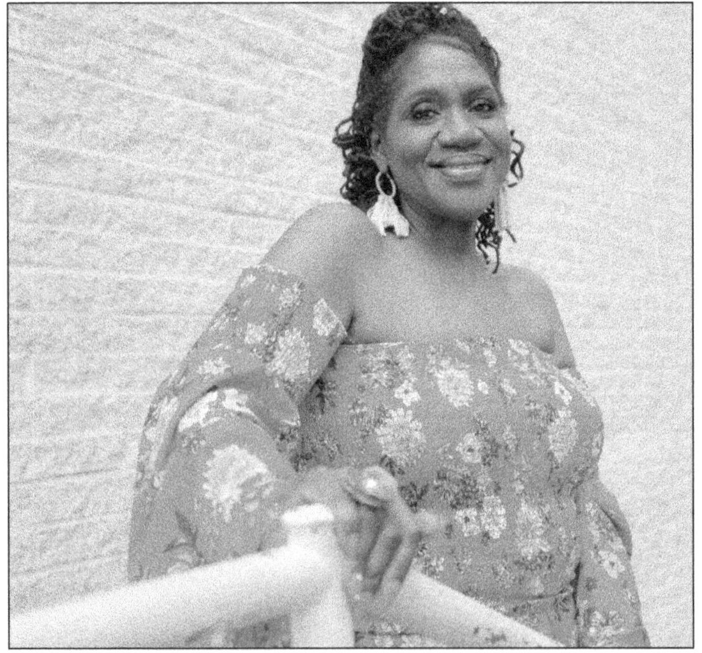

SHARÓN CLARK. Whether performing in America or abroad, Sharón Clark is at home on the stage and in tune with her audience and musicians. An award-winning vocalist, Clark, pictured here at a June 2018 performance at Westminster Presbyterian Church, recently completed a four-month residence in Taiwan and returned to Asia and Europe later in the year for concert and festival performances, including a popular tribute to Sarah Vaughan. (Photograph by Lawrence A. Randall.)

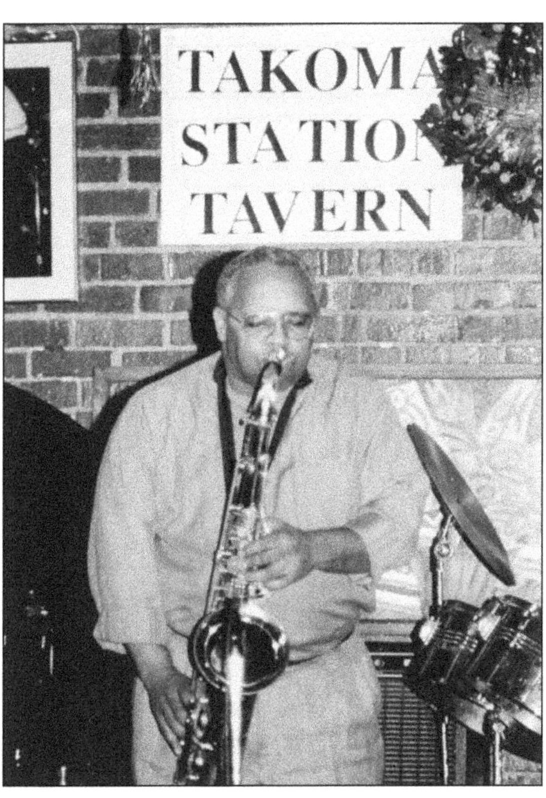

Fred Foss at Takoma Station. Saxophonist Fred Foss performs at a December 18, 1993, benefit for the late Carter Jefferson. Located on Fourth Street NW, Takoma Station Tavern currently hosts a weekly Tuesday Jazz Jam that features some of the top local talent. (Photograph by Michael Wilderman.)

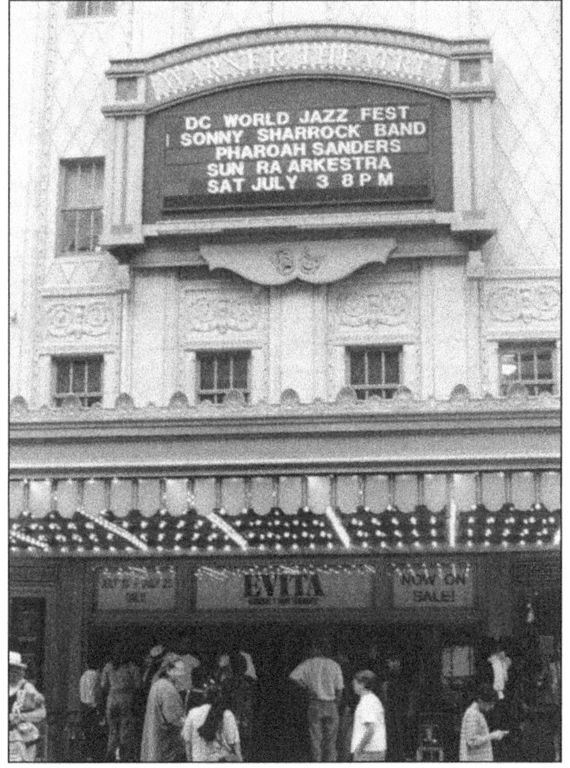

District Curators. The marquee of the Warner Theatre announces District Curators' July 3, 1993, DC World Jazz Festival. Opened in 1924 as a movie palace and home for vaudeville shows, the historic theater closed for renovations in 1989. It reopened in 1992 as a popular performance venue. (Photograph by Michael Wilderman.)

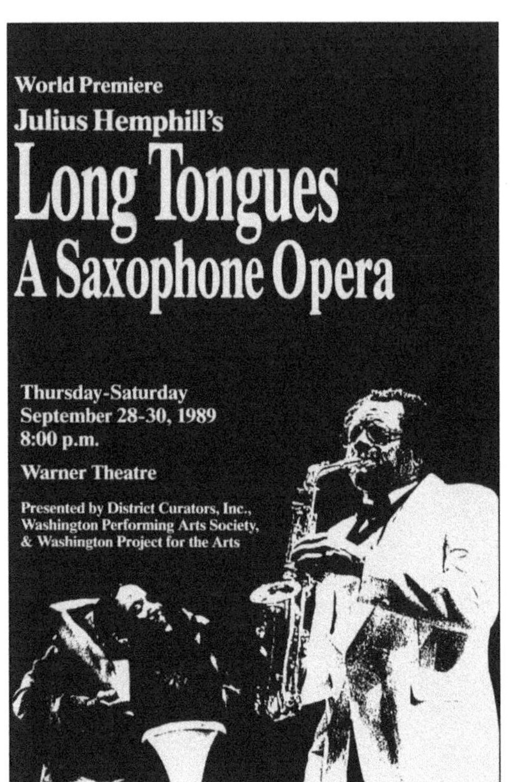

LONGUE TONGUES. In 1987, a *New York Times* article described *Long Tongues: A Saxophone Opera* as "a 75-minute piece for six saxophones, rhythm section, strings, brass and piccolo." Written by Julius Hemphill, who was the main composer for the World Saxophone Quartet, it was set in DC's Bohemian Caverns Club. By September 1989, when the more fully-developed work had its world debut at the Warner Theatre, a *Washington Post* article quoted Hemphill as saying, "Other than the [Village] Vanguard, maybe in New York, the Caverns is really the only jazz club I've ever been in. Everything else seems to be just a club that has jazz in it." (Photograph by Michael Wilderman.)

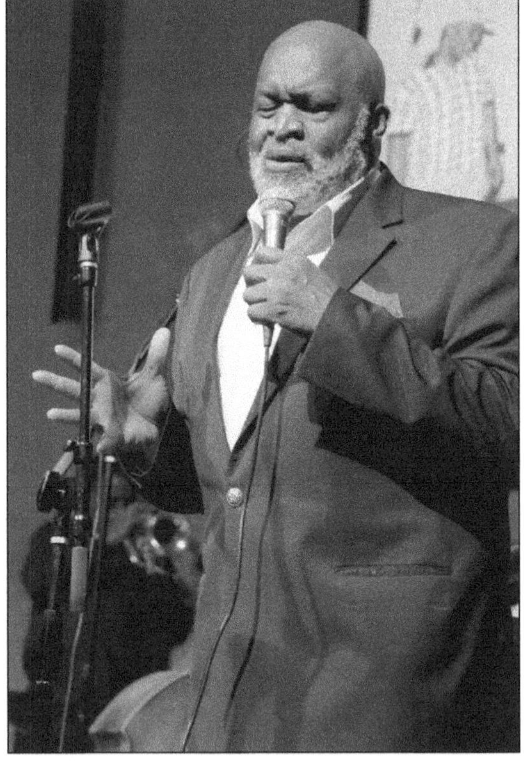

DICK SMITH. A vocalist and former member of the Washington Redskins, Dick Smith is the coordinator and host of Jazz Night at Westminster Presbyterian Church. Pastored by both the Rev. Brian Hamilton and his wife, Rev. Ruth Hamilton, Westminster launched its popular Friday night concert series in 1999. (Photograph by Lawrence A. Randall.)

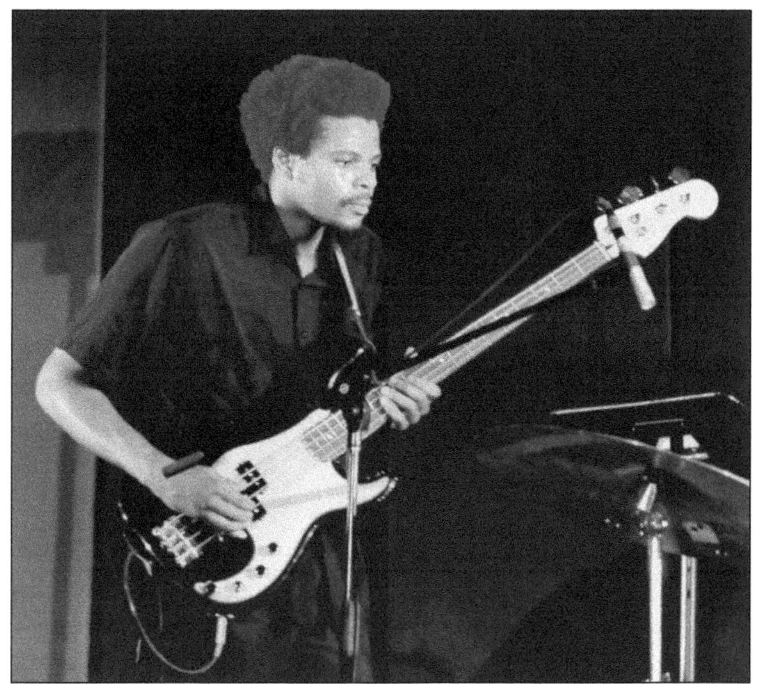

Luke Stewart. Radio programmer, writer, multi-instrumentalist, and concert producer Luke Stuart is shown in a June 12, 2016, performance. For many years, he and others have organized concerts for CapitalBop Inc., a nonprofit organization dedicated to preserving, promoting, and presenting jazz in Washington, DC. (Photograph by Michael Wilderman.)

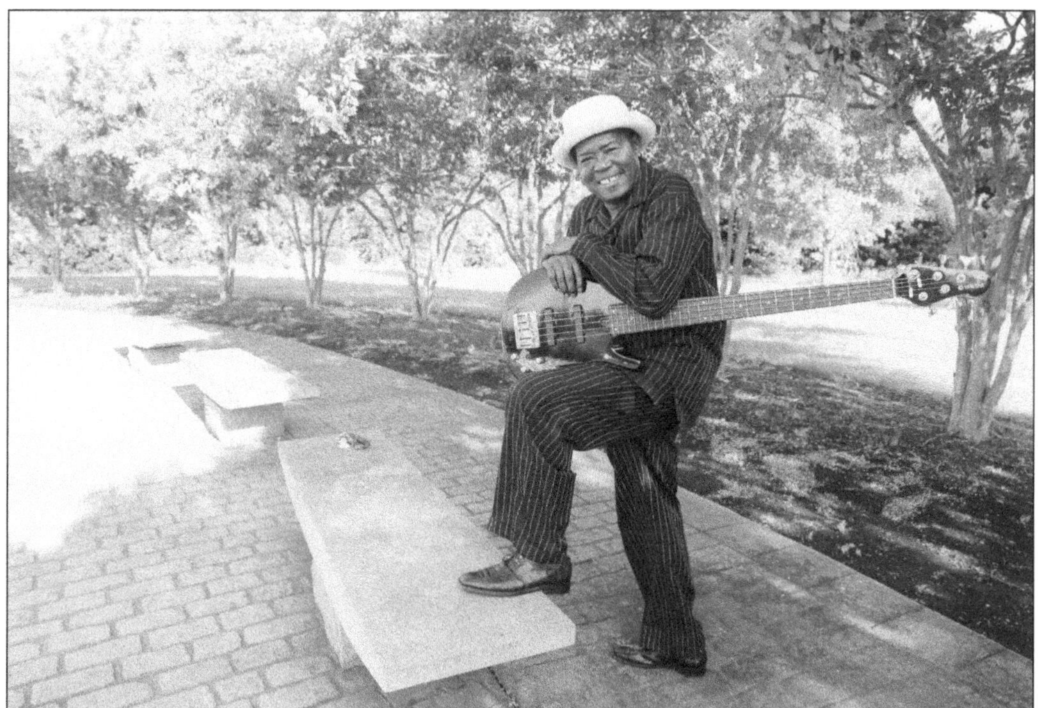

Gary Spencer. Bassist and vocalist Gary Spencer performs throughout the Greater Washington, DC, area. He is a member of DC Legendary Musicians Inc. (Courtesy of Gary Spencer.)

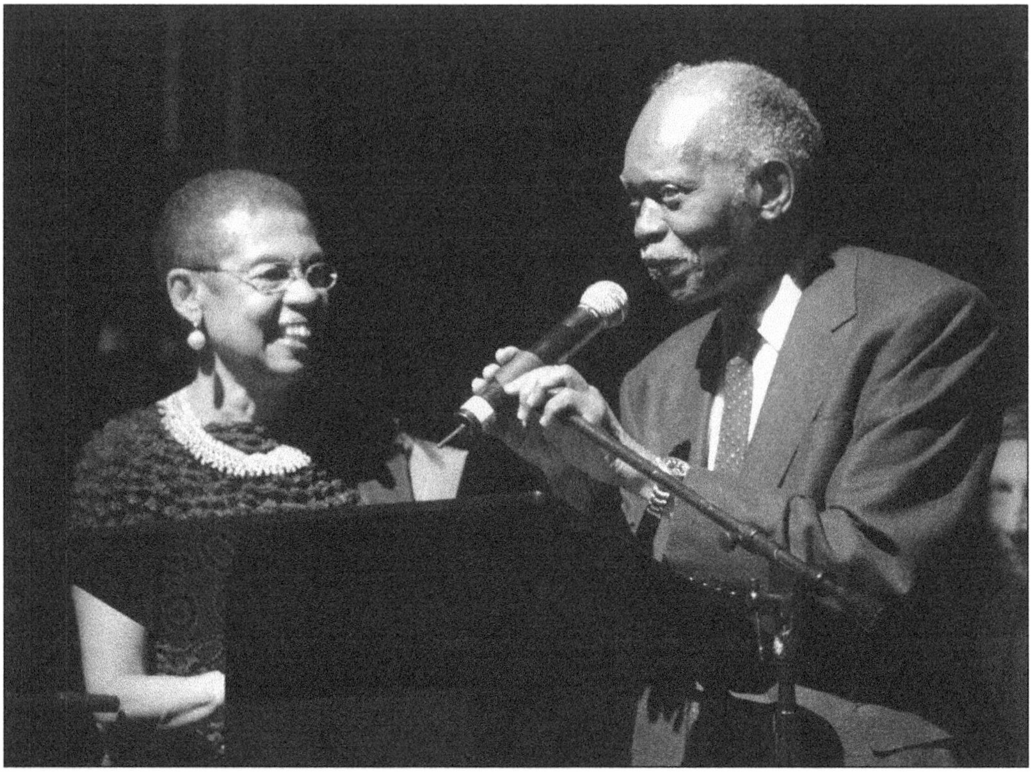

Hank Jones and Congresswoman Eleanor Holmes Norton. A pianist and National Endowment for the Arts Jazz Master, Hank Jones is pictured here with Congresswoman Eleanor Holmes Norton during the Duke Ellington Jazz Festival on September 15, 2007. A frequent guest artist at concerts and festivals around the world, Jones is also the recipient of the Congressional Achievement Award. (Photograph by Michael Wilderman.)

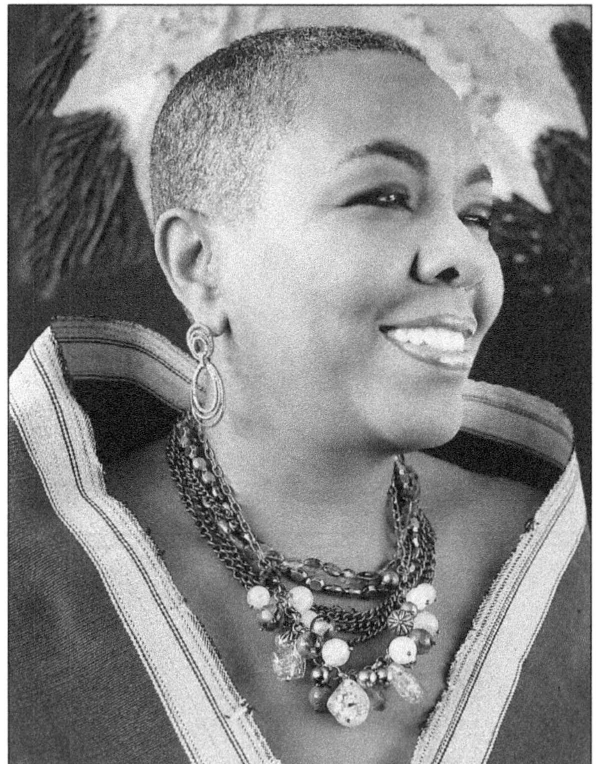

Regennia N. Williams. An award-winning historian and educator, Dr. Regennia N. Williams designed and conducted all of the interviews for the 2017–2018 Washington, DC, Jazz Oral History Project and served as the humanities scholar for the DC Humanities–funded Washington DC Jazz: The Music of the Metropolis and Beyond project. (Photograph by Nathaniel Rhodes; courtesy of Regennia N. Williams.)

Eight

Save the Date
Festivals, Annual Events, Curators, and Producers

When Congress passed House Resolution 57 "respecting the designation of jazz as a rare and valuable national American treasure" in 1987, it formally recognized what was common knowledge for many Washingtonians. In the process, the federal government provided new incentives for more individuals and organizations to lend their support to jazz programming, education, and preservation initiatives. Today, there is no shortage of annual festivals in the Greater Washington, DC, area, including the Mid-Atlantic Jazz Festival and the DC Jazz Festival.

Members of the Congressional Black Caucus, including Washington's own congresswoman, Eleanor Holmes Norton, have played an important role in publicly honoring the top jazz artists for lifetime achievement and their service as cultural ambassadors who take jazz to audiences throughout the global community.

Within the District of Columbia, colleges and universities offer numerous opportunities for students to hear professional artists in performance and to study to become professionals in their own right. The JAZZAlive! series and the Calvin Jones Big Band Festival are mainstays at the University of the District of Columbia. Each year, under the leadership of director Fred Irby, the Howard University Jazz Ensemble produces excellent live performances and professionally produced recordings. In a similar fashion, American University, Georgetown University, Montgomery College, the University of Maryland, Johns Hopkins University, Morgan State University, and George Mason University are among the other postsecondary institutions with jazz programs that train the young jazz lions of today.

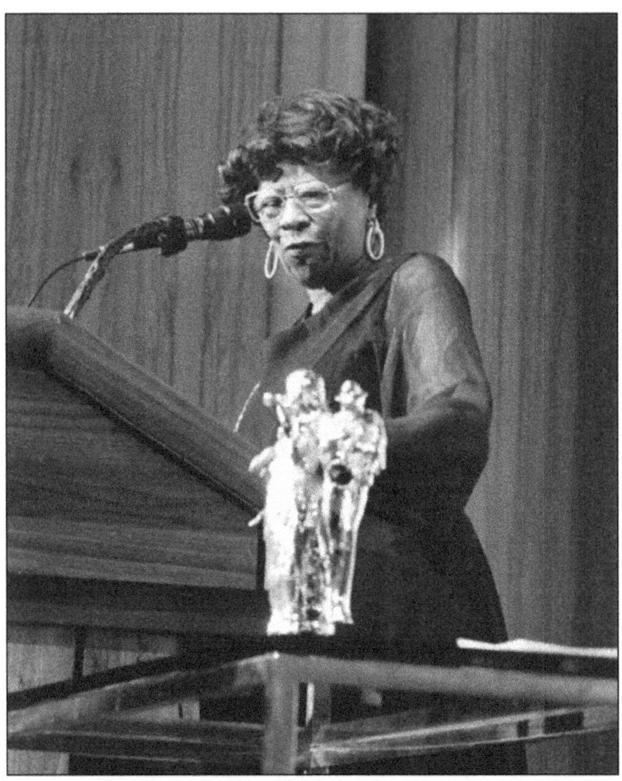

Ella Fitzgerald. Ella Fitzgerald, the "First Lady of Song," is shown here at the October 19, 1989, Congressional Black Caucus / National Endowment for the Arts National Treasure Award gathering in Washington, DC. (Photograph by Michael Wilderman.)

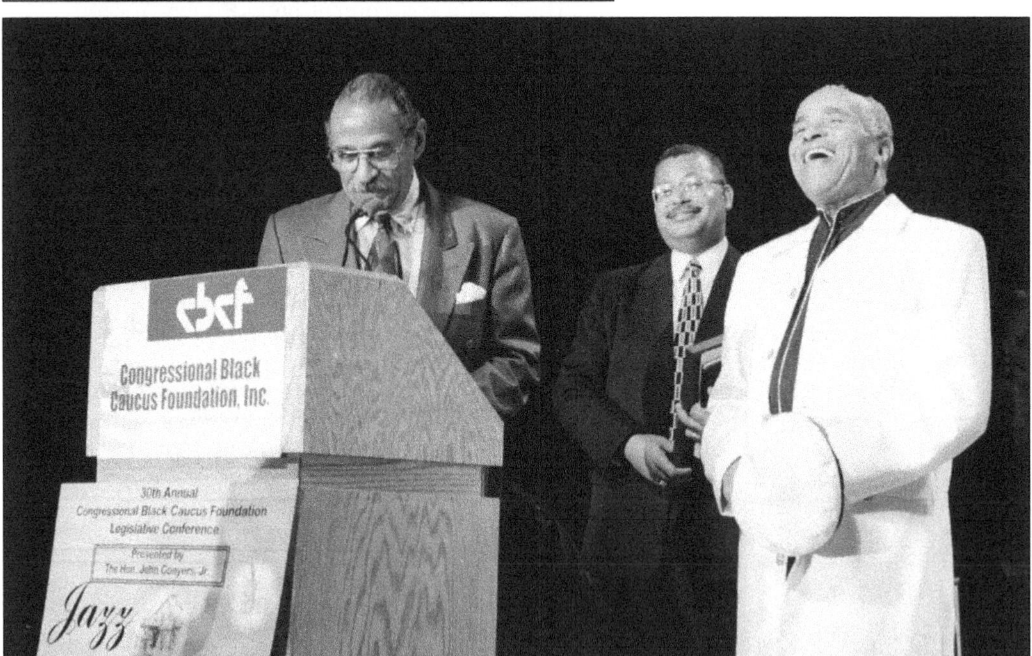

Congressman John Conyers. Michigan congressman John Conyers (at podium) played a crucial role in securing federal support for jazz, including the creation of the Smithsonian Jazz Masterworks Orchestra. He is pictured here as he presents an award to vocalist Jon Hendricks (right), with assistance from Cedric Hendricks, on September 14, 2000. (Photograph by Michael Wilderman.)

Bill Brower and Steve Coleman. Jazz aficionado, writer, and radio programmer Bill Brower (left) interviews saxophonist Steve Coleman during the DC Jazz Festival at the Sixth & I Synagogue, on June 14, 2016. (Photograph by Michael Wilderman.)

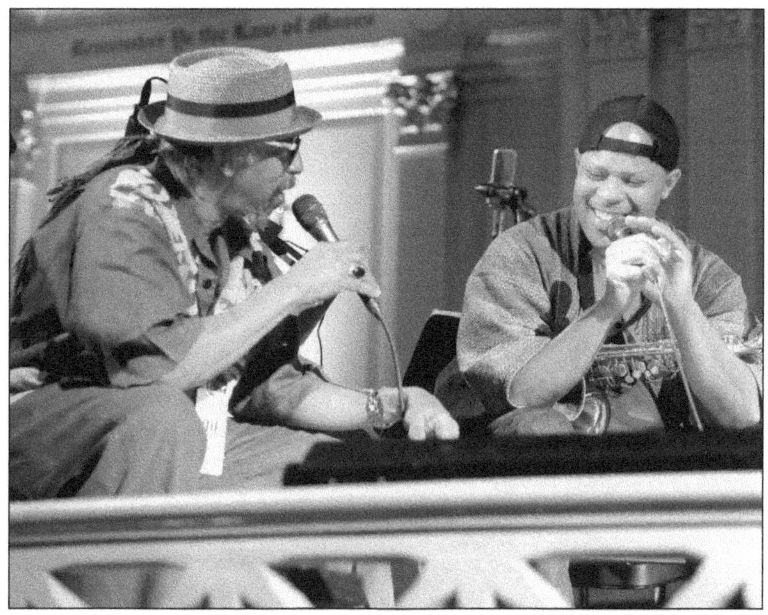

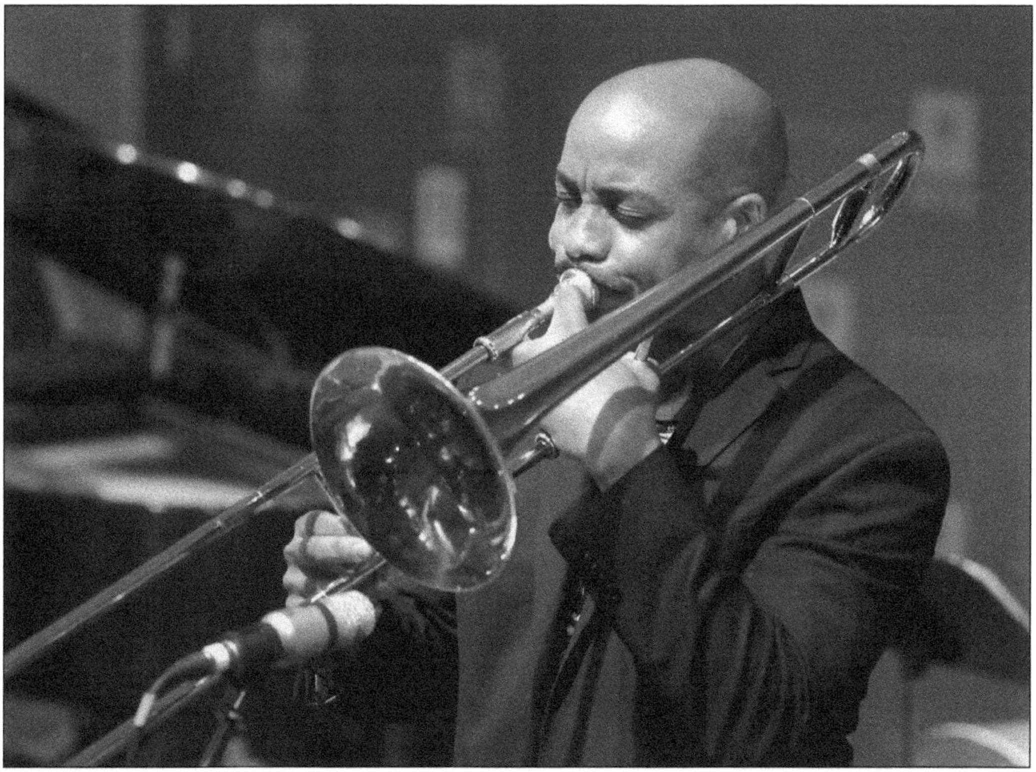

Reginald Cyntje, Jazzfest 2017. A native of the Virgin Islands, trombonist Reginald Cyntje is an alumnus of the University of the District of Columbia and the University of Maryland. In addition to his busy schedule as a performer, Cyntje serves on the faculty of Montgomery College. He is pictured here at the NYU Annex on June 14, 2016. (Photograph by Michael Wilderman.)

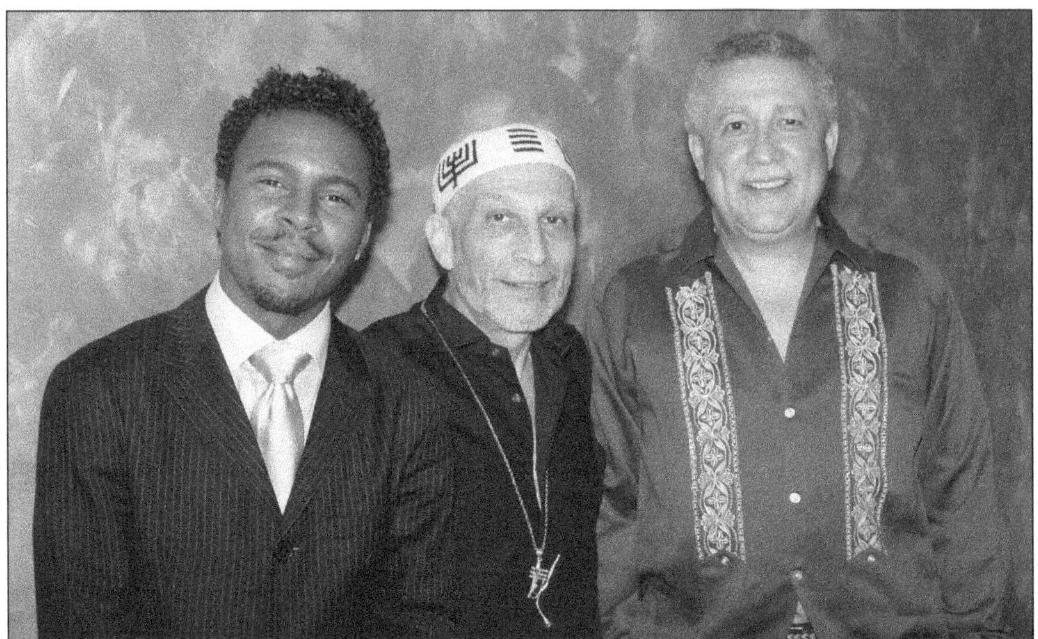

The Duke Ellington Jazz Festival. From left to right, Roy Hargrove, Charles Fishman, and Paquito D'Rivera are shown in this October 4, 2006, photograph from the Duke Ellington Jazz Festival. Fishman launched the Duke Ellington Jazz Festival in the fall of 2005. (Photograph by Michael Wilderman.)

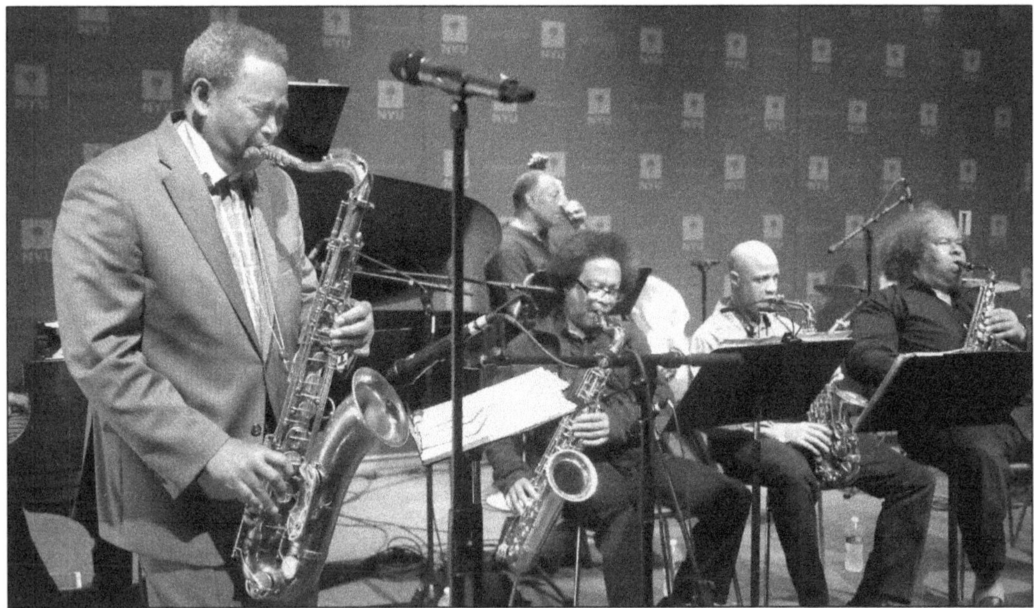

The Odean Pope Sax Choir. In the 2017 CapitalBop coproduced mini-documentary *Odean: The Saxophone Choir at 40*, the North Carolina–born, Philadelphia legend Odean Pope describes himself as "a jazz musician and educator." Others, however, have described him as the musical genius who founded and has led his saxophone choir since 1977. From 1979 until 2002, Pope was a member of the Max Roach Quartet. He is shown here at DC Jazzfest on June 16, 2017. (Photograph by Michael Wilderman.)

Dr. Fred Irby. Trumpeter and distinguished jazz educator Dr. Fred Irby receives an award at the John F. Kennedy Center for the Performing Arts during the DC Jazz Festival on June 13, 2001. (Photograph by Michael Wilderman.)

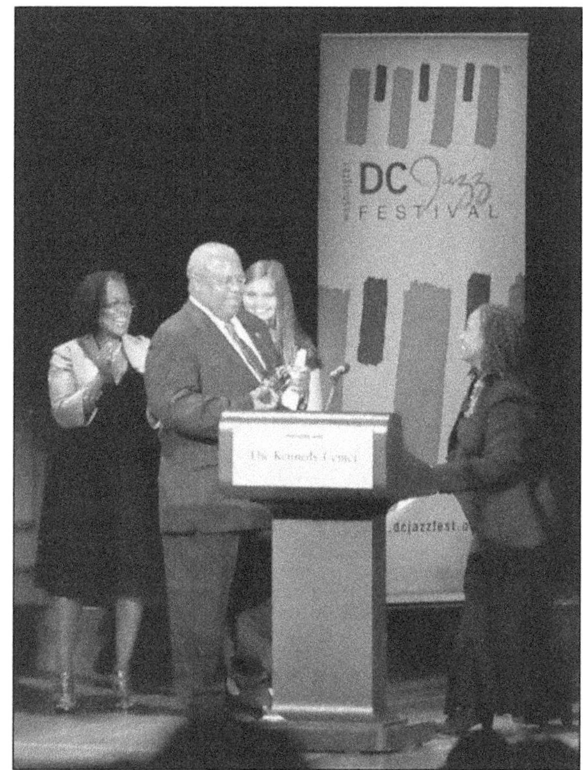

Dexter Gordon with Congressman John Conyers. Members of the Congressional Black Caucus honored saxophonist Dexter Gordon at Howard University on December 2, 1986. (Photograph by Michael Wilderman.)

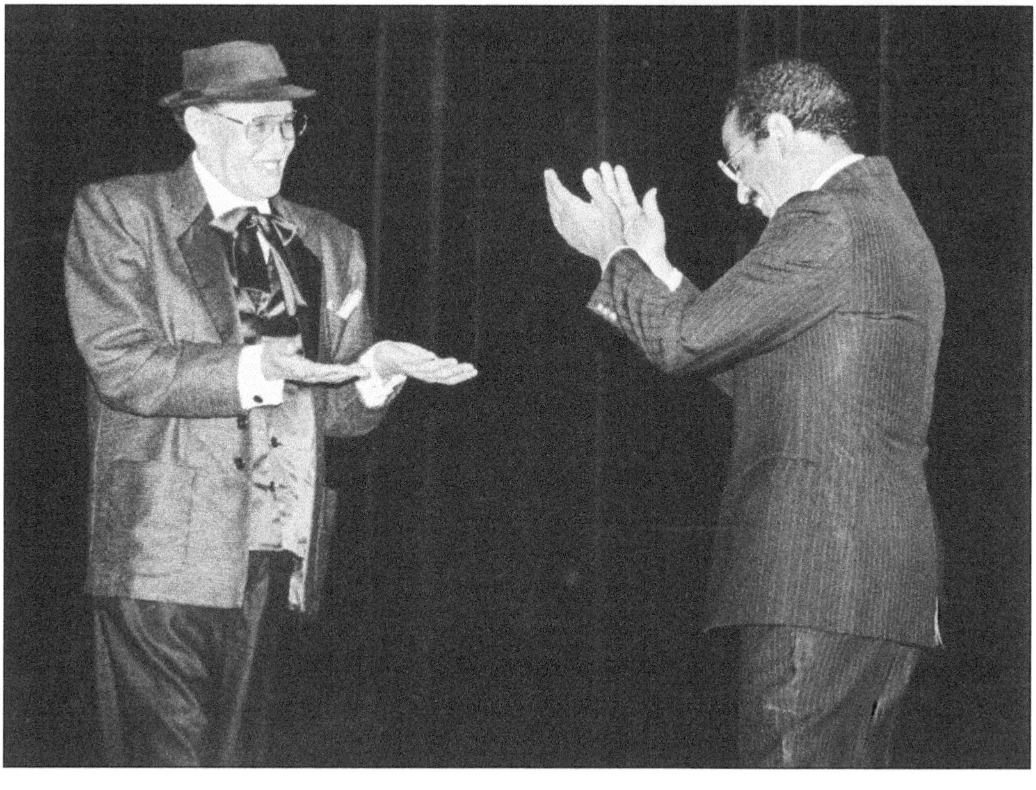

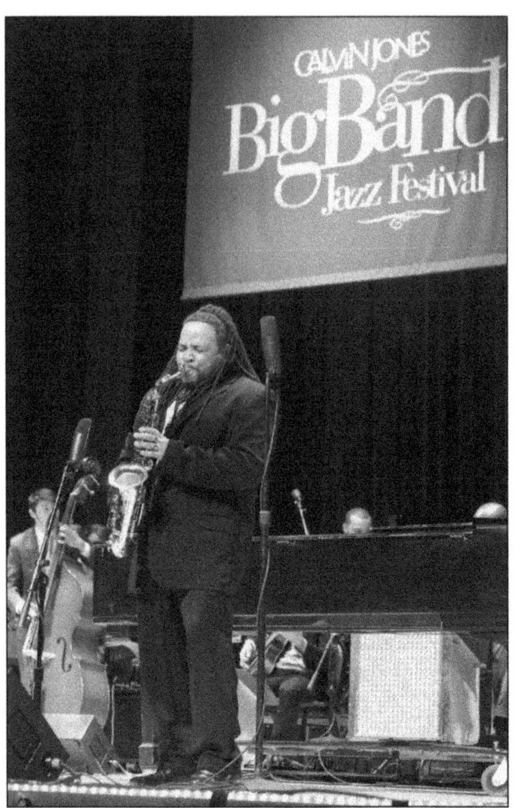

Eddie Baccus and the Calvin Jones Big Band. Saxophonist Eddie Baccus renders a solo performance during an April 7, 2015, Calvin Jones Big Band concert at the University of the District of Columbia (UDC). UDC's Calvin Jones Big Band is named in honor of the longtime faculty member who served as the director of the jazz studies program from 1976 until his death in 2004. Jones was a trombonist, pianist, composer, and arranger. (Photograph by Michael Wilderman.)

Pianist-Director Allyn Johnson with the Calvin Jones Big Band in 2015. Pianist Allyn Johnson is a native Washingtonian and an alumnus of the University of the District of Columbia. After serving as assistant director under Calvin Jones, Johnson succeeded Jones as director of the Calvin Jones Big Band in 2005. Johnson, who also serves as an adjunct professor at UDC, is a member of SUPERNOVA and founder of several ensembles, including Divine Order and Sonic Sanctuary. (Courtesy of the Felix E. Grant Jazz Archives, University of the District of Columbia.)

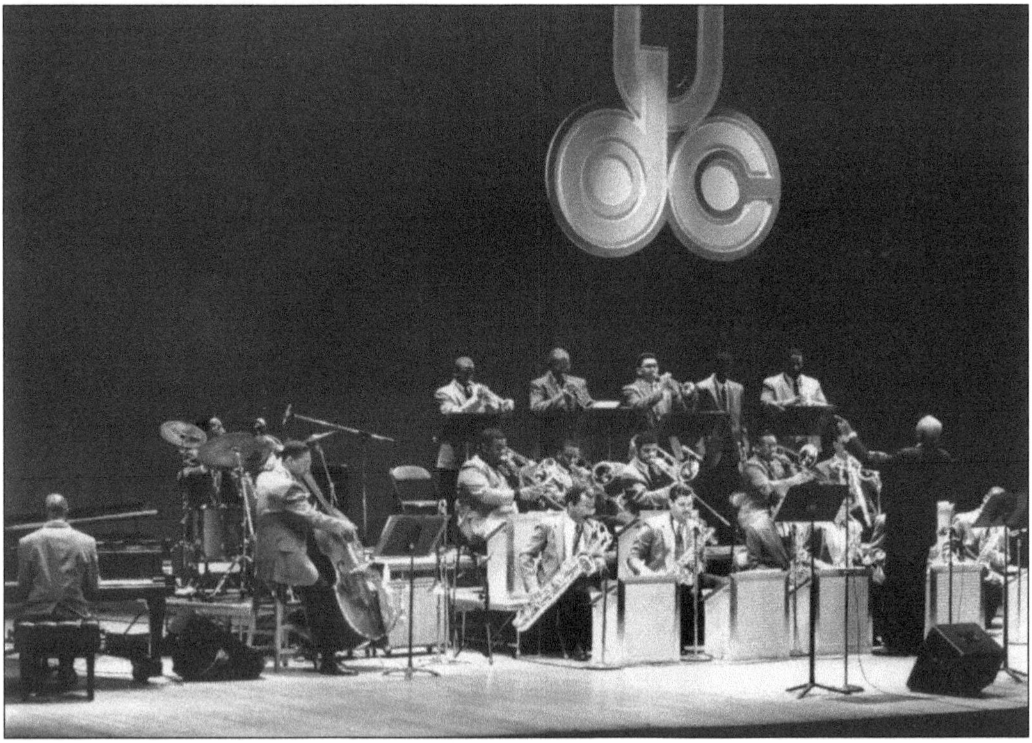

Connaitre Miller. A Kansas native, Prof. Connaitre Miller is a full-time faculty member in the Department of Music at Howard University, coordinator of vocal jazz studies, founder and director of the Afro Blue performing arts ensemble, a solo artist, and a lecturer and workshop clinician. Trained as a concert pianist and with experience teaching in the United States and Australia, in 2013 she received a Jazz Education Achievement Award from *Downbeat* magazine. (Photograph by Lawrence A. Randall.)

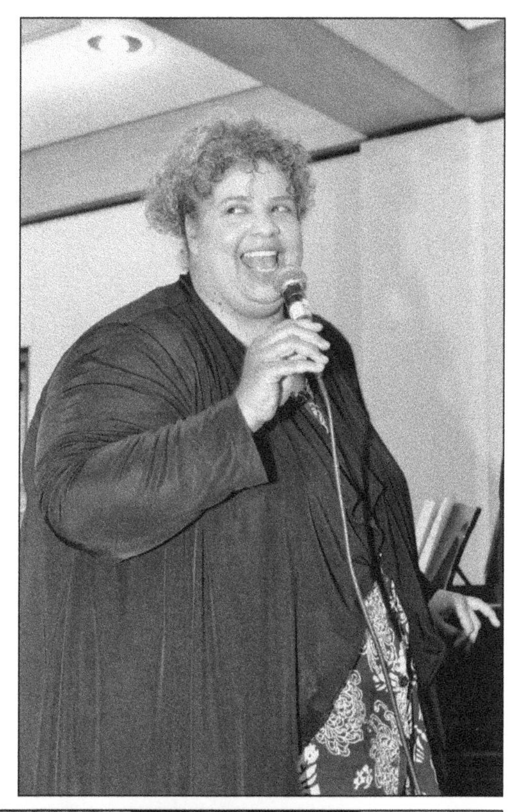

Jazz All-Stars and Pres. Bill Clinton. President and saxophonist William Jefferson Clinton joins the Jazz All-Stars in performing at his January 20, 1993, inaugural ball at the Pension Building. He is seen here with Herbie Hancock, Hilary Clinton, Ron Carter, Illinois Jacquet, Al Grey, Wayne Shorter, Thelonious Monk Jr., and Clark Terry. (Photograph by Michael Wilderman.)

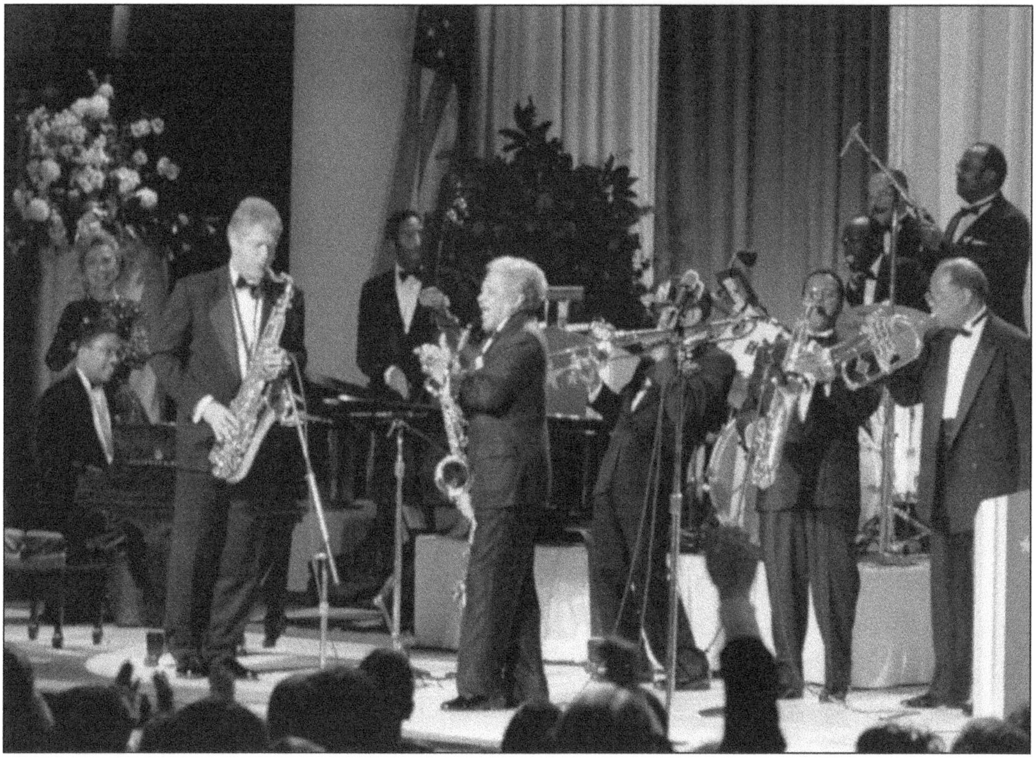

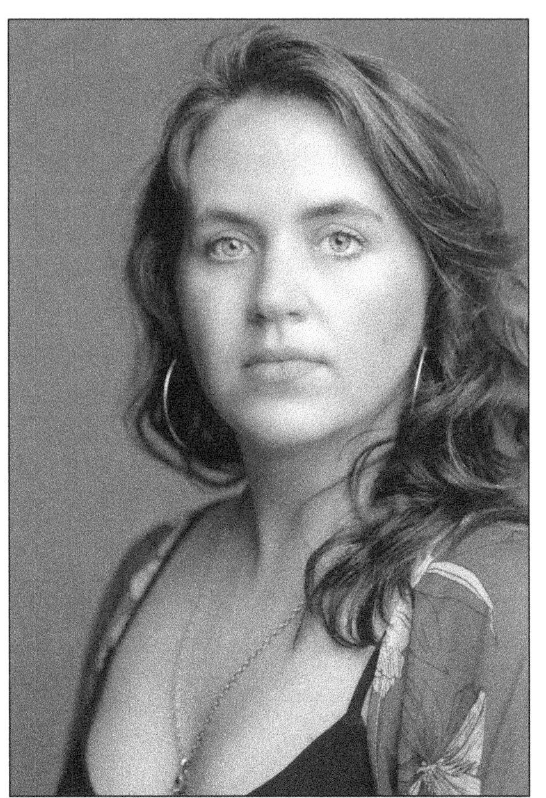

Amy K. Bormet. An alumna of the Duke Ellington School of the Arts, pianist-composer Amy K. Bormet holds a bachelor's degree in jazz studies / piano performance from the University of Michigan and a master's degree in jazz studies from Howard University. The recipient of numerous honors and commissions, her works have been performed by the Smithsonian Jazz Masterworks Orchestra, Afro Blue, and others. In 2011, she founded the Washington Women in Jazz Festival. Each year in March (Women's History Month), the organization sponsors a series of events that are designed to showcase the talents of established and emerging women artists in the District of Columbia. (Photograph by Chris Ubik; courtesy of Amy K. Bormet.)

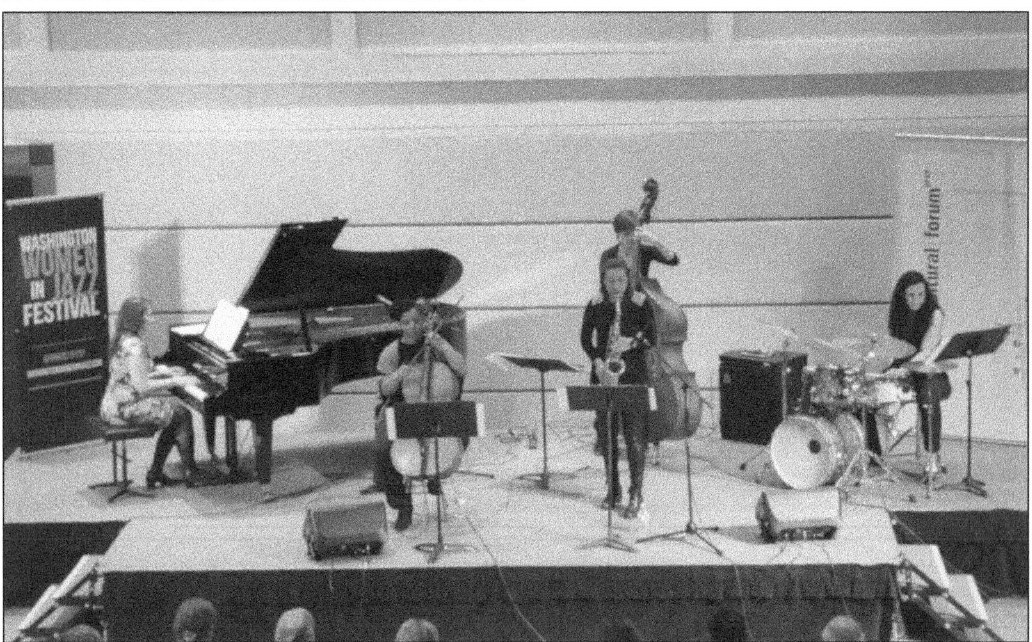

The Washington Women in Jazz Festival. Amy K. Bormet's quintet performs during a 2018 collaboration with the Austrian Cultural Forum. Shown here are Bormet, piano; Judith Ferstl, bass; Ana Barreiro, drums; Shana Tucker, cello; and Sarah Hughes, alto saxophone. (Photograph by Jon Bormet; courtesy of Amy K. Bormet.)

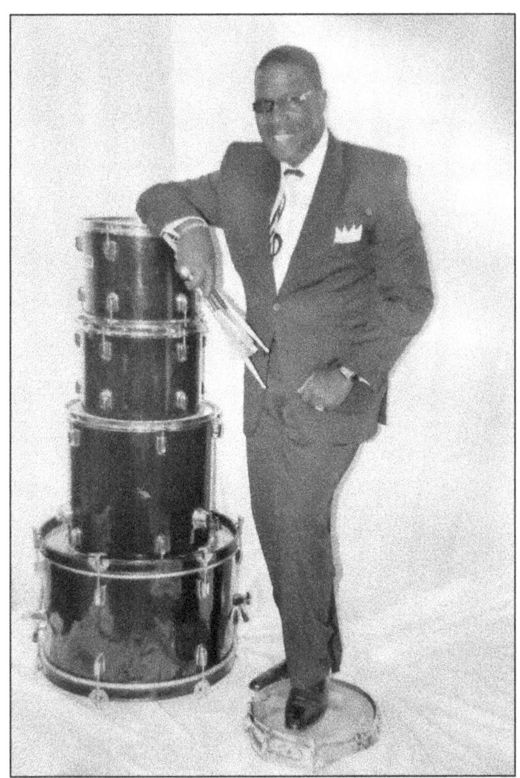

Perry Grayson. Drummer Perry Grayson has performed throughout the Washington, DC, area. He is a member of DC Legendary Musicians Inc. (Courtesy of Perry Grayson.)

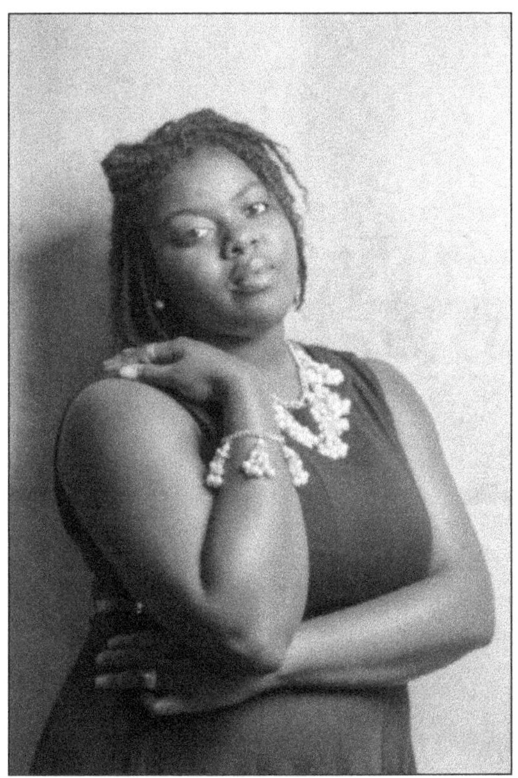

Shacara Rogers. Vocalist Shacara Rogers is both gifted and versatile. A Philadelphia native, she holds both undergraduate and graduate degrees from Howard University, where she perfected her vocal jazz artistry as a student of Jessica Boykin-Settles and Connaitre Miller and served as a soloist with the Howard University Gospel Choir. She has appeared on programs with Terri Lyne Carrington, Dianne Reeves, Geri Allen, Esperanza Spalding, and many other artists. She is the 2014 recipient of the Downbeat Award for Graduate College Outstanding Performance: Vocal Soloist and the first place winner of the 2015 Mid-Atlantic Jazz Festival Vocal Competition, among other honors. (Courtesy of Shacara Rogers.)

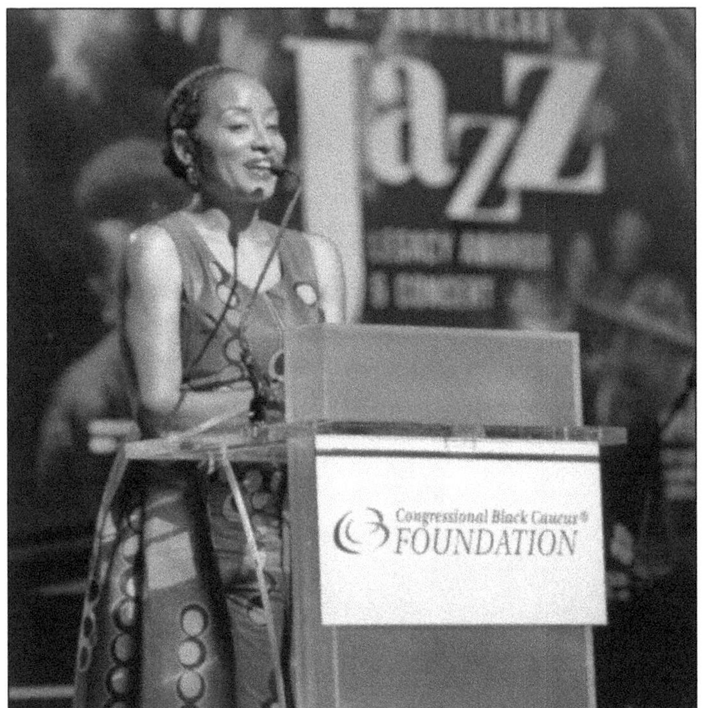

Keanna Faircloth, 2017. WPFW jazz programmer Keanna Faircloth is shown here at the Congressional Black Caucus Annual Legislative Conference and Awards Program. (Photograph by Lawrence A. Randall.)

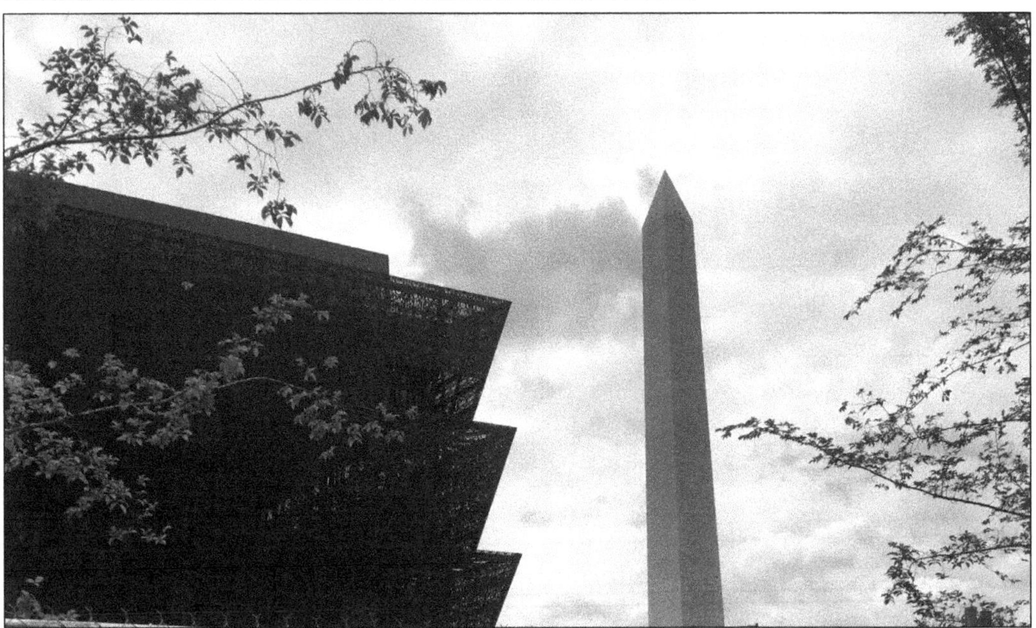

The National Museum of African American History and Culture, 2016. The. National Museum of African American History and Culture (NMAAHC, left) and the Washington Monument are two of the most recognizable landmarks on the National Mall in Washington, DC. NMAAHC, which opened to the public on September 24, 2016, as the 19th museum of the Smithsonian Institution, has already established a track record of producing exhibitions, publications, concerts, and other programs that consider the place of jazz within the larger context of African American history and culture. (Photograph by Regennia N. Williams)

Nine

Smithsonian Jazz

World-Class Programs on the National Mall and Beyond

The curators and archivists of the Smithsonian's National Museum of American History (NMAH) can be thought of as the official custodians of some of the most valuable jazz collections in the world. Among their holdings are manuscript materials and objects that document the careers of Duke Ellington, Ella Fitzgerald, Dizzy Gillespie, John Coltrane, and many others. So rare are some of their materials that scholars travel from across the globe to conduct research there, and the materials are shared with the general public through in-house and touring exhibitions. The museum collaborated with the Smithsonian Institution Traveling Exhibition Service to create a special touring tribute: *Beyond Category: The Musical Genius of Duke Ellington*, which toured the United States from 1993 to 2000. In 2017, with support from the Ella Fitzgerald Charitable Found*ation, the NMAH mounted a centennial exhibition*, The First Lady of Song: Ella Fitzgerald at 100. John Edward Hasse curated both exhibitions.

While it has been suggested that jazz is becoming "the music of the museum," it is worth noting that museums like the NMAH are also taking jazz music to the people. Smithsonian Jazz sponsors a number of initiatives involving students, teachers, and professional musicians, including the annual Jazz Appreciation Month programs and concerts featuring the Smithsonian Jazz Masterworks Orchestra. Founded in 1990, the orchestra has won the applause of American audiences as well as those in African and European nations.

Web-based educational materials are also available, as are transcripts from the National Endowment for the Arts–funded Smithsonian Jazz Oral History Project. Interviewees include pianist and native Washingtonian Shirley Horn and former DC resident Dr. Billy Taylor, architect of many of the John F. Kennedy Center for the Performing Arts' pioneering jazz projects.

Whether performing or teaching at their home on the National Mall, in the shadow of the great pyramids of Egypt, or some other faraway place, the professional members of the Smithsonian Jazz Masterworks Orchestra are following in the Cold War–era footsteps of Duke Ellington, Dizzy Gillespie, Dave Brubeck, and other jazz legends. These performing artists of our time are serving as cultural ambassadors, propagating a message of goodwill, with some 21st-century support from the national government that makes its permanent home in Washington, DC.

This chapter includes images of Smithsonian Jazz Masterworks Orchestra members, conductors, and guest artists in performance, and ends with images of two artists with ties to DC Legendary Musicians Inc. who are among the thousands of DC residents who can take advantage of opportunities to see and hear the Smithsonian Jazz Masterworks Orchestra on a regular basis.

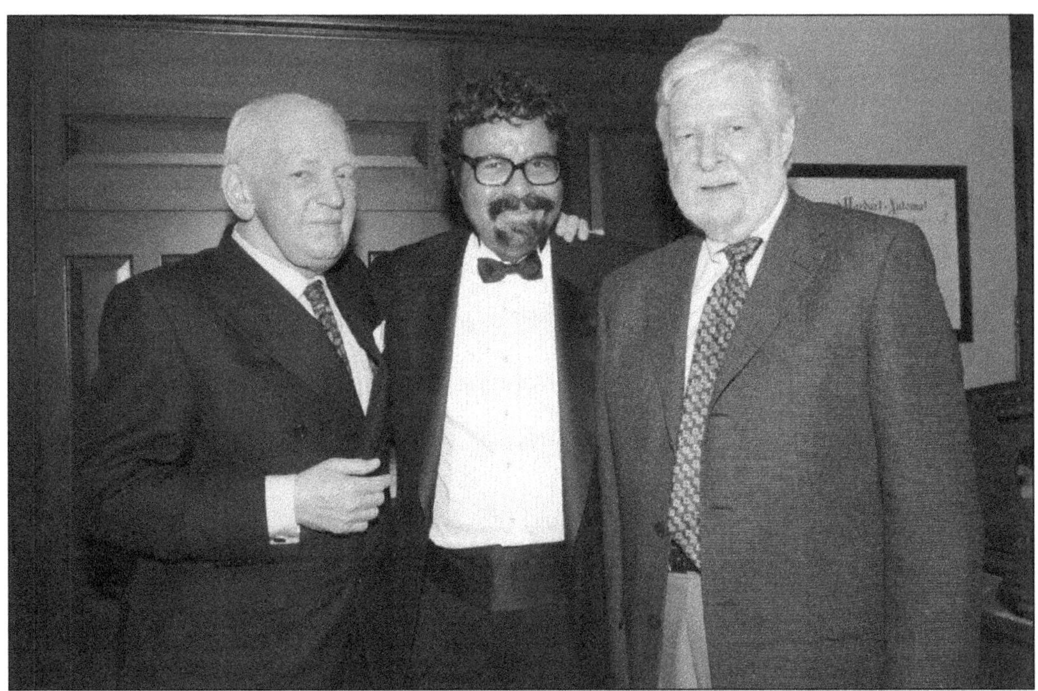

BILL RUSSO, DAVID BAKER, AND BILL HOLMAN. Maestro David Baker (center) is shown here with Bill Russo (left) and Bill Holman. Baker was the founding codirector (with Gunther Schuller) of the Smithsonian Jazz Masterworks Orchestra from 1991 to 1996. In 1996, Baker became the sole director, a position he held until his retirement in 2012. (Courtesy of Smithsonian Jazz.)

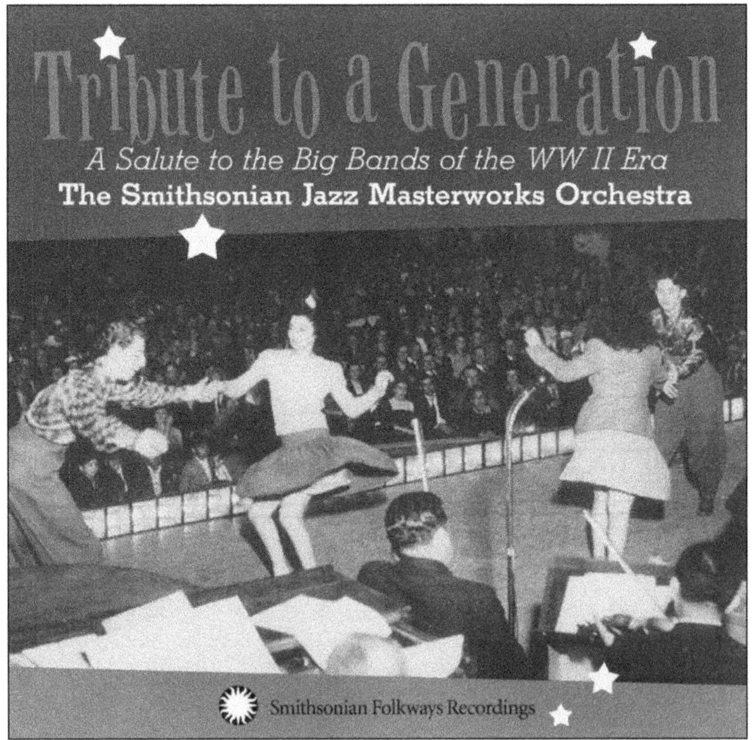

TRIBUTE TO A GENERATION CD COVER. In 2004, the Smithsonian Jazz Masterworks Orchestra released *Tribute to a Generation: A Salute to the Big Bands of the WWII Era* on the Smithsonian Folkways Recordings label. (Courtesy of Smithsonian Jazz.)

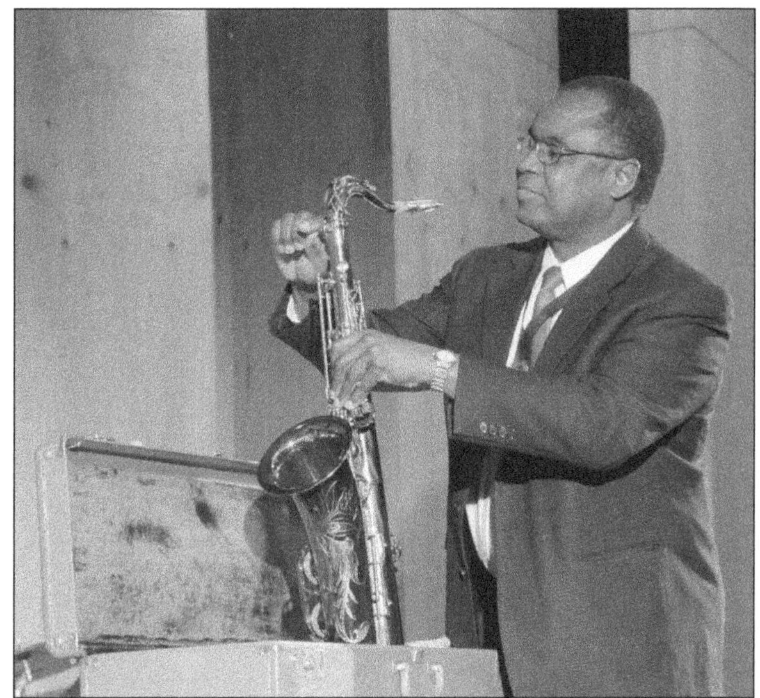

Charlie Young. Saxophonist Charlie Young is a faculty member in the Howard University Department of Music and the artistic director and conductor of the Smithsonian Jazz Masterworks Orchestra. He is pictured here with John Coltrane's saxophone, one of the many jazz-related items in the collections of the National Museum of American History. (Courtesy Smithsonian Jazz.)

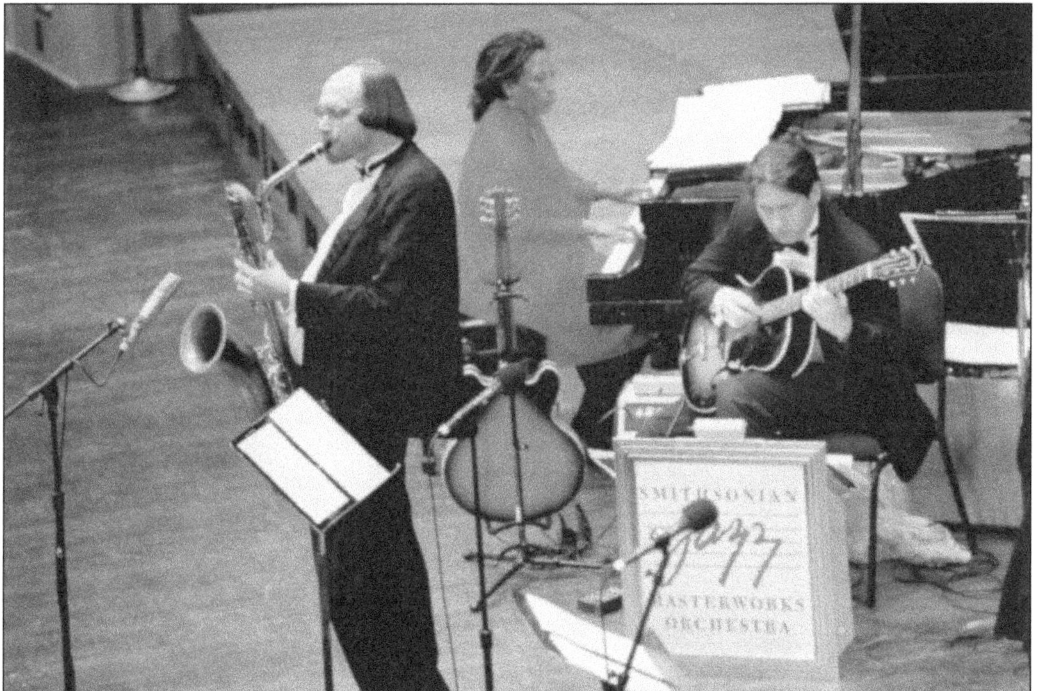

Scott Robinson, Geri Allen, and James Chirillo. Pianist Geri Allen, a Michigan native, attended Howard University as an undergraduate and earned a master's degree in ethnomusicology from the University of Pittsburgh. A prolific and creative composer and arranger, she collaborated with visual artist Carrie Mae Weems and others before her untimely passing in 2017. The guitarist pictured here is James Chirillo, and the saxophonist is Scott Robinson. (Courtesy of Smithsonian Jazz.)

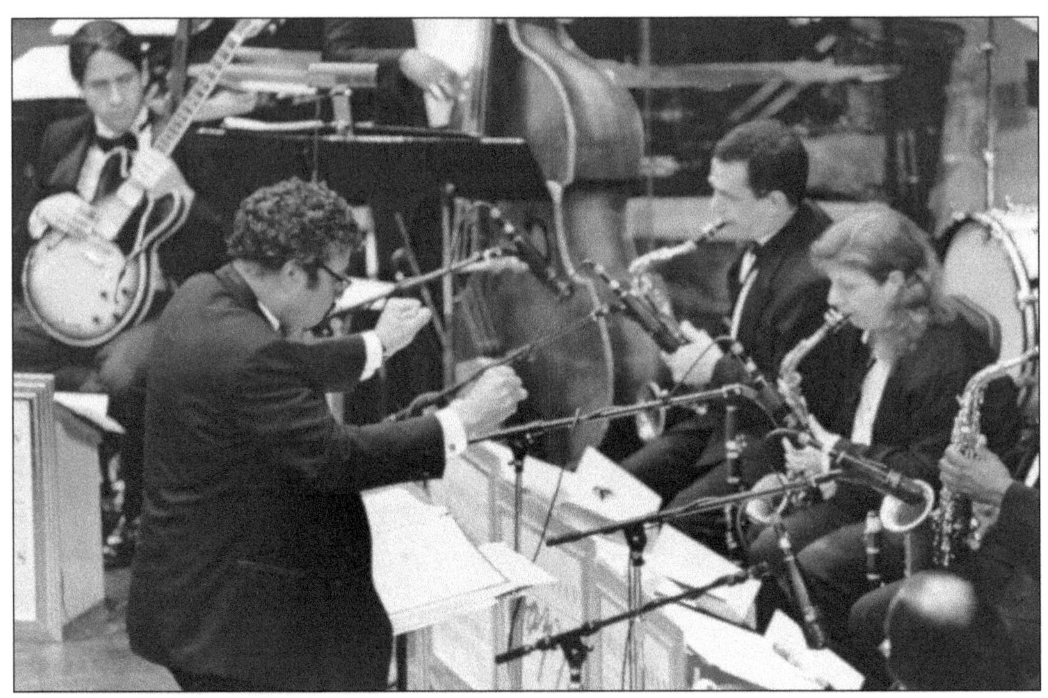

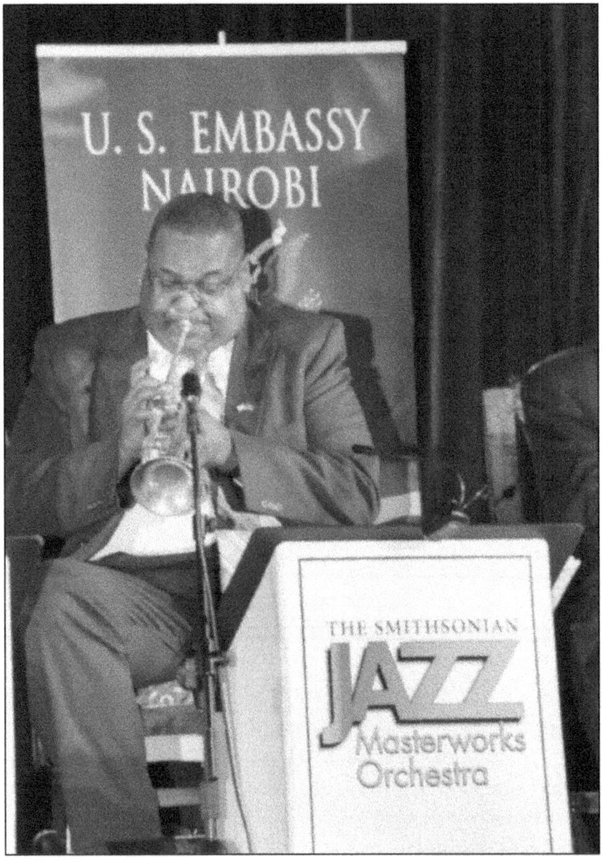

Dr. David Baker Conducting the Smithsonian Jazz Masterworks Orchestra. Indiana native and two-time alumnus of Indiana University, Dr. David Baker went on to join the faculty of his alma mater as the founding director of the jazz studies program. Maestro Baker led the Smithsonian Jazz Masterworks Orchestra for more than 20 years. (Courtesy of Smithsonian Jazz.)

Tom Williams of the Smithsonian Jazz Masterworks Orchestra Octet in Kenya. Under the direction of Charlie Young, the Smithsonian Jazz Masterworks Octet toured Kenya in 2013. The US State Department and the Embassy of Kenya cosponsored this tour. (Courtesy of Smithsonian Jazz.)

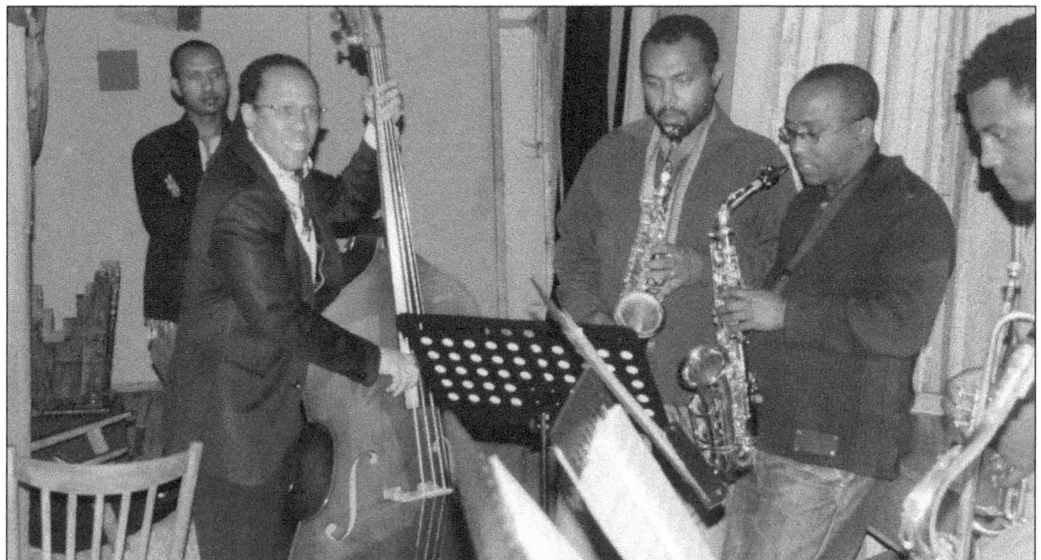

Bassist Michael Bowie, Nairobi, Kenya, 2013. A November 9, 2013, article in *The Star* (Kenya) described the Smithsonian Jazz Masterworks Orchestra Octet's tour as a celebration of 50 years of US-Kenya friendship: "This milestone was marked with a jazz concert presented by the Smithsonian Jazz Masterworks Octet of the National Museum of American History and hosted by the US ambassador Robert Godec." The list of participating musicians included Charlie Young (saxophone), Delores King Williams (vocals), Shelley Carrol (saxophone), Tom Williams (trumpet), John Jensen (trombone), Tony Nalker (piano), Michael Bowie (bass), and Ken Kimery (drums). Bowie is shown here with Kenyan musicians. (Courtesy of Smithsonian Jazz.)

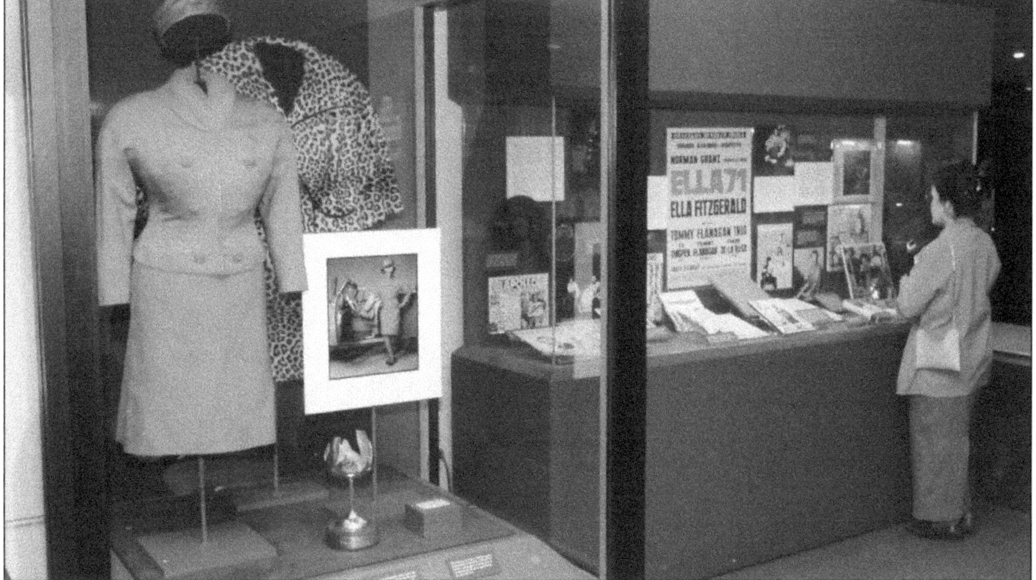

Opening Night at the Smithsonian Institution's Ella Fitzgerald Exhibition. Legendary vocalist Ella Fitzgerald, a Newport News, Virginia, native, rose to the highest heights in the world of jazz and was dearly beloved throughout the mid-Atlantic region and the world. Born in 1917, she was the subject of *The First Lady of Song: Ella Fitzgerald at 100*, a special centenary exhibition that opened at the National Museum of American History in 2017. (Courtesy of Smithsonian Jazz.)

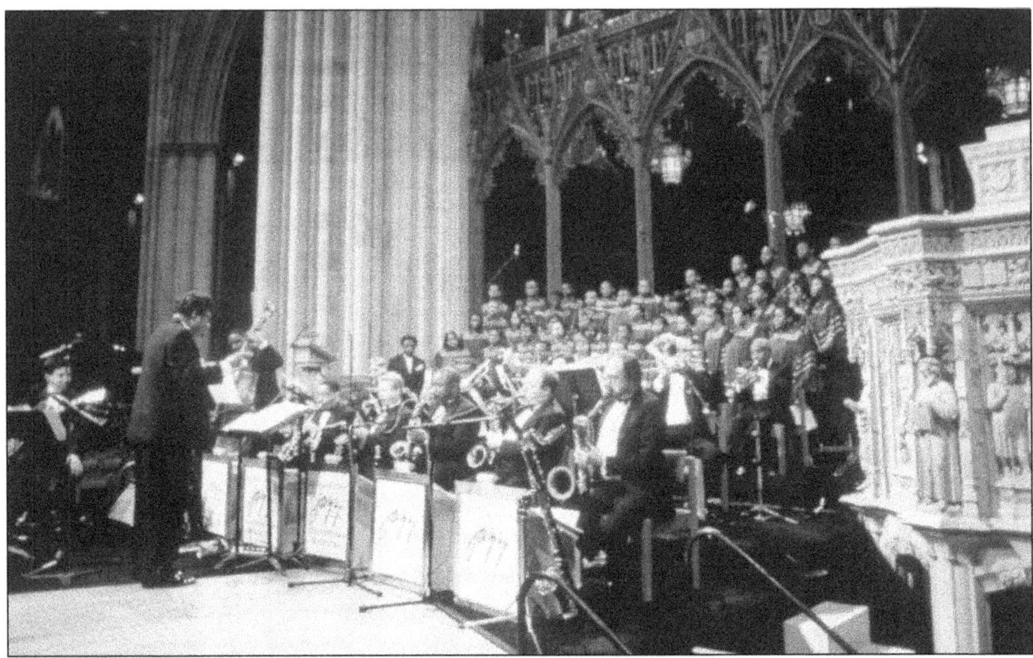

Smithsonian Jazz Masterworks Orchestra at Duke Ellington Centennial Tribute, 1999. In his lifetime, Duke Ellington (1899–1974) performed his liturgical music in the sanctuaries of many religious institutions. On April 29, 1999, the centennial of Ellington's birth, the Smithsonian Jazz Masterworks Orchestra presented *Hallelujah! A Sacred Concert* at the Washington National Cathedral. (Courtesy of Smithsonian Jazz.)

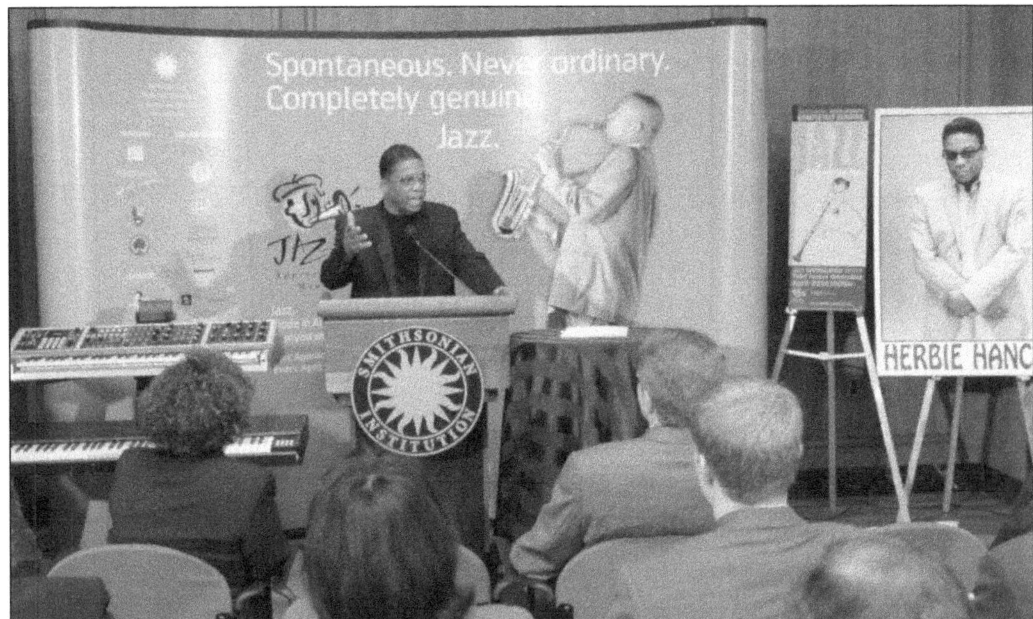

Herbie Hancock Speaking at the National Museum of American History. In April 2004, award-winning pianist and composer Herbie Hancock donated three keyboards to the Smithsonian and delivered the keynote address for Jazz Appreciation Month. (Courtesy of John Edward Hasse.)

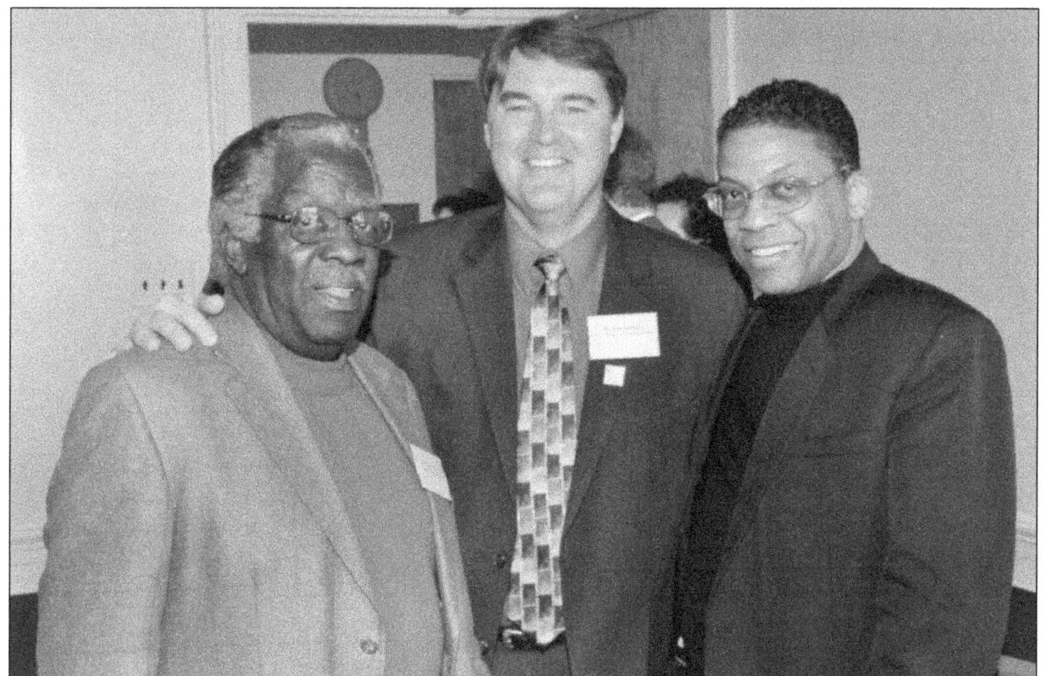

KETER BETTS, KENITH KIMERY, AND HERBIE HANCOCK. Bassist Keter Betts (left) is pictured here with percussionist Kenith Kimery of the Smithsonian Jazz Masterworks Orchestra (center) and keyboard legend and jazz innovator Herbie Hancock. A native of New York, Betts made his home in the Metro DC area for decades and performed and toured with many other well-known jazz artists, including Ella Fitzgerald and Charlie Byrd. (Courtesy of Smithsonian Jazz.)

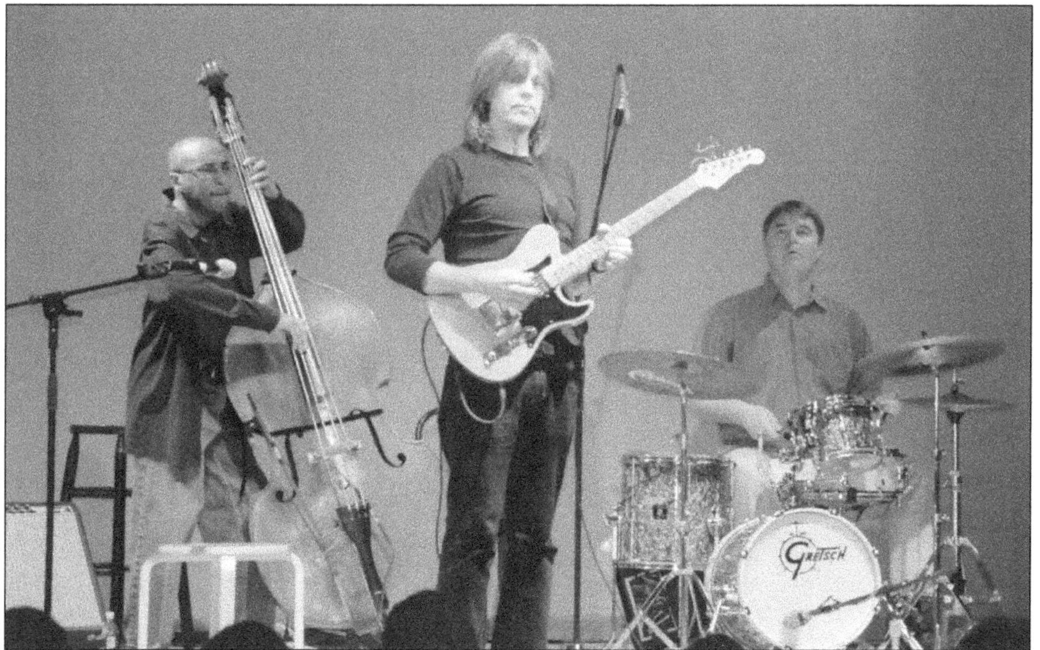

MICHAEL STERN, JAMES KING, AND KEN KIMERY. Guitarist Michael Stern is shown performing with bassist James King and drummer Kenith Kimery. (Courtesy of Smithsonian Jazz.)

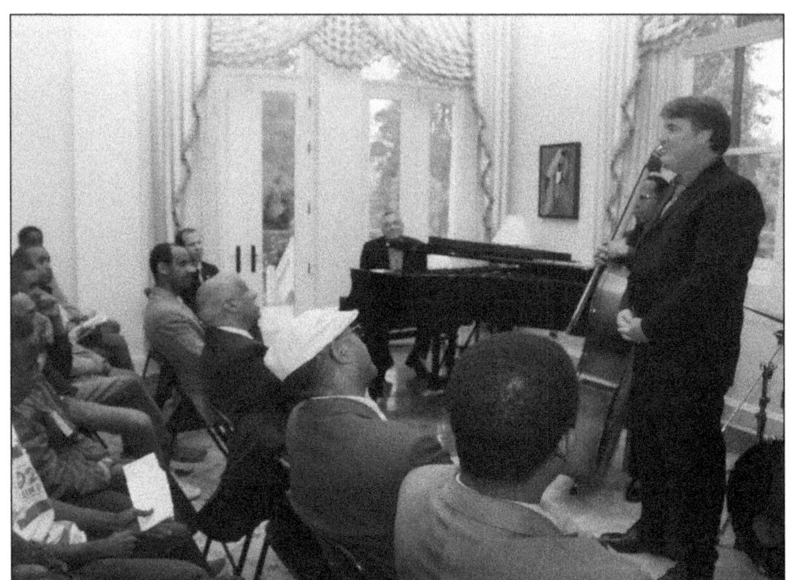

Smithsonian Jazz Masterworks Orchestra Trio in Ethiopia. Executive producer Ken Kimery, bassist Michael Bowie, and pianist Tony Nalker of the Smithsonian Jazz Masterworks Orchestra perform in Ethiopia in 2012. (Courtesy of Smithsonian Jazz.)

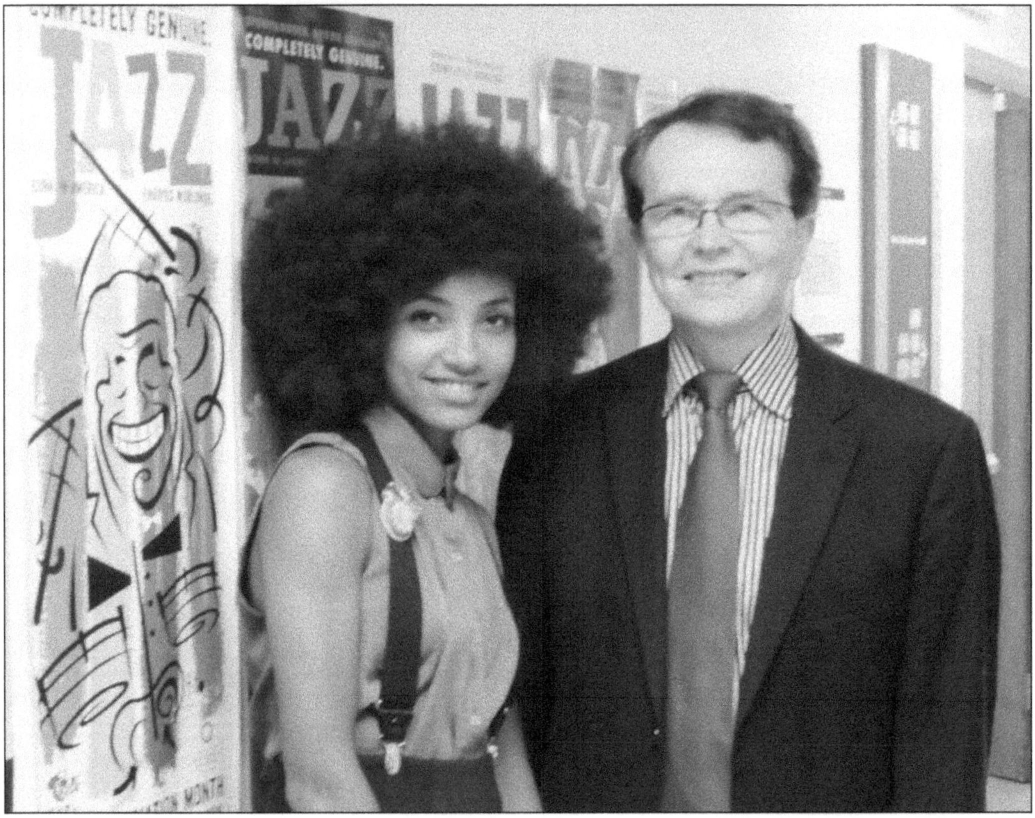

Esperanza Spalding and John Edward Hasse. A pianist, Duke Ellington scholar, and longtime curator at the Smithsonian Institution's National Museum of American History, Dr. John Edward Hasse is the founder of both Jazz Appreciation Month and the Smithsonian Jazz Masterworks Orchestra. Dr. Hasse is pictured here with award-winning bassist and jazz vocalist Esperanza Spalding. (Courtesy of John Edward Hasse.)

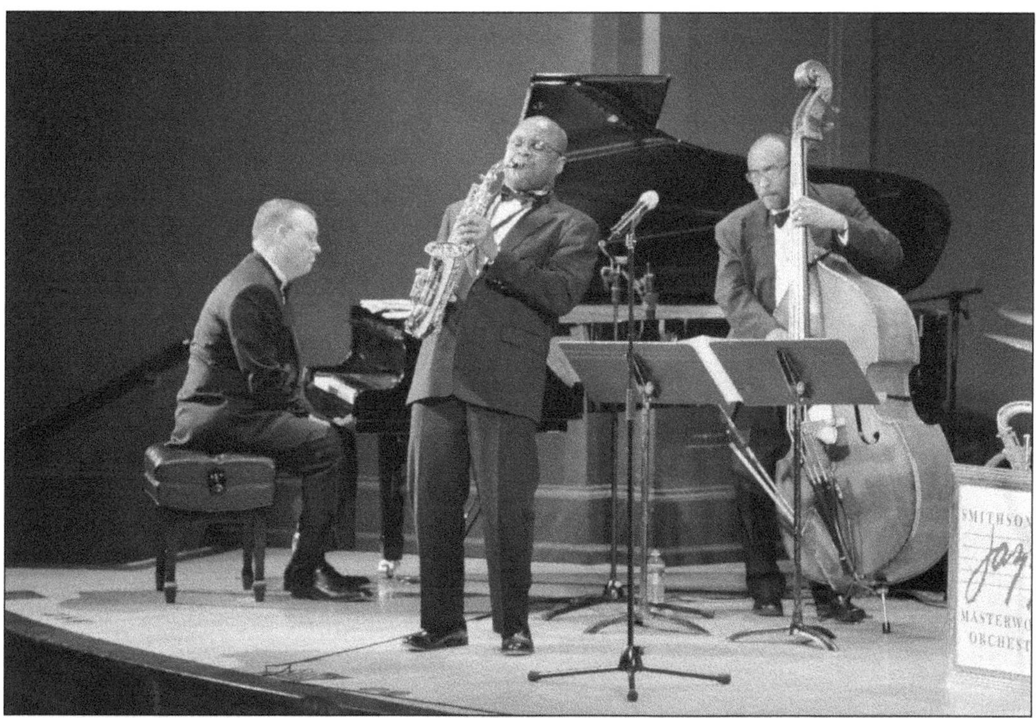

Trio Featuring Charlie Young, Tony Nalker, and James King. Howard University saxophone professor and Smithsonian Jazz Masterworks Orchestra director Charlie Young is joined on stage by pianist Tony Nalker and bassist James King. (Courtesy of Smithsonian Jazz.)

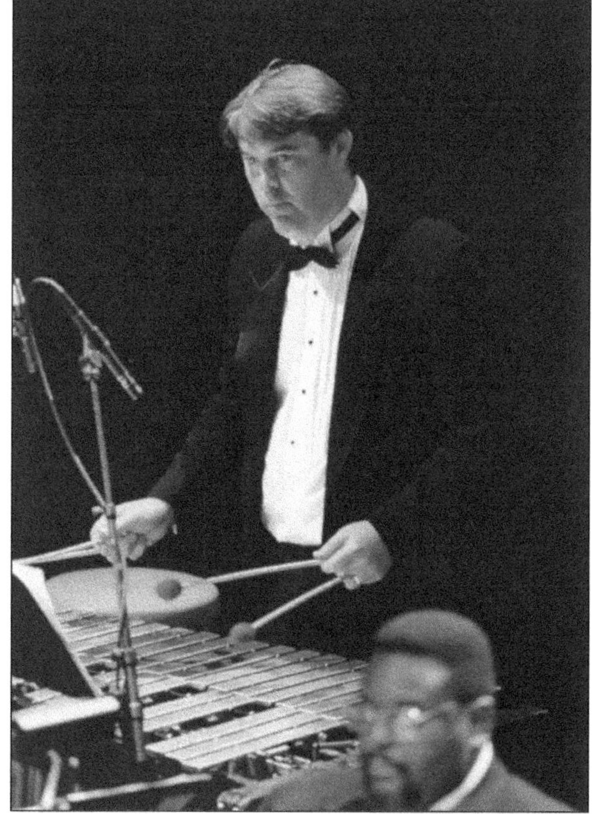

Kennith Kimery on Vibraphone. Drummer and vibraphonist Kennith Kimery serves as the executive director for the Smithsonian Jazz Masterworks Orchestra. Trumpeter Tom Williams is at lower right. (Courtesy of Smithsonian Jazz.)

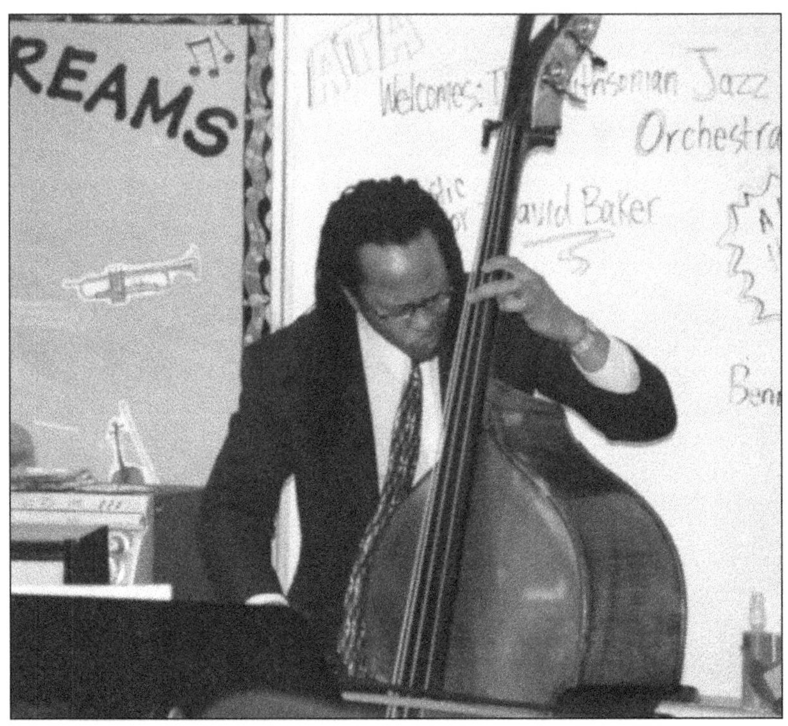

Michael Bowie. Bassist Michael Bowie is a renowned composer, arranger, and educator. At home performing on both the acoustic and electric bass, in addition to his work with the Smithsonian Jazz Masterworks Orchestra, he has taught in District of Columbia Public Schools and toured and recorded with the Harper Brothers, Betty Carter, Sarah Vaughan, Joe Williams, and many others. (Courtesy of Smithsonian Jazz.)

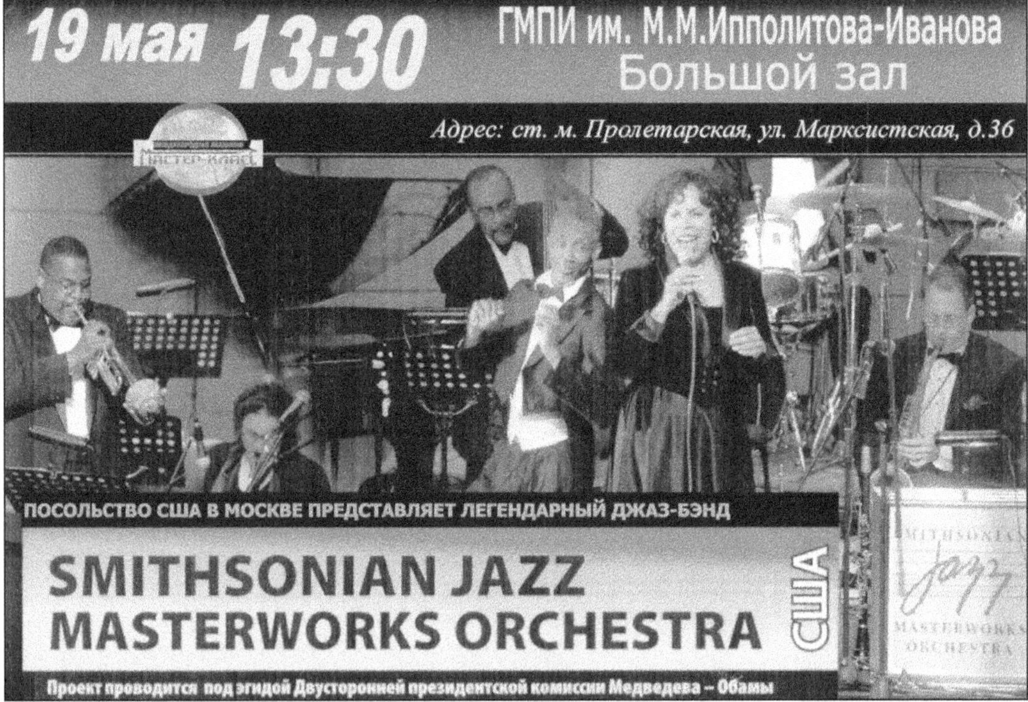

The Smithsonian Jazz Masterworks Orchestra in Russia. This is one of the promotional pieces used during the orchestra's May 2011 tour of Russia. Press materials for the tour listed performances at Spaso House in Moscow, Kazan State Conservatory, the Samara Philharmonic Hall, and the Moscow International House of Music (Courtesy of Smithsonian Jazz.)

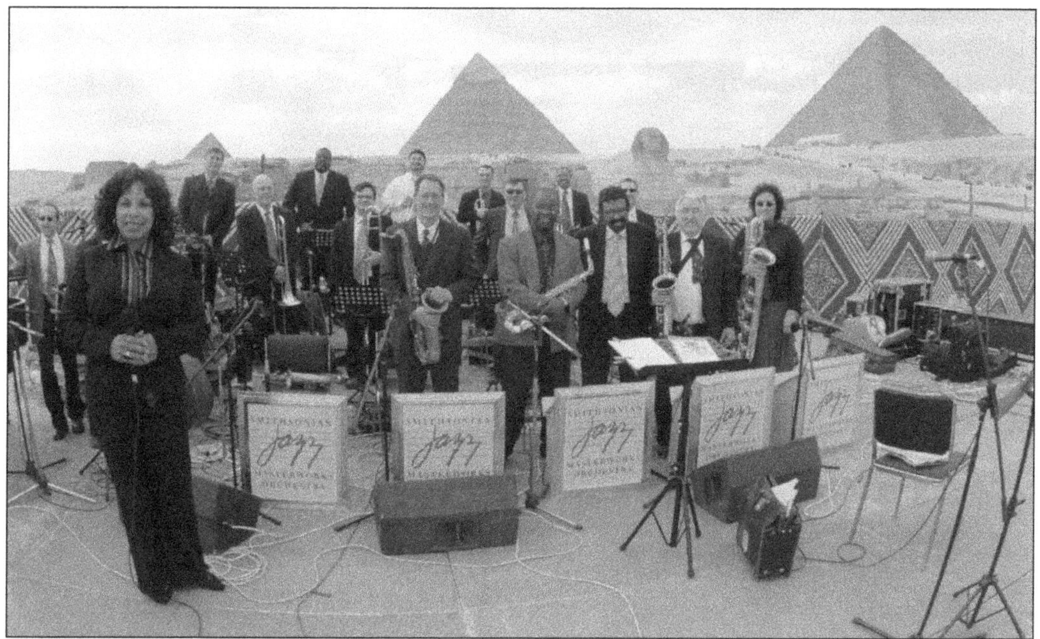

The Smithsonian Jazz Masterworks Orchestra in Egypt. In 2008, the Smithsonian Jazz Masterworks Orchestra performed in Egypt as part of the Jazz on the Nile tour. Sponsors for the tour included the Ministries of Culture and Tourism of Egypt, the US State Department, the Cairo Opera House, and private US and Egyptian companies. (Courtesy of Smithsonian Jazz.)

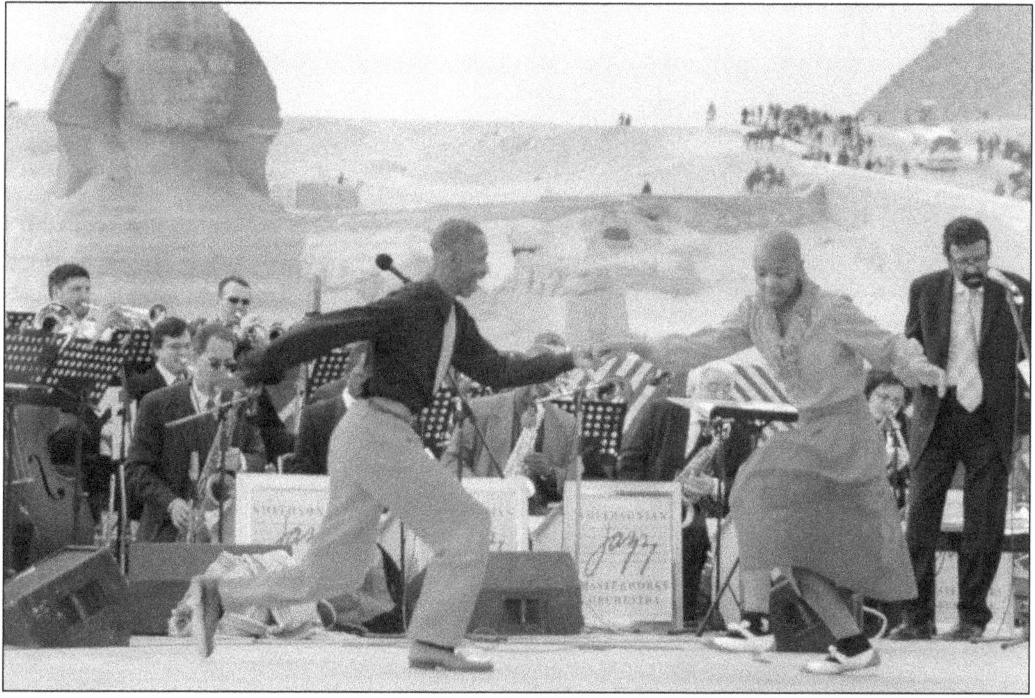

The Smithsonian Jazz Masterworks Orchestra with Dancers in Egypt. Chester Whitmore and Shaunte Johnson, swing and tap dancers, performed with the orchestra as part of the 2008 Jazz on the Nile tour. (Courtesy of Smithsonian Jazz.)

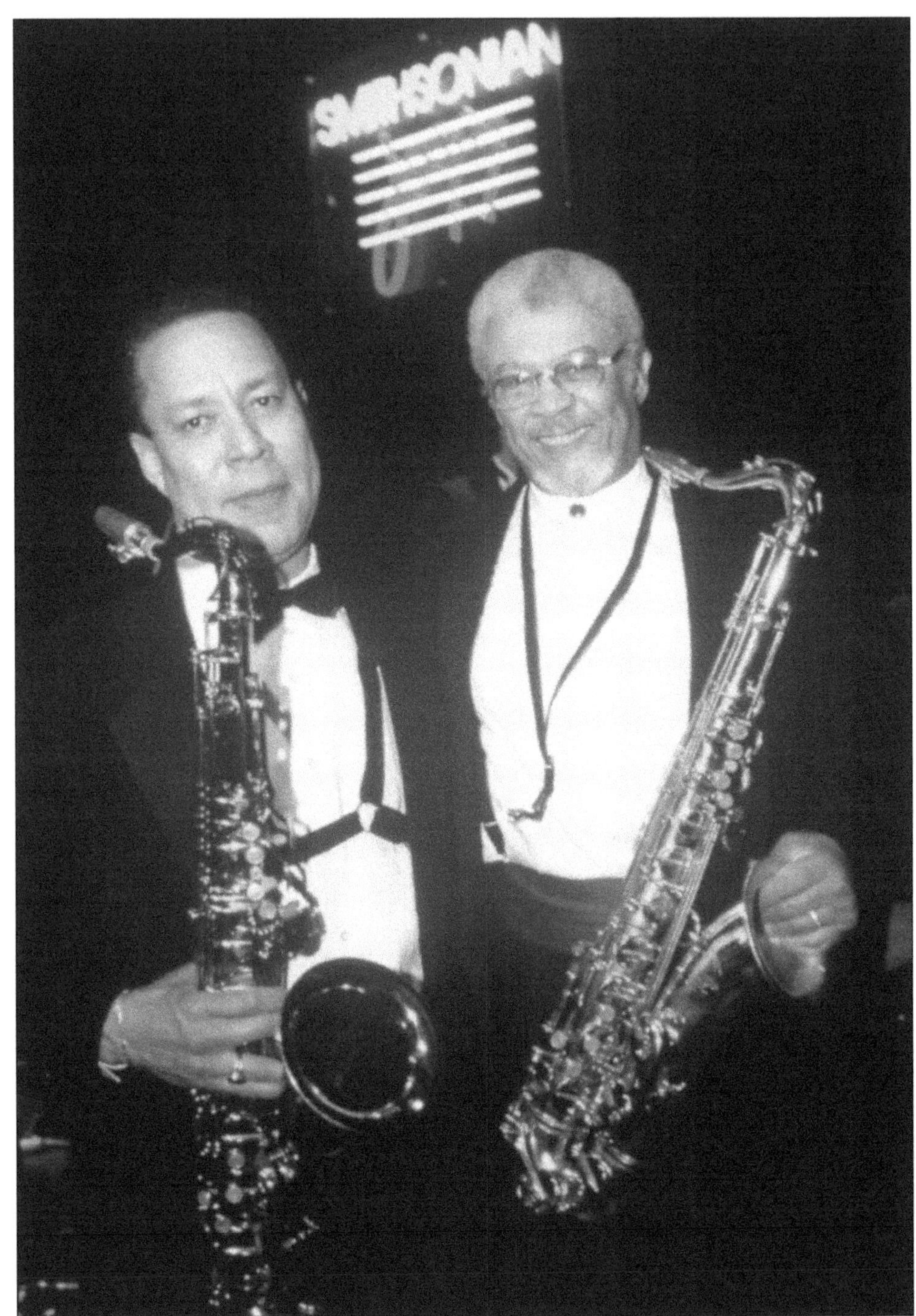

BILL PIERCE AND FRANK FOSTER. Saxophonists Bill Pierce (left) and Frank Foster are two of the many gifted musicians who have performed with the Smithsonian Jazz Masterworks Orchestra. Pierce has worked with a number of outstanding artists, including Art Blakey and the Jazz Messengers in 1980. He has also served as the woodwind department chair at the Berklee College of Music in Boston. The late Frank Foster collaborated with many artists and was a longtime member and later leader of the Count Basie Orchestra, among other groups. (Courtesy of Smithsonian Jazz.)

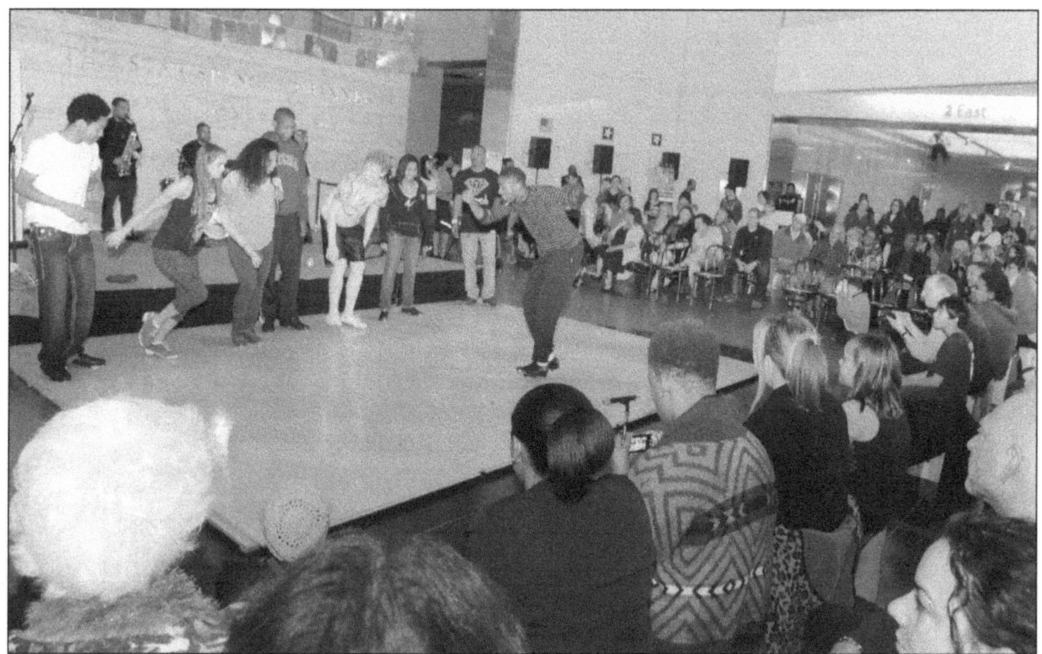

TAP JAM AT THE NATIONAL MUSEUM OF AMERICAN HISTORY. The marriage between movement and jazz and other forms of African American music is described at length in the scholarship of Lawrence Levine and Portia Maultsby and brought to life at the Smithsonian Institution's National Museum of American History and other Washington, DC, venues. (Courtesy of Smithsonian Jazz.)

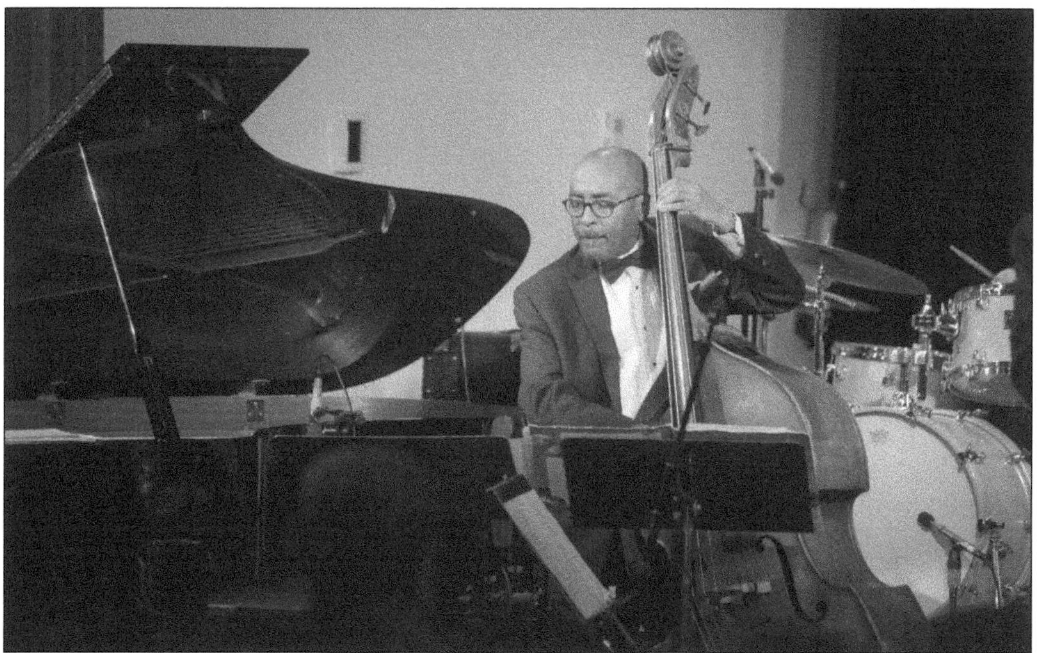

JAMES KING. Bassist James King, a Texas native, has lived and worked in the Washington, DC, area since 1977. In addition to his work with the Smithsonian Jazz Masterworks Orchestra, he has performed with Stanley Turrentine, Roger Wendell "Buck" Hill, and Regina Carter, among others. (Courtesy of Smithsonian Jazz.)

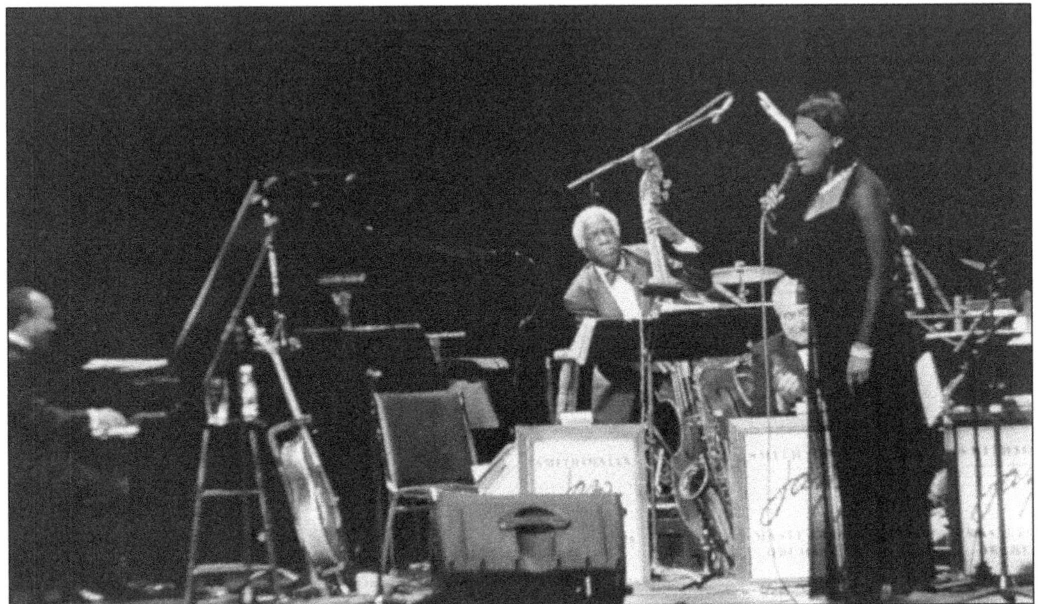

The Smithsonian Jazz Masterworks Orchestra with Keter Betts and Vanessa Rubin. William Thomas "Keter" Betts was a renowned bassist. Betts, along with guitarist Charlie Byrd, is celebrated as a pioneer in bossa nova music. From 1971 to 1993, Betts performed throughout the global community with Ella Fitzgerald. Betts is pictured here with vocalist, native Clevelander, and RCA recording artist Vanessa Ruben. (Courtesy of Smithsonian Jazz.)

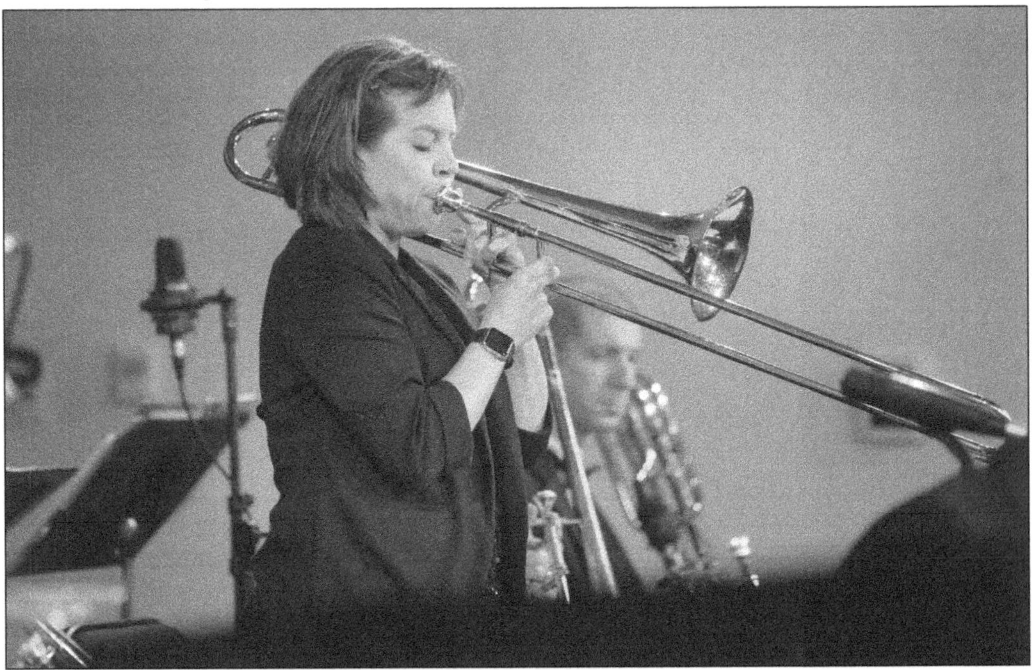

Smithsonian Jazz Masterworks Orchestra Trombonist Jennifer Krupa. Jennifer Krupa is a sought-after concert and studio musician and a frequent performer with the Smithsonian Jazz Masterworks Orchestra. Additionally, she is a member of the US Navy Band Commodores Jazz Ensemble, Sherrie Maricle and the DIVA Jazz Orchestra, and JLQ. (Courtesy of Smithsonian Jazz.)

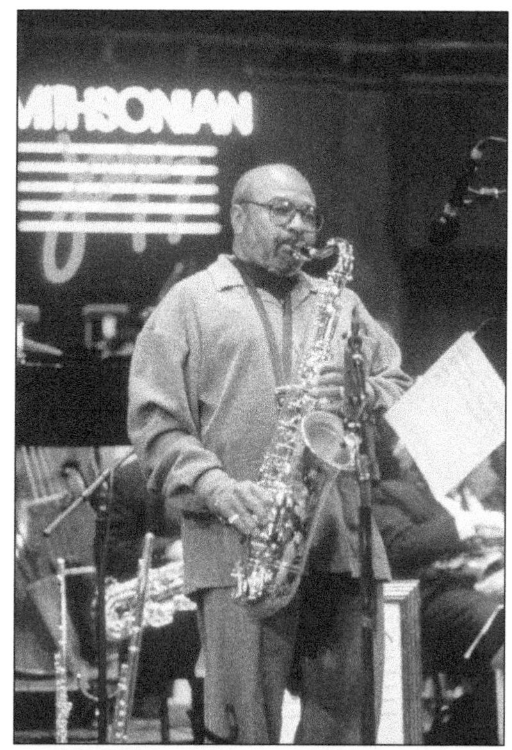

The Smithsonian Jazz Masterworks Orchestra with James Moody. Saxophonist James Moody takes the solo in this performance with the Smithsonian Jazz Masterworks Orchestra. Among his many musical accomplishments, Moody, who was also an accomplished flautist, joined Dizzy Gillespie's bebop big band in 1946 and continued to collaborate with Gillespie off and on, even when he was touring and recording with his own groups. A 2011 Smithsonian blog post suggests that Moody and Gillespie's relationship was based on mutual respect, admiration, and friendship. (Courtesy of Smithsonian Jazz.)

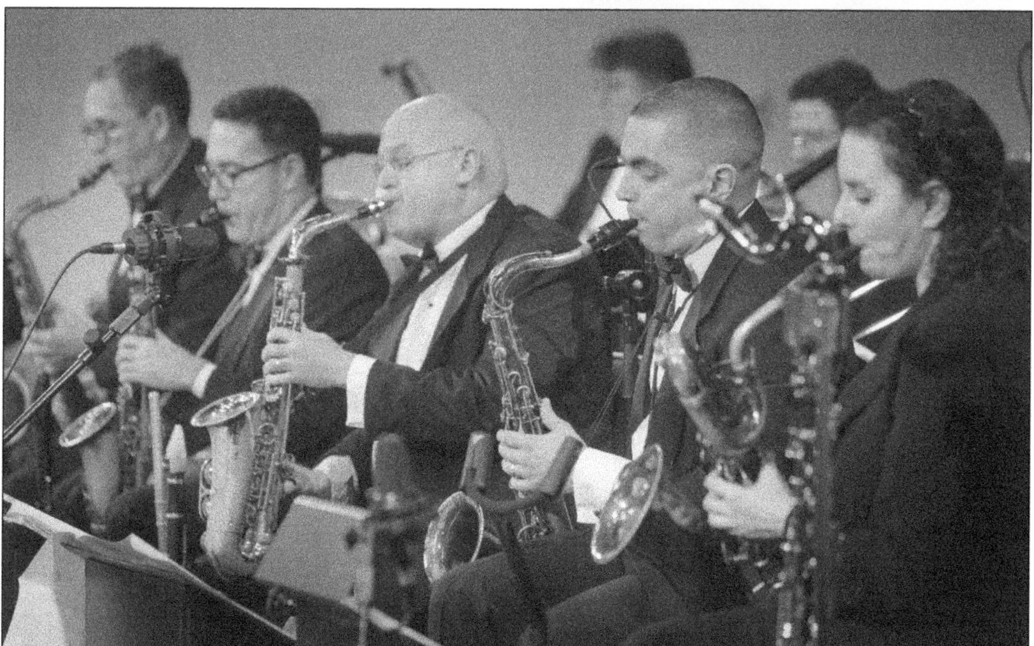

The Smithsonian Jazz Masterworks Orchestra Saxophone Section. Leigh Pilzer (right) is pictured here with other members of the saxophone section of the Smithsonian Jazz Masterworks Orchestra, which includes (from left to right) Scott Silbert, Bill Mulligan, Steve Williams, and Luis Hernandez. Pilzer is also an outstanding leader in the Washington, DC, Women in Jazz Festival community. (Courtesy of Smithsonian Jazz.)

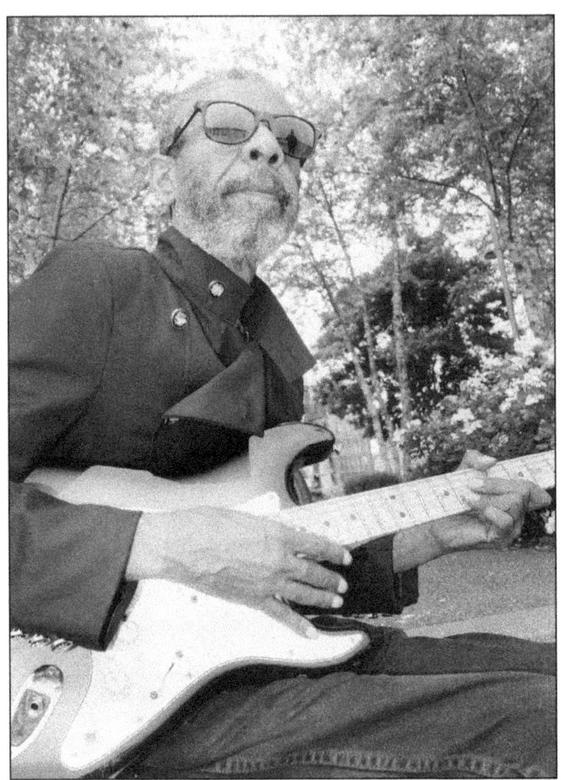

Greg Gaskins. Guitarist Greg Gaskins is shown in 2018 at the Yards Park on the Capitol Riverfront in Washington, DC. Gaskins is a member of DC Legendary Musicians Inc. and former guitarist for the world renowned Manhattans and the Sweet Inspirations. (Photograph by Nathaniel Rhodes; courtesy of DC Legendary Musicians Inc.)

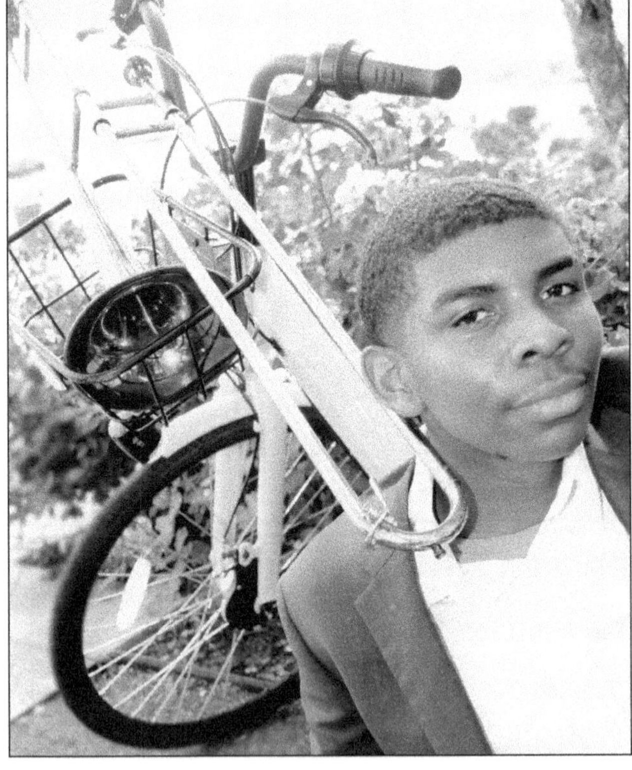

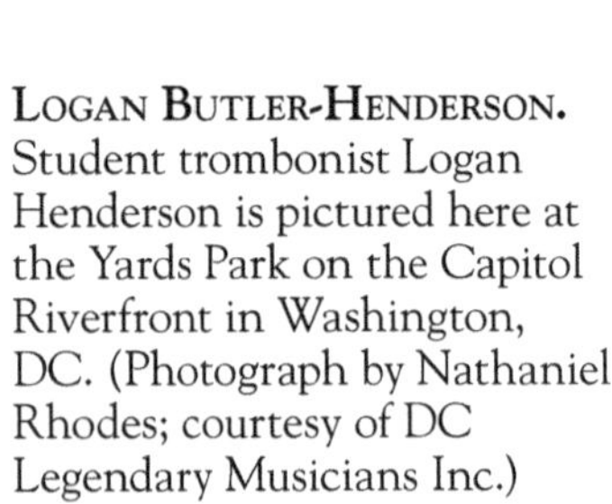

Logan Butler-Henderson. Student trombonist Logan Henderson is pictured here at the Yards Park on the Capitol Riverfront in Washington, DC. (Photograph by Nathaniel Rhodes; courtesy of DC Legendary Musicians Inc.)

Ten

Grand Finale

Nonprofits, Legendary Musicians, Veteran Artists, and Rising Stars

In recent decades, the Duke Ellington School of the Arts has perhaps done more than any other public educational institution in Washington, DC, to transform the lives and launch the careers of some of the city's most gifted jazz artists, including bassist Corcoran Holt. The oral history narrators whose life stories formed an essential part of the primary source evidence used for this text were quick to remind the coauthors, however, that the greater DC area is home to many fine educational institutions and programs that support the training of excellent musicians in general, and jazz musicians in particular.

On the pages of this book, one can certainly find the names and photographs of artists who received their training at the Duke Ellington School of the Arts. Their stories, however, are juxtaposed with those who attended Cardozo High School, the Levine School of Music, Howard University, the University of the District of Columbia, and many others within and outside of the District. For photographer, consultant, and jazz lover Nathaniel Rhodes, "DC is a breeding ground for the world's new ambassadors for jazz."

For more than 10 years, DC Legendary Musicians Inc. has worked to document the rich history of Washington's music and music makers. Under the leadership of founding director Sandra Butler-Truesdale, this 501(c)(3) organization has produced concerts in public and private venues and provided services that are in direct keeping with its mission to preserve, protect, and promote the artistic legacy, contributions and well-being of Washington, DC's professional musicians.

DC Legendary Musicians Inc. reminds members and nonmembers alike that the story of jazz in the Federal City would not be complete without the names of trumpeter and pianist Jimmy Burrell, vocalist Sharón Clark, guitarist David Cole, and vocalist Carl Kokayi Walker. This book gives readers a glimpse of some key moments in the history of Washington, DC, jazz, but this is only the beginning.

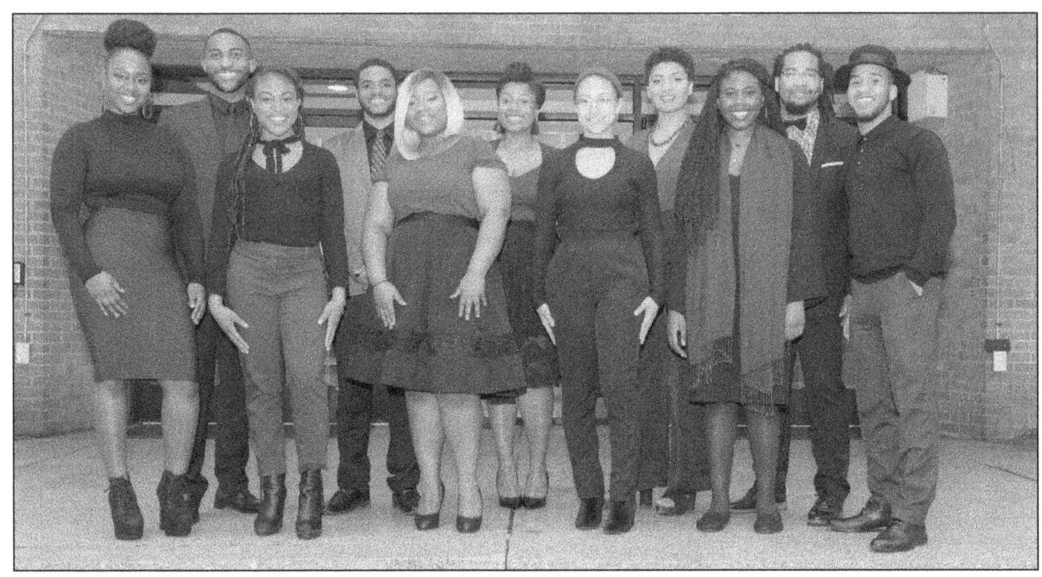

Afro Blue, 2018. Formed in 2002, Howard University's Afro Blue has long been recognized as an excellent vocal ensemble. The group has performed throughout Washington, DC, including at the National Museum of American History, Twins Jazz, and the Congressional Black Caucus Awards Dinner. Afro Blue is the recipient of numerous awards and honors, including the *Downbeat* magazine award for Best College Jazz Group (2003) and *Downbeat's* Best College Jazz Choir award in 2007. Over the years, the group has appeared with Geri Allen, Ron Carter, Jimmy Cobb, and the Smithsonian Jazz Masterworks Orchestra, among others. (Photograph by Lawrence A. Randall.)

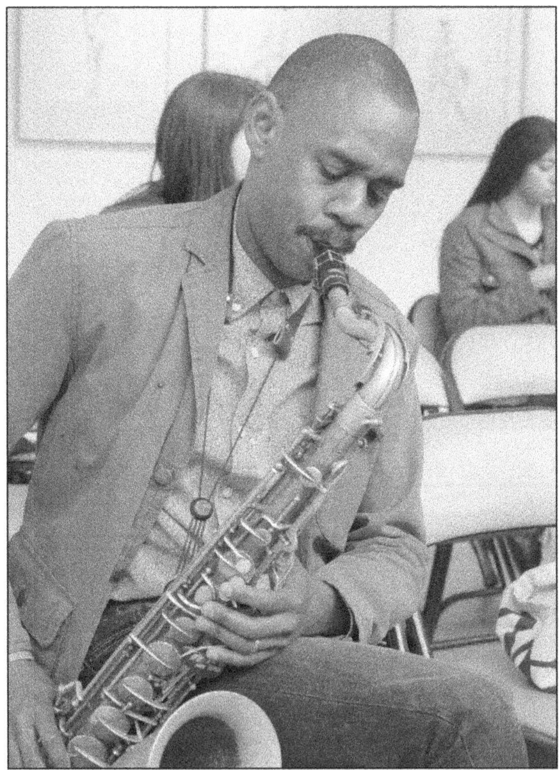

Brian Settles. Saxophonist Brian Settles is a native Washingtonian and an alumnus of the Duke Ellington School of the Arts, where he studied with Davey Yarborough. Settles earned his undergraduate degree from the New School for Jazz and Contemporary Music and his graduate degree in saxophone performance at Howard University, where he studied with Charlie Young, the artistic director and conductor for the Smithsonian Jazz Masterworks Orchestra. Central Studios produced Settles's recordings with Central Union and the Brian Settles Trio. (Photograph by Lawrence A. Randall.)

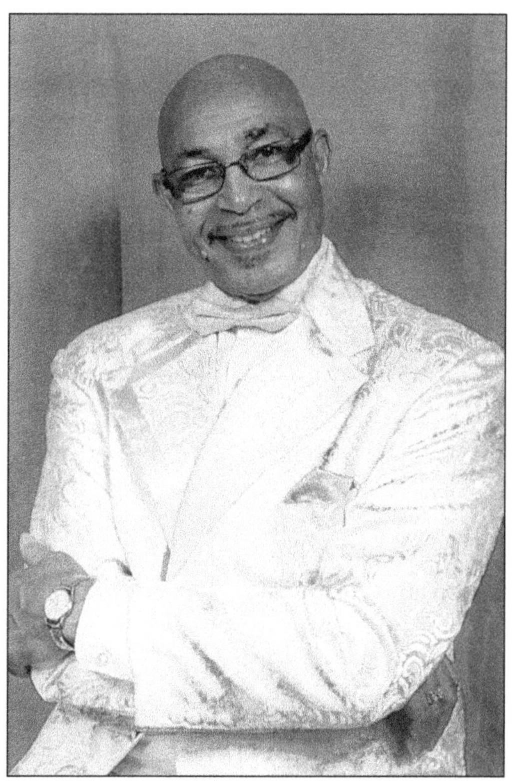

RAY APOLLO ALLEN. Vocalist and recording artist Ray Apollo Allen was a member of the Baltimore-based Orioles for more than nine years. In recent years, his solo vocal style has been described as Motown-inspired and doo-wop, hip-hop, and R&B influenced. (Courtesy of Ray Apollo Allen.)

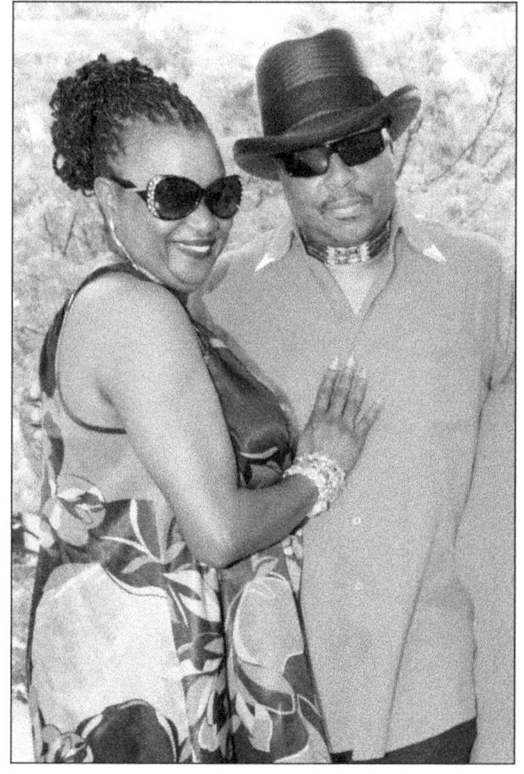

"LADY MARY" AND ADAM "TC" MORTON, 2018. Lady Mary is a soulful singer whose vocal style is influenced by her gospel music roots. Her recording credits include work with Jacques "Saxman" Johnson and two solo albums. Concert appearances include billings with such artists as the Temptations, and she has performed locally at Blues Alley and other DC venues. Her husband, Adam "TC" Morton, is the drummer in her six-piece Indahouse band and an accomplished musician in his own right. TC received his formal postsecondary training at Federal City College. His long list of performance credits includes work with Liberation Road, Seduction, and many others. (Photograph by Lawrence A. Randall.)

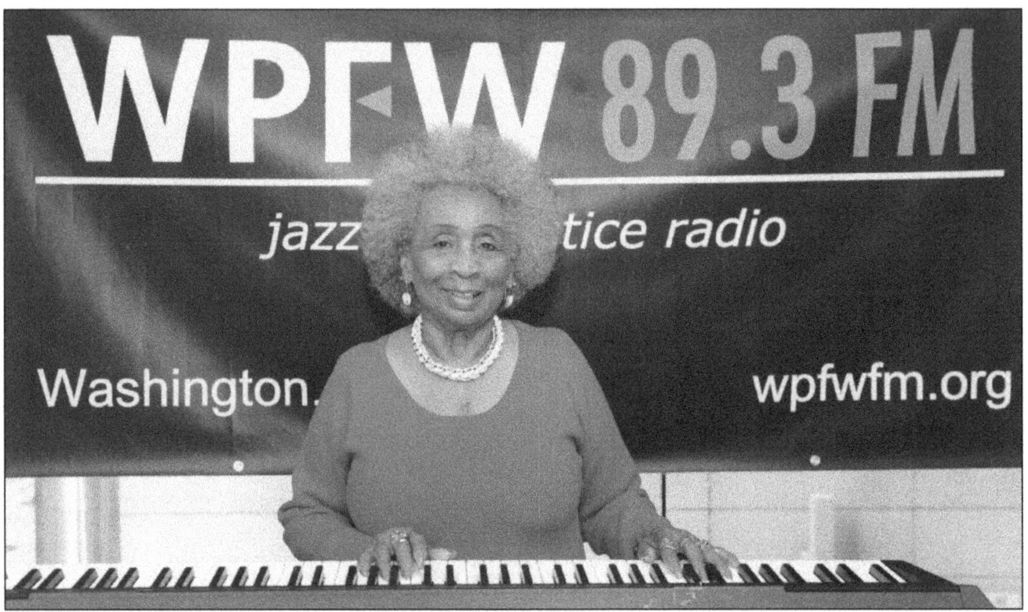

Sandra Butler-Truesdale, 2018. A Howard University alumna, the Rev. Dr. Sandra Butler-Truesdale is an associate minister at the Metropolitan African Methodist Episcopal Church, the founder and director of DC Legendary Musicians Inc., and a programmer at WPFW. She also served as chair of the Howard Theatre Restoration Community Committee and promoted, produced, and coordinated the acts for the Howard Theatre's 100-year celebration and the theater's reopening. She was interviewed for the 2017–2018 Washington, DC, Jazz Oral History Project. (Photograph by Lawrence A. Randall.)

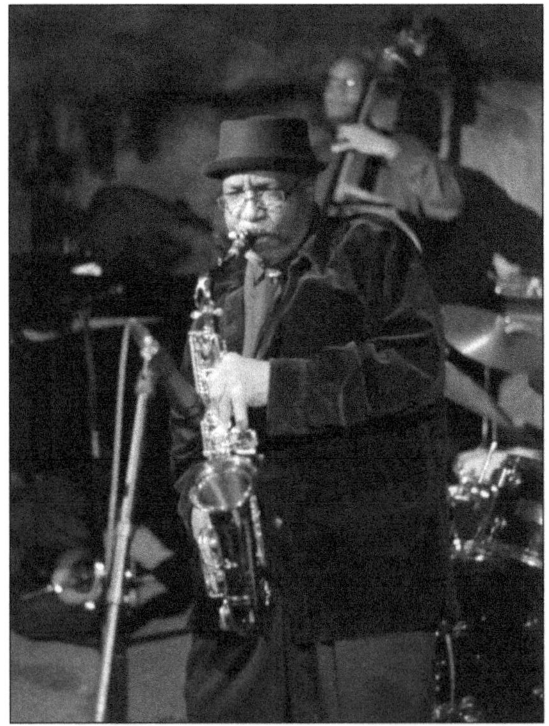

Ron Sutton Jr., 1963–2018. Ron Sutton Jr., a beloved saxophonist, was a native Washingtonian who loved jazz. The son of well-known radio programmer and jazz aficionado Ron Sutton Sr., he began his career as a teenager at the Duke Ellington School of the Arts. Sutton was among a cohort of young musicians who came of age in DC in the late 1970s and went on to apprentice with some of jazz's mid-century greats. Raised in a musical family, Sutton also studied with saxophonist Fred Foss. His playing was built upon the bebop vernacular of Charlie Parker, and reflected his training in DC's tradition-steeped jazz community. His soloing was always heartfelt and charged with energy. He died of a heart attack at the Washington Hospital Center on Sunday, September 19, 2018. (Courtesy of Sandra Butler-Truesdale.)

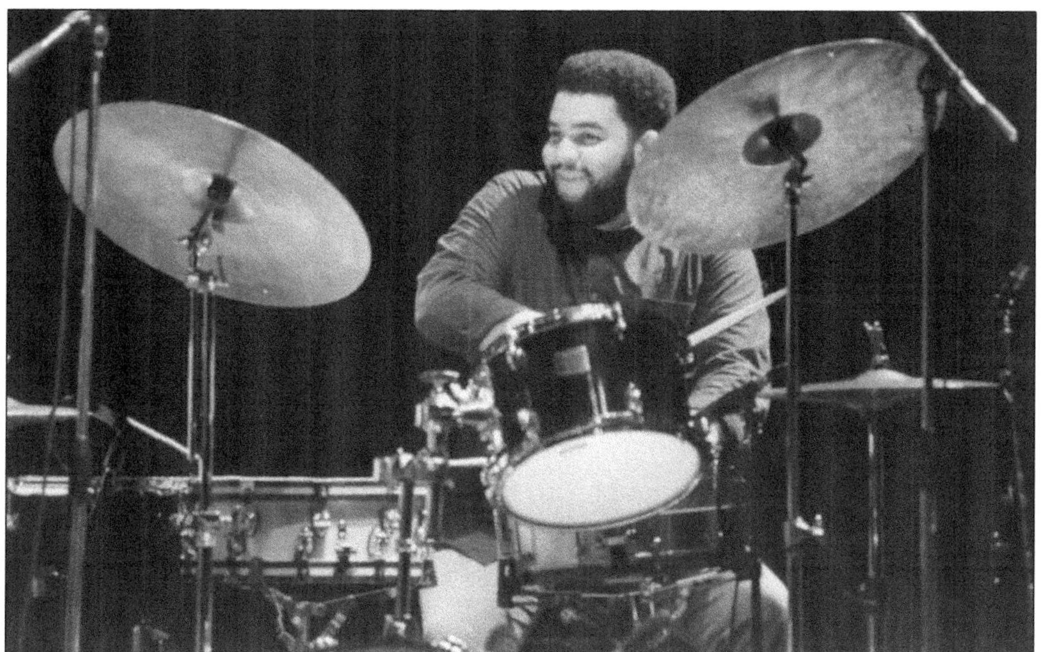

Kush Abadey. Drummer Kush Abadey is an award-winning artist and bandleader who has performed and/or recorded with Ravi Coltrane and Terrance Blanchard, among others. His talents have allowed him to perform at the White House, the Kennedy Center, and in concerts and festivals all over the world. He has studied with some of the top percussionists, including faculty members at Berklee College of Music, where he was the recipient of a Presidential Scholarship. He was interviewed for the 2017–2018 Washington, DC, Jazz Oral History Project. (Courtesy of Kush Abadey.)

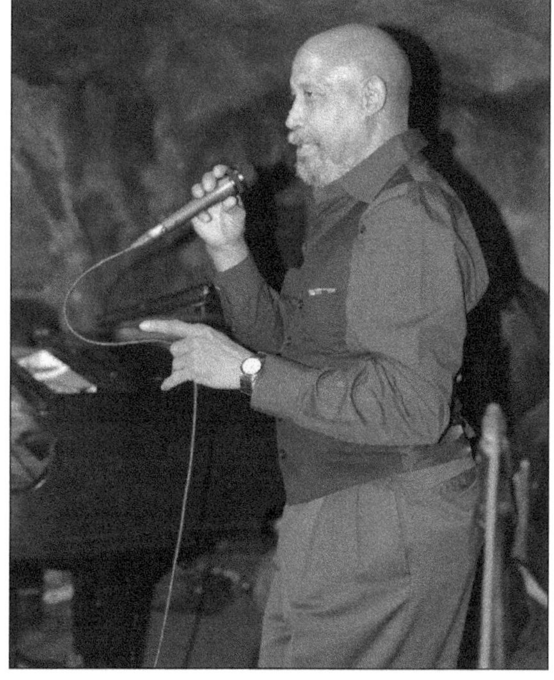

George Victor Johnson. Washington native George Victor Johnson is a vocalist, actor, and composer. Growing up in the nation's capital, he was exposed to a variety of musical genres at home, at school, and while singing in his church choir. While performing at Bill Harris's Pigfoot Club, he met pianist John Malachi, who would play an important role in his musical life for more than a decade. He has appeared at Twins Lounge, Twins Jazz, Takoma Station, Blues Alley, and many other local, national, and international venues. (Photograph by Lawrence A. Randall.)

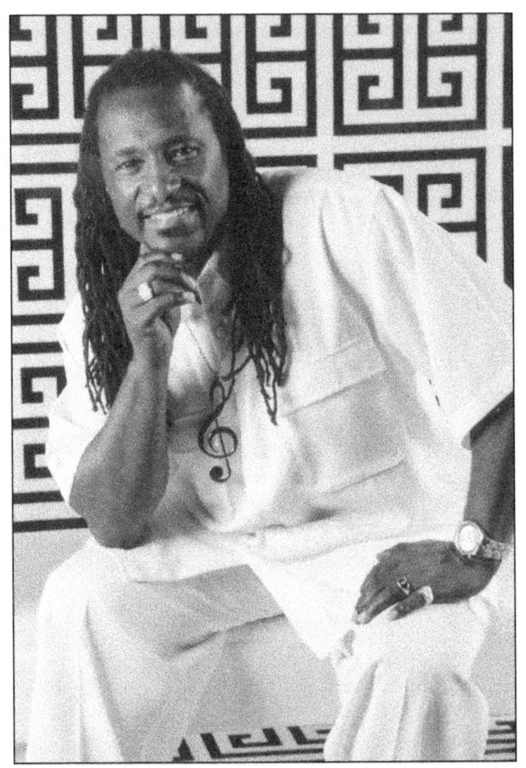

MELVIN CALDWELL. Keyboard artist and vocalist Melvin Caldwell has enjoyed a lifetime of making music. He is at home both with the choral and quartet-style religious music, which is steeped in the traditions of the black church, and the R&B traditions that are intimately linked to these musical styles. (Courtesy of Melvin Caldwell.)

DC CONGRESSMAN THE REV. WALTER FAUNTROY WITH STUDIO BAND. In May 2017, the Rev. Walter Fauntroy, a former congressman (second from right), was the guest of honor at a fundraiser hosted by DC Legendary Musicians Inc. The event, held at Busboys and Poets, featured performances by DC Legendary Musicians Inc. members and remarks by Congresswoman Eleanor Holmes Norton, Reverend Fauntroy, and others. In the weeks following the fundraiser, Reverend Fauntroy joined some of his musician friends at a studio session with blues guitarist Memphis Gold (far right). Also pictured are, from left to right, Tony Foster, Omar Ashaka, Melvin Caldwell, and Perry Grayson. (Courtesy of Sandra Butler-Truesdale.)

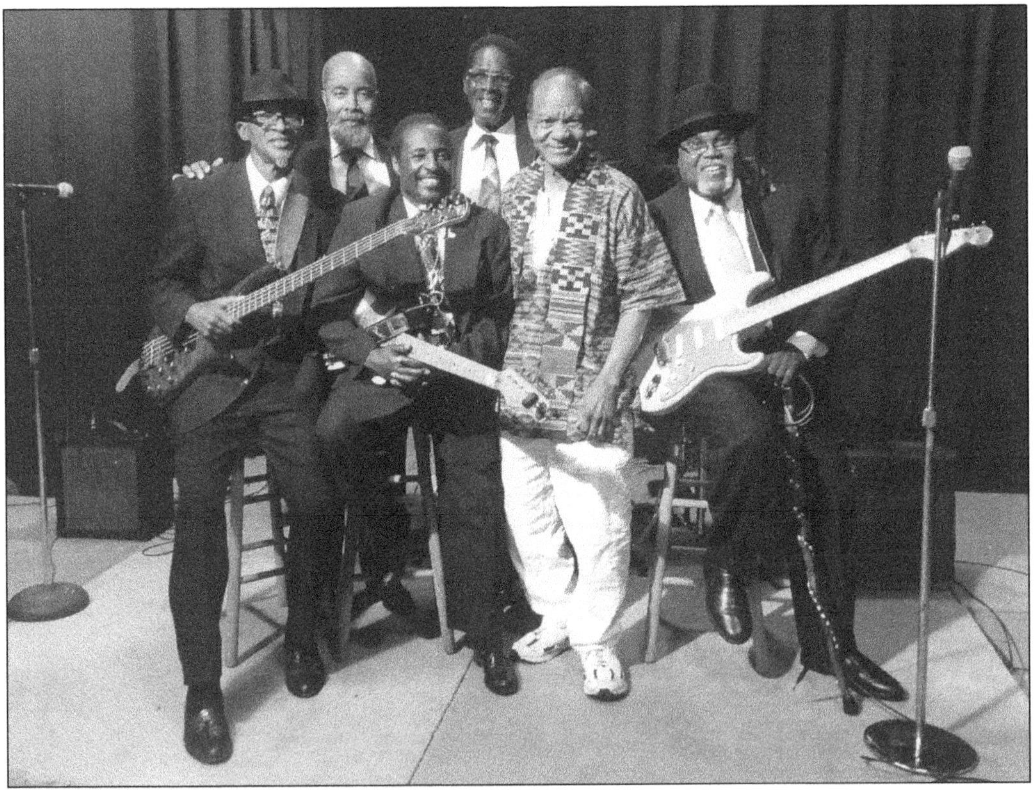

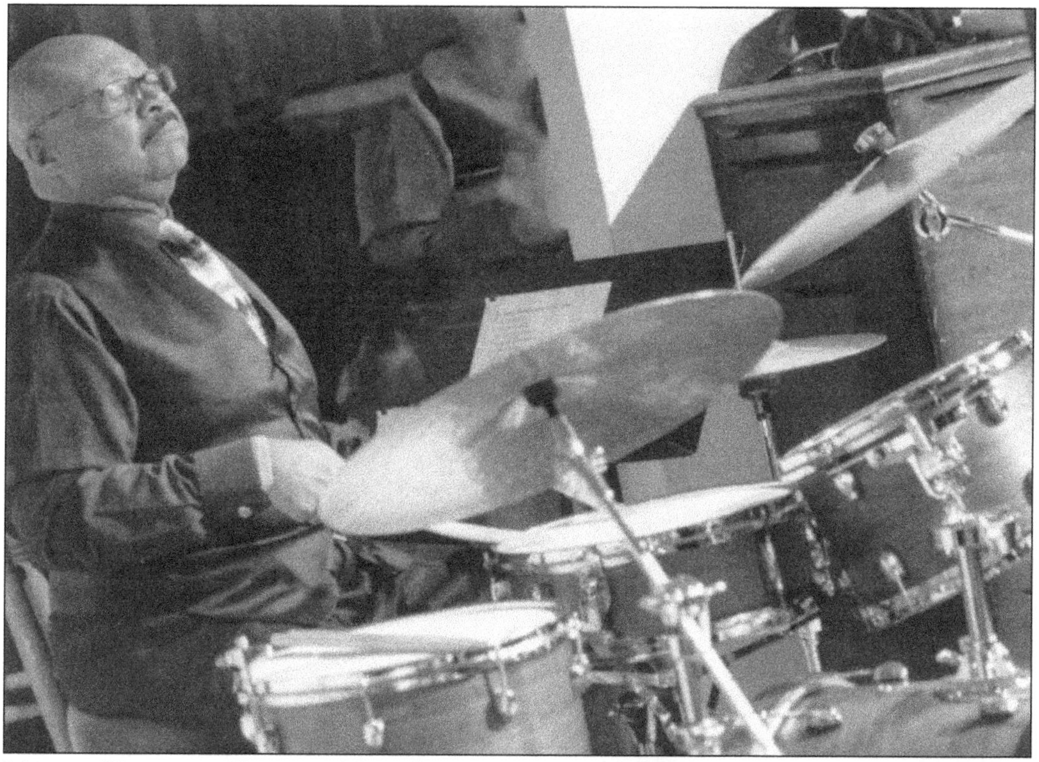

MANUEL KELLOUGH. Drummer Manuel "Manny" Kellough is an alumnus of the University of Southern California, where he earned his bachelor's degree in jazz studies. His performance credits include work with Ray Charles, Barry White, Carmen McCrae, Larry Graham, and Billy Preston, with whom he performed for 25 years. He currently serves as the resident jazz musician for Celebrity Cruise Lines. Kellough was interviewed for the 2017–2018 Washington, DC, Jazz Oral History Project. (Courtesy of Manuel Kellough.)

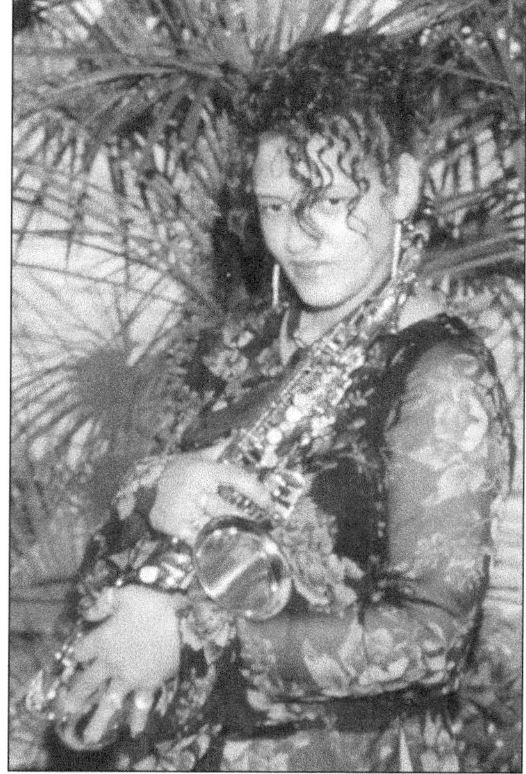

THE REV. DR. GINGER CORNWELL. The Rev. Dr. Ginger Cornwell is a saxophonist, vocalist, and public speaker. She came of age in Maryland with aspirations of becoming a radio announcer and went on to study communications at Howard University. She has played saxophone for more than 20 years and performed her own brand of gospel saxophone in the United States, the Caribbean, and Korea. Cornwell was interviewed for the 2017–2018 Washington, DC, Jazz Oral History Project. (Courtesy of the Reverend Dr. Ginger Cornwell.)

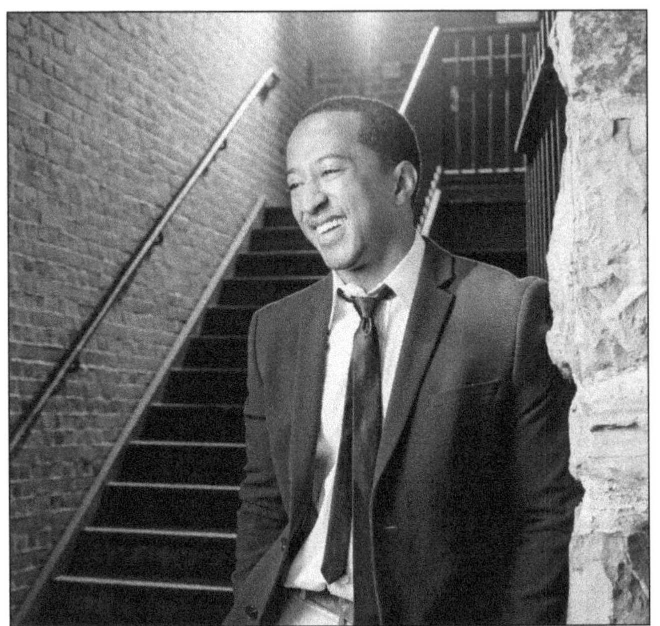

Mark Meadows. Pianist Mark Meadows describes himself as "genreless." Adept at performing the works of jazz pioneer Ferdinand "Jelly Roll" Morton, the Motown sound, his own compositions, and everything in between, Meadows is popular with audiences at home and abroad, having headlined at Jazz at Lincoln Center and toured and performed in Central Africa and Russia. The son of a jazz and gospel musician and a product of the United Methodist Church, he holds degrees from Johns Hopkins University. Meadows was interviewed for the 2017–2018 Washington, DC, Jazz Oral History Project. (Courtesy of Mark Meadows.)

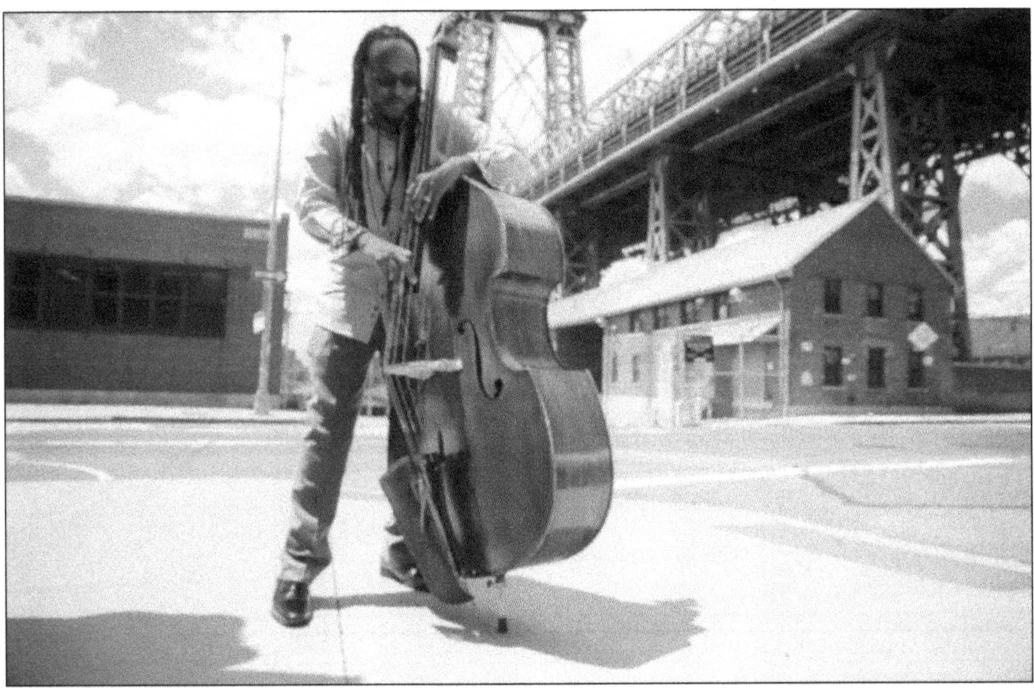

Corcoran Neal Holt. Bassist and percussionist Corcoran Neal Holt is an alumnus of Washington, DC's Duke Ellington School of the Arts, the Shenandoah Conservatory, and Queens College. A busy artist with 17 years of professional experience, Holt includes Keter Betts, Ron Carter, Christian McBride, Ray Brown, Steve Novosel, Reggie Workman, and David Yarborough on the list of great musicians who inspired him and helped him find his own voice as an artist. Based in New York, in recent years he has performed with the Kenny Garrett Quintet and the Corcoran Holt Quintet and Ensemble. Holt was interviewed for the 2017–2018 Washington, DC, Jazz Oral History Project. (Courtesy of Corcoran Holt.)

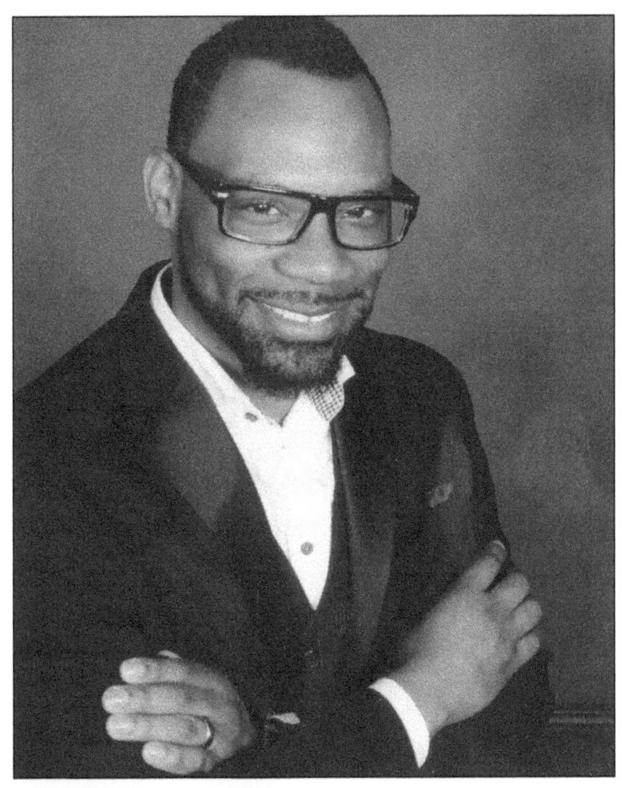

Jawoed Mosché Snowden. Washington-based trombonist Jawoed Mosché Snowden came of age in the United House of Prayer for All People, listening to, falling in love with the music of, and, eventually, performing with the renowned shout bands of that faith community. Snowden has performed in numerous churches, clubs, and other venues and special events, including the Millennium Stage at the John F. Kennedy Center for the Performing Arts, Ben's Next Door, and the DC Funk Parade. Snowden was interviewed for the 2017–2018 Washington, DC, Jazz Oral History Project. (Courtesy of Jawoed Mosché Snowden.)

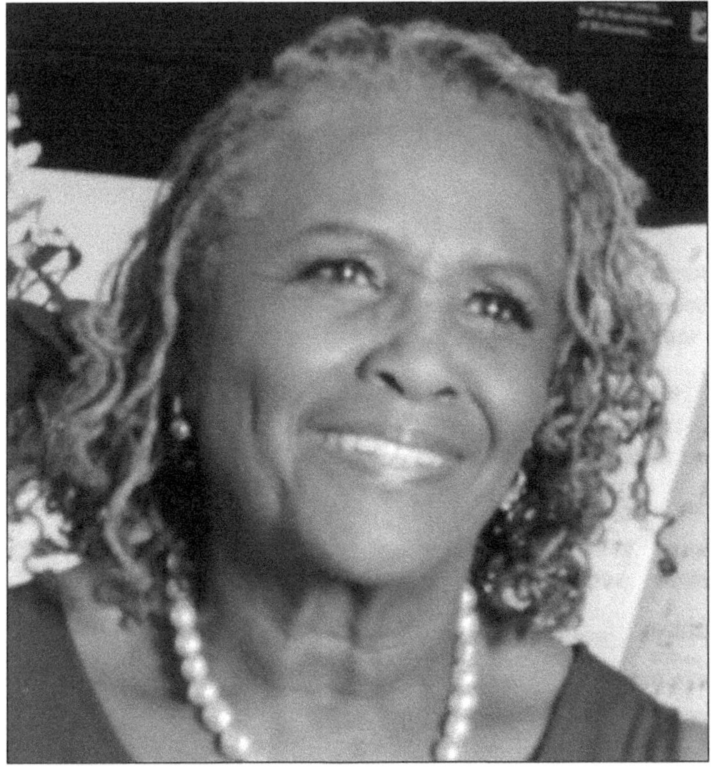

Queen Esther Marrow, 2016. A legendary vocalist and an incredibly versatile performing artist, Queen Esther Marrow has delighted audiences across the country and around the world for more than 50 years. From her childhood experiences with the music of the United House of Prayer for all People and her early solo performances in Duke Ellington's historic 1965 "Sacred Concert" through her annual European tours with the Harlem Gospel Singers, she is, as Duke Ellington would say, "beyond category." In 2016, Regennia N. Williams interviewed Marrow for the Praying Grounds Oral History Project. (Photograph by Nathaniel Rhodes.)

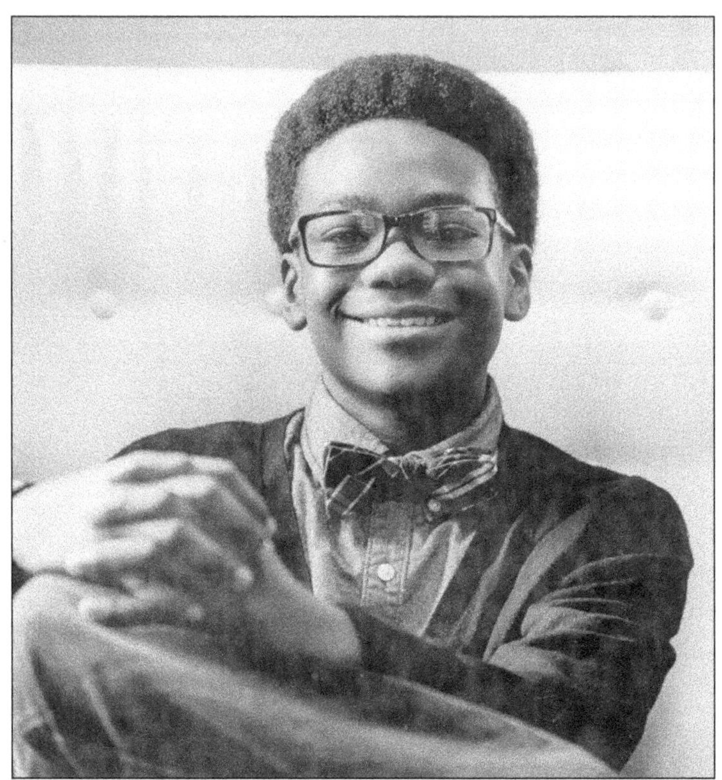

JE'LAN HARWELL, 2017. At the tender age of 14, blues guitarist Je'Lan Harwell is a rising star on the local music scene. The product of a musical family, Harwell was introduced to guitar music by his grandfather. Harwell was interviewed for the 2017–2018 Washington, DC, Jazz Oral History Project. (Courtesy of Je'Lan Harwell.)

NIA ELAINE MARIE ALSOP, 2017. Baltimore native Nia Elaine Marie Alsop has lived in Washington, DC, since 2005, when she was only one year old. A gifted young singer, she studied privately with jazz vocalist Denyse Pearson and did ensemble work with the Children's Chorus of Washington. She has also completed summer enrichment training with Theatre Lab, Step Africa, and Girls Rock. As a student at Stuart-Hobson Middle School, she performed in productions of *Into the Woods* and *Willy Wonka*. Alsop was interviewed for the 2017–2018 Washington, DC, Jazz Oral History Project, and is a student at the Duke Ellington School of the Arts. (Courtesy of Kelly Elaine Navies.)

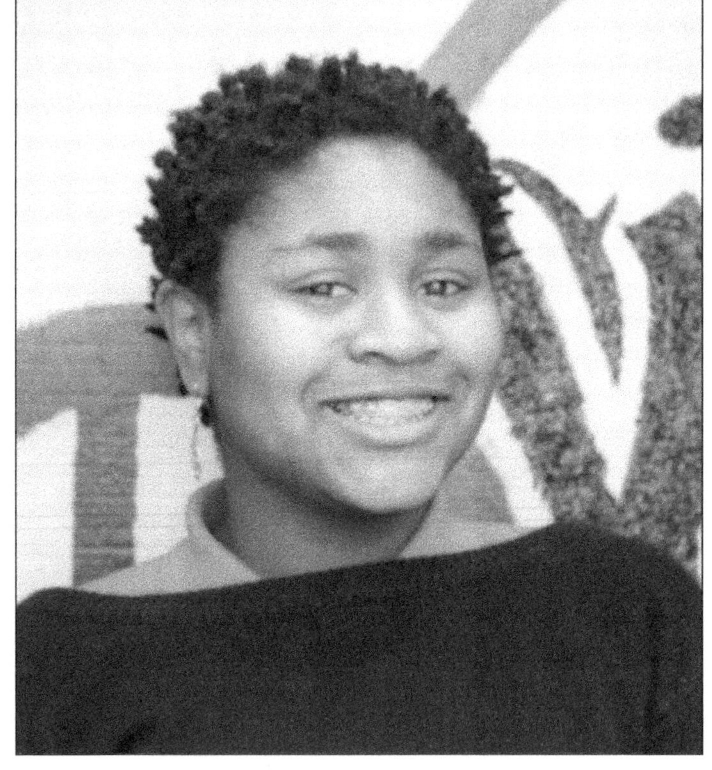

Bibliography

Bennett, Tracey Gold. *Washington, DC: 1861–1962*. Charleston, SC: Arcadia Publishing, 2006.

———. *Washington, DC: 1963–2006*. Charleston, SC: Arcadia Publishing, 2007.

Burnim, Mellonee V. and Portia K. Maultsby, eds. *African American Music: An Introduction*. New York, NY: Routledge, 2015.

Cohen, Harvey. *Duke Ellington's America*. Chicago, IL: University of Chicago Press, 2010.

Du Bois, William Edward Burghardt, with an introduction by Arnold Rampersad. *The Souls of Black Folk*. New York, NY: Oxford University Press, 2007. (Originally published 1903.)

Enstice, Wayne and Janis Stockhouse. *Jazzwomen: Conversations with Twenty-One Musicians*. Bloomington, IN: Indiana University Press, 2004.

Floyd, Samuel A. Jr. *The Power of Black Music: Interpreting Its History from Africa to the United States*. New York, NY: Oxford University Press, 1995.

Gioia, Ted. *The History of Jazz*. New York, NY: Oxford University Press, 2011.

History of Jazz: Oxygen for the Ears. Directed by Stefan Immler. Giganova Productions, 2012.

Jackson, Maurice and Blair A. Ruble, eds. *DC Jazz: Stories of Jazz Music in Washington, DC*. Washington, DC: Georgetown University Press, 2018.

Jazz Ambassadors, The. Directed by Hugo Berkeley. Antelope Films, Normal Life Pictures, and Thirteen/WNET, 2018.

Levine, Lawrence. *Black Culture and Black Consciousness: Afro-American Folk Thought from Slavery to Freedom*. New York, NY: Oxford University Press, 1978.

McCalla, James. *Jazz: A Listener's Guide*. Englewood Cliffs, NJ: Prentice-Hall, 1982.

Ruble, Blair A. *The Muse of Urban Delirium: How the Performing Arts Paradoxically Transform Conflict Ridden Cities into Centers of Cultural Innovation*. Washington, DC: New Academia Publishing, 2017.

———. *Washington's U Street: A Biography*. Baltimore, MD: Johns Hopkins University Press, 2012.

Sales, Grover. *Jazz: America's Classical Music*. Englewood Cliffs, NJ: Prentice Hall, 1984.

Sapp, Jane, ed. *The Smithsonian Collection of Classic Jazz* (revised edition). Washington, DC: The Smithsonian Institution, 1987.

Southern, Eileen. *The Music of Black Americans: A History* (third edition). New York, NY: W.W. Norton & Company, 1997.

Teachout, Terry. *Duke: A Life of Duke Ellington*. New York, NY: Penguin Group, 2013.

Ward, Geoffrey C. and Ken Burns. *Jazz: A History of America's Music*. New York, NY: Alfred A. Knopf, 2000.

Williams, Paul Kelsey. *Greater U Street*. Charleston, SC: Arcadia Publishing, 2002.

www.ingramcontent.com/pod-product-compliance
Lightning Source LLC
LaVergne TN
LVHW060627110826
845147LV00015B/951
* 9 7 8 1 4 6 7 1 2 7 8 3 7 *